# SUBSIDIA BIBLICA

18

subsidia biblica – 18

JOSEPH A. FITZMYER, S.J.

# The Biblical Commission's Document
# "The Interpretation of the Bible in the Church"

## Text and Commentary

EDITRICE PONTIFICIO ISTITUTO BIBLICO — ROMA 1995

The text of the Document of the Pontifical Biblical Commission, "The Interpretation of the Bible in the Church", is reprinted with permission of the Libreria Editrice Vaticana.

IMPRIMI POTEST

Romae, die 4 Octobris 1994

R. P. KLEMENS STOCK, S.J.

*Rector Pontificii Instituti Biblici*

ISBN 88-7653-605-1

EDITRICE PONTIFICIO ISTITUTO BIBLICO
Piazza della Pilotta 35 - 00187 Roma, Italia

# PRESENTATION

When I asked Fr. Fitzmyer to write a commentary on "The Interpretation of the Bible in the Church" he demurred, pleading conflict of interest. After all, he was a member of the Pontifical Biblical Commission which prepared the document. But I explained that I did not have a critical commentary in mind (in which case his demurrer might have been warranted), but a commentary which was clarificatory. And for such a commentary he would be well qualified, not only by reason of his membership in the commission, but also because of his considerable experience and expertise in the study of the Bible.

This is not to say that critical comments on the document would be out of place. On the contrary, the very quality of "The Interpretation of the Bible in the Church" demands them. In the few months in which the document has been in circulation it has won wide acclaim. But of course there have been negative observations as well. Critical comments are needed to prepare the way for what is hoped will be a new edition some years hence. In this way the document can better fulfill its potential for giving authoritative guidance to those who would search the Scriptures with the help of some of the Church's leading scholars.

\* \* \*

I wish to thank Don Nicolò Suffi, S.D.B., Director of the Libreria Editrice Vaticana, for giving permission to use the English text of the document of the Pontifical Biblical Commission, "The Interpretation of the Bible in the Church", in the present publication.

James Swetnam, S.J.
Editor, "Subsidia Biblica"
Rome, November 1, 1994

# PREFACE

The purpose of this commentary is to supply a brief explanation of topics that appear in the Biblical Commission's recent document, *The Interpretation of the Bible in the Church*[1]. The document bears the date, 15 April 1993, which was the time when the French original was completed on the basis of comments received from the Sacred Congregation for the Doctrine of the Faith and from the Holy Father, Pope John Paul II. It was published by the Libreria Editrice Vaticana only on 18 November 1993, the centenary of the encyclical of Pope Leo XIII on biblical studies, *Providentissimus Deus*. The delay in publication allowed for the translation of the document into various other languages, English, German, Italian, Portuguese, and Spanish, which were published simultaneously with the French original.

When the Biblical Commission's document was finally completed, Pope John Paul II summoned the College of Cardinals resident in Rome, the diplomatic corps, the professors of the Biblical Institute, and the members of the Biblical Commission to a solemn audience in the Sala Clementina on Friday, 23 April 1993, at which he delivered an allocution, which commemorated the hundredth anniversary of the encyclical of Pope Leo XIII and the fiftieth anniversary of the encyclical of Pope Pius XII, *Divino afflante Spiritu* of 1943, and commented on the new document of the Biblical Commission[2]. This audience thus solemnized the anniversaries of the two encyclicals on biblical interpretation and gave papal approval of the Commission's document.

---

[1] Commission Biblique Pontificale, *L'Interprétation de la Bible dans l'Eglise* (Vatican City: Libreria Editrice Vaticana, 1993). The document was also issued by the same publisher in English, *The Interpretation of the Bible in the Church*. It has been reprinted in *Origins* 23/29 (6 January 1994) 497-524. It is also available in pamphlet form under the same English title: Washington, DC: United States Catholic Conference, 1994 (ISBN 1-155586-806-1) and Boston MA: St. Paul Books & Media, 1994.

[2] See *Osservatore Romano*, Saturday, 24 April 1993, p. 1. An English translation of the allocution appeared in the weekly English edition of *Osservatore Romano* of 28 April 1993, pp. 3-4, 6. Cf. *Documentation Catholique* 90 (1993) 503-8. It is also found in the booklet, *The Interpretation of the Bible in the Church* (Vatican City: Libreria Editrice Vaticana, 1993) 7-21. It is not included, however, in the reprint of the document published by *Origins*.

Part of the purpose of this commentary is to supply bibliographical references to the topics discussed in the document. In this regard, however, I have had to be selective. No attempt has been made to cover the matter exhaustively, but it is hoped that those items mentioned will guide the interested reader to further works.

The document is lengthy, and it is not possible to comment on every phrase in it. Moreover, in some instances it is not possible to say more than what the text says. At times I have attempted to comment at some length on a paragraph or sentence, when I judged that that was called for. When, however, my commentary says little more than what is in the document, the reader will realize that the latter needs little further explanation.

My thanks are due to the following persons who have helped me in various ways in the writing and publication of this commentary: James Swetnam, S.J., the editor of the series, who first suggested the idea of a commentary and has helped with many comments on its text; J.-N. Aletti, S.J, P. Grech, O.S.A., who have read parts of the commentary and suggested improvements on them; and B. Byrne, S.J., J. R. Donahue, S.J., and A. Dulles, S.J. for help on various problems. To all of them I am grateful.

Joseph A. Fitzmyer, S.J.
Professor Emeritus, Biblical Studies
The Catholic University of America
Resident at:
Jesuit Community, Georgetown University
Washington, DC 20057

# TABLE OF CONTENTS

PRESENTATION (James Swetnam, S.J.) ..................... v

PREFACE (Joseph A. Fitzmyer, S.J.) ..................... vii

TABLE OF CONTENTS ...................................... ix

ABBREVIATIONS ......................................... xiii

ADDRESS OF HIS HOLINESS POPE JOHN PAUL II ...... 1

Introduction ........................................... 1

I.   From "Providentissimus Deus" to "Divino afflante Spiritu"   2

II.  The Harmony between Catholic Exegesis and the Mystery of
     the Incarnation ..................................... 4

III. The New Document of the Biblical Commission .......... 8

Conclusion ............................................. 10

PREFACE TO THE BIBLICAL COMMISSION DOCUMENT
(Joseph Cardinal Ratzinger) ............................ 13

PONTIFICAL BIBLICAL COMMISSION: THE INTERPRE-
TATION OF THE BIBLE IN THE CHURCH (TEXT) ...... 15

PONTIFICAL BIBLICAL COMMISSION: THE INTERPRE-
TATION OF THE BIBLE IN THE CHURCH (COMMENTA-
RY BY JOSEPH A. FITZMYER, S.J.) ................... 15

N.B. The Text is placed at the top of each page, with the corresponding
Commentary immediately below. Hence the page references for
Text and Commentary coincide.

**Introduction** ............................................... 15

A. The State of the Question Today ........................ 15

B. The Purpose of This Document ........................ 24


**I. Methods and Approaches for Interpretation** ................ 26

A. The Historical Critical Method ......................... 26
  1. History of the Method ............................ 26
  2. Principles ....................................... 37
  3. Description ...................................... 38
  4. Evaluation ...................................... 44

B. New Methods of Literary Analysis ..................... 50
  1. Rhetorical Analysis ............................. 53
  2. Narrative Analysis .............................. 58
  3. Semiotic Analysis .............................. 63

C. Approaches Based on Tradition ....................... 67
  1. The Canonical Approach ......................... 68
  2. Approach through Recourse to Jewish Traditions of Inter-
     pretation ....................................... 74
  3. Approach by the History of the Influence of the Text
     (*Wirkungsgeschichte*) .......................... 79

D. Approaches That Use the Human Sciences .............. 82
  1. The Sociological Approach ....................... 83
  2. The Approach through Cultural Anthropology ......... 87
  3. Psychological and Psychoanalytical Approach ........ 89

E. Contextual Approaches ............................... 92
  1. The Liberationist Approach ...................... 92
  2. The Feminist Approach .......................... 96

F. Fundamentalist Interpretation ........................ 101


**II. Hermeneutical Questions** .......................... 109

A. Philosophical Hermeneutics .......................... 109
  1. Modern Perspectives ............................ 111
  2. Usefulness for Exegesis ........................ 114

B. The Meaning of Inspired Scripture .................... 117
  1. The Literal Sense .............................. 119
  2. The Spiritual Sense ............................ 124
  3. The Fuller Sense .............................. 130

**III. Characteristics of Catholic Interpretation** ................  132

A. Interpretation in the Biblical Tradition ..................  133
   1. Re-Readings (*Relectures*) ...........................  134
   2. Relationships between the Old Testament and the New  ..  136
   3. Some Conclusions .................................  140

B. Interpretation in the Tradition of the Church ..............  142
   1. Formation of the Canon ...........................  143
   2. Patristic Exegesis ...............................  145
   3. The Roles of Various Members of the Church in Interpre-
      tation .........................................  150

C. The Task of the Exegete .........................  155
   1. Principal Guidelines .............................  155
   2. Research ......................................  157
   3. Teaching .....................................  158
   4. Publications ...................................  160

D. Relationships with Other Theological Disciplines ..........  161
   1. Theology and Presuppositions regarding Biblical Texts  ..  161
   2. Exegesis and Systematic Theology ...................  163
   3. Exegesis and Moral Theology ......................  164
   4. Differing Points of View and Necessary Interaction ......  166

**IV. Interpretation of the Bible in the Life of the Church** ........  170

A. Actualization .................................  170
   1. Principles ....................................  171
   2. Methods .....................................  173
   3. Limits .......................................  175

B. Inculturation .................................  176

C. Use of the Bible ...............................  179
   1. In the Liturgy ................................  179
   2. *Lectio Divina* ...............................  181
   3. In Pastoral Ministry ...........................  183
   4. In Ecumenism ...............................  186

**Conclusion** ......................................  189

Select Bibliography ...............................  193

Indexes ..........................................  195
   1. Biblical ......................................  195
   2. Modern Authors ..............................  200
   3. Topical ......................................  207

# ABBREVIATIONS

| | |
|---|---|
| AAR | American Academy of Religion |
| AARTTS | American Academy of Religion, Texts in Translation Series |
| *AAS* | *Acta Apostolicae Sedis* |
| AB | Anchor Bible |
| *ABD* | D. N. Freedman et al. (eds.), *The Anchor Bible Dictionary* (6 vols.; New York: Doubleday, 1992) |
| ACW | Ancient Christian Writers |
| AnBib | Analecta Biblica |
| *ANEP* | J. B. Pritchard (ed.), *The Ancient Near East in Pictures Relating to the Old Testament* (Princeton, NJ: Princeton University, 1954) |
| *ANESTP* | J. B. Pritchard (ed.), *The Ancient Near East: Supplementary Texts and Pictures Relating to the Old Testament* (Princeton, NJ: Princeton University, 1969) |
| *ANET* | J. B. Pritchard (ed.), *Ancient Near Eastern Texts Relating to the Old Testament* (Princeton, NJ: Princeton University, 1950) |
| *ASS* | *Acta Sanctae Sedis* |
| BETL | Bibliotheca ephemeridum theologicarum lovaniensium |
| BGBH | Beiträge zur Geschichte der biblischen Hermeneutik |
| BGPTM | Beiträge zur Geschichte der Philosophie und Theologie des Mittelalters |
| BHT | Beiträge zur historischen Theologie |
| *Bib* | *Biblica* |
| *BLit* | *Bibel und Liturgie* |
| *BRev* | *Bible Review* |
| *CBQ* | *Catholic Biblical Quarterly* |
| CBQMS | Catholic Biblical Quarterly Monograph Series |
| CCLat | Corpus christianorum, Series latina |
| *CivCatt* | *Civiltà cattolica* |
| *ConcJ* | *Concordia Journal* |
| *DBSup* | *Dictionnaire de la Bible, Supplément* |
| DS | H. Denzinger and A. Schönmetzer, *Enchiridion symbolorum* (ed. 32; Barcelona: Herder, 1963) |
| *EB* | *Enchiridion biblicum: Documenti della chiesa sulla Sacra Scrittura: Edizione bilingue* (Bologna: Edizioni Dehoniane, 1993) |
| *ESBNT* | J. A. Fitzmyer, *Essays on the Semitic Background of the New Testament* (London: Chapman, 1971; repr., Missoula, MT: Scholars, 1974) |

| | |
|---|---|
| *ETL* | *Ephemerides theologicae lovanienses* |
| FC | Fathers of the Church |
| FRLANT | Forschungen zur Religion und Literatur des Alten und Neuen Testaments |
| GCS | Griechische christliche Schriftsteller |
| HKAT | Handkommentar zum Alten Testament |
| HTS | Harvard Theological Studies |
| *IBS* | *Irish Biblical Studies* |
| *IKZ "Communio"* | *Internationale kirchliche Zeitschrift: "Communio"* |
| *ITQ* | *Irish Theological Quarterly* |
| *JANES* | *Journal of the Ancient Near Eastern Society* |
| *JBL* | *Journal of Biblical Literature* |
| *JES* | *Journal of Ecumenical Studies* |
| *JNSL* | *Journal of Northwest Semitic Languages* |
| *JR* | *Journal of Religion* |
| *JSNT* | *Journal for the Study of the New Testament* |
| JSNTSup | Supplement to *JSNT* |
| *JSOT* | *Journal for the Study of the Old Testament* |
| JSOTSup | Supplement to *JSOT* |
| *KD* | *Kerygma und Dogma* |
| *KJV* | *King James Version* (of the Bible) |
| LCL | Loeb Classical Library |
| *MTZ* | *Münchener theologische Zeitschrift* |
| *NJBC* | R. E. Brown et al. (eds.), *The New Jerome Biblical Commentary* (Englewood Cliffs, NJ: Prentice Hall, 1990) |
| *NRSV* | *The New Revised Standard Version* (of the Bible) |
| *NRT* | *La nouvelle revue théologique* |
| NTL | New Testament Library |
| *NTS* | *New Testament Studies* |
| OCT | Oxford Classical Texts |
| PG | J. Migne (ed.), Patrologia graeca |
| PL | J. Migne (ed.), Patrologia latina |
| *RB* | *Revue biblique* |
| *RHPR* | *Revue d'histoire et de philosophie religieuses* |
| *RSR* | *Recherches de science religieuse* |
| *RSS* | *Rome and the Study of Scripture* (7th ed.; St. Meinrad, IN: Grail, 1962) |
| *RTL* | *Revue théologique de Louvain* |
| *RTP* | *Revue de théologie et de philosophie* |
| SBLDS | Society of Biblical Literature Dissertation Series |
| SBLRBS | Society of Biblical Literature Resources for Biblical Study |
| SBLSCS | Society of Biblical Literature Septuagint and Cognate Studies |
| SBT | Studies in Biblical Theology |
| SC | Sources chrétiennes |
| SNTSMS | Studiorum Novi Testamenti Societas Monograph Series |
| *SPatav* | *Studia patavina* |
| SubBib | Subsidia biblica |

| | |
|---|---|
| *TBT* | *The Bible Today* |
| *TD* | *Theology Digest* |
| *TJT* | *Toronto Journal of Theology* |
| *TP* | *Theologie und Philosophie* |
| *TQ* | *Theologische Quartalschrift* |
| *TS* | *Theological Studies* |
| *VDom* | *Verbum domini* |
| *VT* | *Vetus Testamentum* |
| VTSup | Supplements to *VT* |
| *ZAW* | *Zeitschrift für die alttestamentliche Wissenschaft* |
| *ZNW* | *Zeitschrift für die neutestamentliche Wissenschaft* |

# HIS HOLINESS, POPE JOHN PAUL II
## ADDRESS
## ON THE INTERPRETATION
## OF THE BIBLE IN THE CHURCH*

*This address was given Friday, the 23rd of April, 1993, during the course of an audience commemorating the centenary of the encyclical of Leo XIII, "Providentissimus Deus" and the fiftieth anniversary of the encyclical of Pius XII, "Divino afflante Spiritu", both dedicated to Biblical studies.*

*The audience was held in the Sala Clementina of the Vatican Palace, in the presence of cardinals, the Diplomatic Corps accredited to the Holy See, the Pontifical Biblical Commission and professors of the Pontifical Biblical Institute.*

*During the course of the audience, Cardinal Joseph Ratzinger presented the Pope with the document of the Biblical Commission on the interpretation of the Bible in the Church.*

\* \* \*

Your Eminences,
Your Excellencies, the Heads of Diplomatic Missions,
Members of the Pontifical Biblical Commission,
Professors of the Pontifical Biblical Institute,

1. I wholeheartedly thank Cardinal Ratzinger for the sentiments he expressed a few moments ago in presenting the document prepared by the Pontifical Biblical Commission on the interpretation of the Bible in the Church. I joyfully accept this document, the fruit of a collegial work undertaken on Your Eminence's initiative, and perseveringly continued over several years. It responds to a heartfelt concern of mine, for the interpretation of Sacred Scripture is of capital importance for the Christian faith and the Church's life. As the Council well reminded us: "In the

* English translation from *L'Osservatore Romano*, weekly edition in English, 28 April 1993, pp. 3, 4, 6. The Holy Father's address was given in French.

sacred books the Father who is in heaven comes lovingly to meet his children, and talks with them. And such is the force and power of the word of God that it can serve the Church as her support and vigour, and the children of the Church as strength for their faith, food for the soul, and a pure and lasting source of spiritual life" (*Dei Verbum*, 21). For men and women today the manner in which biblical texts are interpreted has immediate consequences for their personal and community relationship with God, and it is also closely connected with the Church's mission. A vital problem is at issue and deserves all your attention.

2. Your work is finishing at a very opportune moment, for it provides me with the opportunity to celebrate with you two richly significant anniversaries: the centenary of the Encyclical *Providentissimus Deus*, and the 50th anniversary of the Encyclical *Divino afflante Spiritu*, both concerned with biblical questions. On 18 November 1893, Pope Leo XIII, very attentive to intellectual problems, published his Encyclical on scriptural studies with the goal, he wrote, "of encouraging and recommending them" as well as "orienting them in a way that better corresponds to the needs of the time" (*Enchiridion Biblicum*, 82). Fifty years later, Pope Pius XII gave Catholic exegetes further encouragement and new directives in his Encyclical *Divino afflante Spiritu*. Meanwhile, the papal Magisterium showed its constant concern for scriptural problems through numerous interventions. In 1902, Leo XIII established the Biblical Commission; in 1909, Pius X founded the Biblical Institute. In 1920, Benedict XV celebrated the 1500th anniversary of St Jerome's death with an Encyclical on the interpretation of the Bible. The strong impetus thus given to biblical studies was fully confirmed at the Second Vatican Council so that the whole Church benefited from it. The Dogmatic Constitution *Dei Verbum* explains the work of Catholic exegetes and invites pastors and the faithful to take greater nourishment from the word of God contained in the Scriptures.

Today I want to highlight some aspects of the teaching of these two Encyclicals and the permanent validity of their orientation through changing circumstances, in order to profit more from their contribution.

## I. From "Providentissimus Deus" to "Divino afflante Spiritu"

3. First, one notes an important difference in these two documents, namely, the polemical, or to be more exact, the apologetic part of the two Encyclicals. In fact, both appear concerned to answer attacks on the Catholic interpretation of the Bible, but these attacks did not follow the same direction. On the one hand, *Providentissimus Deus* wanted especially to protect Catholic interpretation of the Bible from the attacks of

rationalistic science; on the other hand, *Divino afflante Spiritu* was primarily concerned with defending Catholic interpretation from attacks that opposed the use of science by exegetes and that wanted to impose a non-scientific, so-called "spiritual" interpretation of Sacred Scripture.

This radical change of perspective was obviously due to the circumstances. *Providentissimus Deus* appeared in a period marked by vicious polemics against the Church's faith. Liberal exegesis gave important support to these polemics, for it made use of all the scientific resources, from textual criticism to geology, including philology, literary criticism, history of religions, archaeology and other disciplines besides. On the other hand, *Divino afflante Spiritu* was published shortly after an entirely different polemic arose, particularly in Italy, against the scientific study of the Bible. An anonymous pamphlet was widely circulated to warn against what it described as "a very serious danger for the Church and souls: the critico-scientific system in the study and interpretation of Sacred Scripture, its disastrous deviations and aberrations".

4. In both cases the reaction of the Magisterium was significant, for instead of giving a purely defensive response, it went to the heart of the problem and thus showed (let us note this at once) the Church's faith in the mystery of the incarnation.

Against the offensive of liberal exegesis, which presented its allegations as conclusions based on the achievements of science, one could have reacted by anathematizing the use of science in biblical interpretation and ordering Catholic exegetes to hold to a "spiritual" explanation of the texts.

*Providentissimus Deus* did not take this route. On the contrary, the Encyclical earnestly invites Catholic exegetes to acquire genuine scientific expertise so that they may surpass their adversaries in their own field. "The first means of defence", it said, "is found in studying the ancient languages of the East as well as the practice of scientific criticism" (*EB*, 118). The Church is not afraid of scientific criticism. She distrusts only preconceived opinions that claim to be based on science, but which in reality surreptitiously cause science to depart from its domain.

Fifty years later, in *Divino afflante Spiritu* Pope Pius XII could note the fruitfulness of the directives given by *Providentissimus Deus*: "Due to a better knowledge of the biblical languages and of everything regarding the East, ... a good number of the questions raised at the time of Leo XIII against the authenticity, antiquity, integrity and historical value of the Sacred Books... have now been sorted out and resolved" (*EB*, 546). The work of Catholic exegetes "who correctly use the intellectual weapons employed by their adversaries" (562) has borne its fruit. It is for this very reason that *Divino afflante Spiritu* seems less concerned than *Providentissimus Deus* to fight against the positions of rationalistic exegesis.

5. However, it became necessary to respond to attacks coming from the supporters of a so-called "mystical" exegesis (*EB*, 552), who sought to have the Magisterium condemn the efforts of scientific exegesis. How did the Encyclical respond? It could have limited itself to stressing the usefulness and even the necessity of these efforts for defending the faith, which would have favoured a kind of dichotomy between scientific exegesis, intended for external use, and spiritual interpretation, reserved for internal use. In *Divino afflante Spiritu*, Pius XII deliberately avoided this approach. On the contrary, he vindicated the close unity of the two approaches, on the one hand emphasizing the "theological" significance of the literal sense, methodically defined (*EB*, 551), and on the other, asserting that, to be recognized as the sense of a biblical text, the spiritual sense must offer proof of its authenticity. A merely subjective inspiration is insufficient. One must be able to show that it is a sense "willed by God himself", a spiritual meaning "given by God" to the inspired text (*EB*, 552-553). Determining the spiritual sense then, belongs itself to the realm of exegetical science.

Thus we note that, despite the great difference in the difficulties they had to face, the two Encyclicals are in complete agreement at the deepest level. Both of them reject a split between the human and the divine, between scientific research and respect for the faith, between the literal sense and the spiritual sense. They thus appear to be in perfect harmony with the mystery of the incarnation.

## II. The Harmony between Catholic Exegesis and the Mystery of the Incarnation

6. The strict relationship uniting the inspired biblical texts with the mystery of the incarnation was expressed by the Encyclical *Divino afflante Spiritu* in the following terms: "Just as the substantial Word of God became like men in every respect except sin, so too the words of God, expressed in human languages, became like human language in every respect except error" (*EB*, 559). Repeated almost literally by the conciliar Constitution *Dei Verbum* (13), this statement sheds light on a parallelism rich in meaning.

It is true that putting God's words into writing, through the charism of scriptural inspiration, was the first step towards the incarnation of the Word of God. These written words, in fact, were an abiding means of communication and communion between the chosen people and their one Lord. On the other hand, it is because of the prophetic aspect of these words that it was possible to recognize the fulfilment of God's plan when "the Word became flesh and made his dwelling among us" (*Jn* 1:14). After the heavenly glorification of the humanity of the Word made flesh, it is again due to written words that his stay among us is attested to in an abiding way. Joined to the inspired writings of the first covenant, the inspired writings of the new covenant are a verifiable means of communication and communion between the believing people and God, the Father, Son and Holy Spirit. This means certainly can never be separated from the stream of spiritual life that flows from the Heart of Jesus crucified and which spreads through the Church's sacraments. It has nevertheless its own consistency precisely as a written text which verifies it.

7. Consequently, the two Encyclicals require that Catholic exegetes remain in full harmony with the mystery of the incarnation, a mystery of the union of the divine and the human in a determinate historical life. The earthly life of Jesus is not defined only by the places and dates at the beginning of the first century in Judea and Galilee, but also by his deep roots in the long history of a small nation of the ancient Near East, with its weaknesses and its greatness, with its men of God and its sinners, with its slow cultural evolution and its political misadventures, with its defeats and its victories, with its longing for peace and the kingdom of God. The Church of Christ takes the realism of the incarnation seriously, and this is why she attaches great importance to the "historico-critical" study of the Bible. Far from condemning it, as those who support "mystical" exegesis would want, my Predecessors vigorously approved. "Artis criticae disciplinam", Leo XIII wrote, "quippe percipiendae penitus hagiographorum sententiae perutilem, *Nobis vehementer probantibus*, nostri (exegetae, scilicet, catholici) excolant" (Apostolic Letter *Vigilantiae*, establishing the Biblical Commission, 30 October 1902: *EB*, 142). The same "vehemence" in the approval and the same adverb ("vehementer") are found in *Divino afflante Spiritu* regarding research in textual criticism (cf. *EB*, 548).

8. *Divino afflante Spiritu*, we know, particularly recommended that exegetes study the *literary genres* used in the Sacred Books, going so far as to say that Catholic exegesis must "be convinced that this part of its task cannot be neglected without serious harm to Catholic exegesis" (*EB*, 560). This recommendation starts from the concern to understand the meaning of the texts with all the accuracy and precision possible and, thus, in their historical, cultural context. A false idea of God and the incarnation presses a certain number of Christians to take the opposite approach. They tend to believe that, since God is the absolute Being, each of his words has an absolute value, independent of all the conditions of human language. Thus, according to them, there is no room for studying these conditions in order to make distinctions that would relativize the significance of the words. However, that is where the illusion occurs and the mysteries of scriptural inspiration and the incarnation are really rejected, by clinging to a false notion of the Absolute. The God of the Bible is not an absolute Being who, crushing everything he touches, would suppress all differences

and all nuances. On the contrary, he is God the Creator, who created the astonishing variety of beings "each according to its kind", as the Genesis account says repeatedly (*Gn* 1). Far from destroying differences, God respects them and makes use of them (cf. *1 Cor* 12:18, 24, 28). Although he expresses himself in human language he does not give each expression a uniform value, but uses its possible nuances with extreme flexibility and likewise accepts its limitations. That is what makes the task of exegetes so complex, so necessary and so fascinating! None of the human aspects of language can be neglected. The recent progress in linguistic, literary and hermeneutical research have led biblical exegesis to add many other points of view (rhetorical, narrative, structuralist) to the study of literary genres; other human sciences, such as psychology and sociology, have likewise been employed. To all this one can apply the charge which Leo XIII gave the members of the Biblical Commission: "Let them consider nothing that the diligent research of modern scholars will have newly found as foreign to their realm; quite the contrary, let them be alert to adopt without delay anything useful that each period brings to biblical exegesis" (*Vigilantiae: EB*, 140). Studying the human circumstances of the word of God should be pursued with ever renewed interest.

9. Nevertheless, this study is not enough. In order to respect the coherence of the Church's faith and of scriptural inspiration, Catholic exegesis must be careful not to limit itself to the human aspects of the biblical texts. First and foremost, it must help the Christian people more clearly perceive the word of God in these texts so that they can better accept them in order to live in full communion with God. To this end it is obviously necessary that the exegete himself perceive the divine word in the texts. He can do this only if his intellectual work is sustained by a vigorous spiritual life.

Without this support, exegetical research remains incomplete; it loses sight of its main purpose and is confined to secondary tasks. It can even become a sort of escape. Scientific study of the merely human aspects of the texts can make the exegete forget that the word of God invites each person to come out of himself to live in faith and love.

On this point the Encyclical *Providentissimus Deus* recalls the special nature of the Sacred Books and their consequent need for interpretation: "The Sacred Books", he said "cannot be likened to ordinary writings, but, since they have been dictated by the Holy Spirit himself and have extremely serious contents, mysterious and difficult in many respects, we always need, in order to understand and explain them, the coming of the same Holy Spirit, that is, his light and grace, which must certainly be sought in humble prayer and preserved by a life of holiness" (*EB*, 89). In a shorter formula, borrowed from St Augustine, *Divino afflante Spiritu* expressed the same requirement: "Orent ut intelligant!" (*EB*, 569).

Indeed, to arrive at a completely valid interpretation of words inspired by the Holy Spirit, one must first be guided by the Holy Spirit and it is necessary to pray for that, to pray much, to ask in prayer for the interior light of the Spirit and docilely accept that light, to ask for the love that alone enables one to understand the language of God, who "is love" (*1 Jn* 4:8, 16). While engaged in the very work of interpretation, one must remain in the presence of God as much as possible.

10. Docility to the Holy Spirit produces and reinforces another attitude needed for the correct orientation of exegesis: fidelity to the Church. The Catholic exegete does not entertain the individualist illusion leading to the belief that one can better understand the biblical texts outside the community of believers. The contrary is true, for these texts have not been given to individual researchers "to satisfy their curiosity or provide them with subjects for study and research" (*Divino afflante Spiritu: EB*, 566); they have been entrusted to the community of believers, to the Church of Christ, in order to nourish faith and guide the life of charity. Respect for this purpose conditions the validity of the interpretation. *Providentissimus Deus* recalled this basic truth and observed that, far from hampering biblical research, respect for this fact fosters its authentic progress (cf *EB*, 108-109). It is comforting to note that recent studies in hermeneutical philosophy have confirmed this point of view and that exegetes of various confessions have worked from similar perspectives by stressing, for example, the need to interpret each biblical text as part of the scriptural canon recognized by the Church, or by being more attentive to the contributions of patristic exegesis.

Being faithful to the Church, in fact, means resolutely finding one's place in the mainstream of the great Tradition that, under the guidance of the Magisterium, assured of the Holy Spirit's special assistance, has recognized the canonical writings as the word addressed by God to his people and has never ceased meditating on them and discovering their inexhaustible riches. The Second Vatican Council asserted this again: "All that has been said about the manner of interpreting Scripture is ultimately subject to the judgment of the Church, which exercises the divinely conferred commission and ministry of watching over and interpreting the word of God" (*Dei Verbum*, 12).

It is nevertheless true — the Council also states this, repeating an assertion of *Providentissimus Deus* — that it "is the task of exegetes to work, according to these rules, towards a better understanding and explanation of the meaning of Sacred Scripture in order that their research may help the Church to form a firmer judgment" (*Dei Verbum*, 12; cf. *Providentissimus Deus: EB*, 109: "ut, quasi praeparato studio, iudicium Ecclesiae maturetur").

11. In order better to carry out this very important ecclesial task,

exegetes will be keen to remain close to the preaching of God's word, both
by devoting part of their time to this ministry and by maintaining relations
with those who exercise it and helping them with publications of pastoral
exegesis (cf. *Divino afflante Spiritu: EB*, 551). Thus they will avoid becoming lost in the complexities of abstract scientific research which dis-
tances them from the true meaning of the Scriptures. Indeed, this meaning
is inseparable from their goal, which is to put believers into a personal
relationship with God.

### III. The New Document of the Biblical Commission

12. In these perspectives, *Providentissimus Deus* stated, "a vast field
of research is open to the personal work of each exegete" (*EB*, 109). Fifty
years later, *Divino afflante Spiritu* again made the same encouraging
observation: "There are still many points, some very important, in the
discussion and explanation of which the intellectual penetration and talent
of Catholic exegetes can and should be freely exercised" (*EB*, 565).

What was true in 1943 remains so even in our day, for advances in
research have produced solutions to certain problems and, at the same
time, new questions to be studied. In exegesis, as in other sciences, the
more one pushes back the limits of the unknown, the more one enlarges
the area to be explored. Less than five years after the publication of *Divino afflante Spiritu*, the discovery of the Qumran scrolls shed the light of
a new day on a great number of biblical problems and opened up other
fields of research. Since then, many discoveries have been made and new
methods of investigation and analysis have been perfected.

13. It is this changed situation that has made a new examination of
the problems necessary. The Pontifical Biblical Commission has worked
on this task and today presents the fruit of its work, entitled *L'interprétation de la Bible dans l'Église*.

What is striking on first reading this document is the *spirit of openness*
in which it was conceived. The methods, approaches and interpretations
practised today in exegesis have been examined and, despite occasionally
serious reservations which must be stated, one acknowledges in almost
every case, the presence of valid elements for an integral interpretation of
the biblical text.

For Catholic exegesis does not have its own exclusive method of interpretation, but starting with the historico-critical basis freed from its
philosophical presuppositions or those contrary to the truth of our faith, it
makes the most of all the current methods by seeking in each of them the
"seeds of the Word".

14. Another characteristic feature of this synthesis is its *balance and
moderation*. In its interpretation of the Bible, it knows how to harmonize

the diachronic and the synchronic by recognizing that the two are mutually complementary and indispensable for bringing out all the truth of the text and for satisfying the legitimate demands of the modern reader.

Even more importantly, Catholic exegesis does not focus its attention on only the human aspects of biblical Revelation, which is sometimes the mistake of the historico-critical method, or on only the divine aspects, as fundamentalism would have it; it strives to highlight both of them as they are united in the divine "condescension" (*Dei Verbum*, 13), which is the basis of all Scripture.

15. Lastly, one will perceive the document's stress on the fact that *the biblical Word is at work speaking universally, in time and space*, to all humanity. If "the words of God... are like human language" (*Dei Verbum*, 13), it is so that they may be understood by all. They must not remain distant, "too mysterious and remote for you.... For the word is very near to you, already in your mouths and in your hearts; you have only to carry it out" (*Dt* 30:11, 14).

This is the aim of biblical interpretation. If the first task of exegesis is to arrive at the authentic sense of the sacred text or even at its different senses, it must then communicate this meaning to the recipient of Sacred Scripture, who is every human person, if possible.

The Bible exercises its influence down the centuries. A constant process of actualization adapts the interpretation to the contemporary mentality and language. The concrete, immediate nature of biblical language greatly facilitates this adaptation, but its origin in an ancient culture causes not a few difficulties. Therefore, biblical thought must always be translated anew into contemporary language so that it may be expressed in ways suited to its listeners. This translation, however, should be faithful to the original and cannot force the texts in order to accommodate an interpretation or an approach fashionable at a given time. The word of God must appear in all its splendour, even if it is "expressed in human words" (*Dei Verbum*, 13).

Today the Bible has spread to every continent and every nation. However, in order for it to have a profound effect, there must be *inculturation* according to the genius proper to each people. Perhaps nations less marked by the deviances of modern Western civilization will understand the biblical message more easily than those who are already insensitive as it were to the action of God's word because of secularization and the excesses of demythologization.

In our day, a great effort is necessary, not only on the part of scholars and preachers, but also those who popularize biblical thought: they should use every means possible — and there are many today — so that the universal significance of the biblical message may be widely acknowledged and its saving efficacy may be seen everywhere.

Thanks to this document, the interpretation of the Bible in the Church will be able to obtain new vigour for the good of the whole world, so that the truth may shine forth and stir up charity on the threshold of the third millennium.

## Conclusion

16. Finally, I have the joy of being able, as were my Predecessors, Leo XIII and Pius XII, to offer to Catholic exegetes, and in particular, to you, the members of the Pontifical Biblical Commission, both my thanks and encouragement.

I cordially thank you for the excellent work you have accomplished in service to the word of God and the People of God: a work of research, teaching and publication; an aid to theology, to the liturgy of the word and to the ministry of preaching; initiatives fostering ecumenism and good relations between Christians and Jews; involvement in the Church's efforts to respond to the aspirations and difficulties of the modern world.

To this I add my warm encouragement for the next step to be taken. The increasing complexity of the task requires everyone's effort and a broad interdisciplinary cooperation. In a world where scientific research is taking on greater importance in many domains, it is indispensable for exegetical science to find its place at a comparable level. It is one of the aspects of inculturating the faith which is part of the Church's mission in connection with accepting the mystery of the incarnation.

May you be guided in your research by Jesus Christ, the incarnate Word of God, who opened the minds of his disciples to the understanding of the Scriptures (*Lk* 24:45). May the Virgin Mary serve as a model for you not only by her generous docility to the word of God, but also and especially by her way of accepting what was said to her! St Luke tells us that Mary reflected in her heart on the divine words and the events that took place, "*symbállousa en tê kardía autês*" (*Lk* 2:19). By welcoming the Word she is the model and mother of disciples (cf. *Jn* 19:27). Therefore, may she teach you fully to accept the word of God, not only in intellectual research but also with your whole life!

In order that your work and your activity may make the light of the Scriptures shine ever more brightly, I wholeheartedly give you my Apostolic Blessing.

PONTIFICAL BIBLICAL COMMISSION

# THE INTERPRETATION OF THE BIBLE IN THE CHURCH

# PREFACE
## TO THE BIBLICAL COMMISSION DOCUMENT

The study of the Bible is, as it were, the soul of theology, as the Second Vatican Council says, borrowing a phrase from Pope Leo XIII (*Dei Verbum*, 24). This study is never finished; each age must in its own way newly seek to understand the sacred books. In the history of interpretation the rise of the historical-critical method opened a new era. With it, new possibilities for understanding the biblical word in its originality opened up. Just as with all human endeavor, though, so also this method contained hidden dangers along with its positive possibilities: the search for the original can lead to putting the word back into the past completely so that it is no longer taken in its actuality. It can result that only the human dimension of the word appears as real, while the genuine author, God, is removed from the reach of a method which was established for understanding human reality. The application of a "profane" method to the Bible necessarily led to discussion. Everything that helps us better to understand the truth and to appropriate its representations is helpful and worthwhile for theology. It is in this sense that we must seek how to use this method in theological research. Everything that shrinks our horizon and hinders us from seeing and hearing beyond that which is merely human must be opened up. Thus the emergence of the historical-critical method set in motion at the same time a struggle over its scope and over its proper configuration which is by no means finished as yet.

In this struggle the teaching office of the Catholic Church has taken up positions several times. First, Pope Leo XIII, in his encyclical *Providentissimus Deus* of 18 November 1893, plotted out some markers on the exegetical map. At a time when liberalism was extremely sure of itself and much too intrusively dogmatic, Leo XIII was forced to express himself in a rather critical way, even though he did not exclude that which was positive from the new possibilities. Fifty years later, however, because of the fertile work of great Catholic exegetes, Pope Pius XII, in his encyclical *Divino afflante Spiritu* of 30 September 1943, was able to provide largely positive encouragement toward making the modern methods of understanding the Bible fruitful. The constitution on divine revelation of the Second Vatican Council, *Dei Verbum*, of 18 November 1965, adopted all of this. It provided us with a synthesis, which substantially remains, between the lasting insights of patristic theology and the new methodological understanding of the moderns.

In the meantime, this methodological spectrum of exegetical work has broadened in a way which could not have been envisioned thirty years ago. New methods and new approaches have appeared, from structuralism to materialistic, psychoanalytic and liberation exegesis. On the other hand, there are also new attempts to recover patristic exegesis and to include renewed forms of a spiritual interpretation of scripture. Thus the Pontifical Biblical Commission took as its task an attempt to take the bearings of Catholic exegesis in the present situation one hundred years after *Providentissimus Deus* and fifty years after *Divino afflante Spiritu*. The Pontifical Biblical Commission, in its new form after the Second Vatican Council, is not an organ of the teaching office, but rather a commission of scholars who, in their scientific and ecclesial responsibility as believing exegetes, take positions on important problems of scriptural interpretation and know that for this task they enjoy the confidence of the teaching office. Thus the present document was established. It contains a well-grounded overview of the panorama of present-day methods and in this way offers to the inquirer an orientation to the possibilities and limits of these approaches. Accordingly, the text of the document inquires into how the meaning of scripture might become known — this meaning in which the human word and God's word work together in the singularity of historical events and the eternity of the everlasting Word which is contemporary in every age. The biblical word comes from a real past. It comes not only from the past, however, but at the same time from the eternity of God and it leads us into God's eternity, but again along the way through time, to which the past, the present and the future belong. I believe that this document is very helpful for the important questions about the right way of understanding Holy Scripture, and that it also helps us to go further. It takes up the paths of the encyclicals of 1893 and 1943 and advances them in a fruitful way. I would like to thank the members of the Biblical Commission for the patient and frequently laborious struggle in which this text grew little by little. I hope that the document will have a wide circulation so that it becomes a genuine contribution to the search for a deeper assimilation of the word of God in Holy Scritpure.

Rome, on the feast of St. Matthew the Evangelist 1993.

JOSEPH Cardinal RATZINGER

# THE INTERPRETATION OF THE BIBLE IN THE CHURCH
## TEXT

## INTRODUCTION

The interpretation of biblical texts continues in our own day to be a matter of lively interest and significant debate. In recent years the discussions involved have taken on some new dimensions. Granted the fundamental importance of the Bible for Christian faith, for the life of the Church and for relations between Christians and the faithful of other religions, the Pontifical Biblical Commission has been asked to make a statement on this subject.

### A. The State of the Question Today

The problem of the interpretation of the Bible is hardly a modern phenomenon, even if at times that is what some would have us believe. The Bible itself bears witness that its interpretation can be a difficult matter. Alongside texts that are perfectly clear, it contains passages of some obscurity. When reading certain prophecies of Jeremiah, Daniel pondered

---

## THE INTERPRETATION OF THE BIBLE IN THE CHURCH
### COMMENTARY

The Introduction of the document, *The Interpretation of the Bible in the Church*, sets forth two things, the state of the question today (A), and the purpose of the document (B).

Section A seeks to explain why the Bible, a monument of world culture and a highly esteemed piece of world literature, needs to be interpreted or explained for readers of today. Even for those who reckon with the Bible as the Word of God couched in human language, it is a

at length over their meaning (*Dn* 9:2). According to the Acts of the Apostles, an Ethiopian of the first century found himself in the same situation with respect to a passage from the book of Isaiah (*Isa* 53:7-8) and recognized that he had need of an interpreter (*Acts* 8:30-35). The Second Letter of Peter insists that "no prophecy of Scripture is a matter of private interpretation" (*2 Pet* 1:20) and it also observes that the letters of the Apostle Paul contain "some difficult pasages, the meaning of which the ignorant and untrained distort, as they do also in the case of the other Scriptures, to their own ruin" (*2 Pet* 3:16).

The problem is, therefore, quite old. But it has been accentuated with

---

collection of writings not composed in the wording of today. It came into being during more than a millennium, and its final redaction took place almost two thousand years ago. No matter how well it is translated into modern vernaculars, it still remains a book conceived and composed in ancient times. Hence it calls for modern readers to retroject themselves in time for a proper comprehension of it, even though it is still meant to bring God's word to them today. The tension that exists between what it meant and what it means, between its ancient composition and its present destination creates the difficulty of understanding it.

Passages in the Bible itself at times reveal this very difficulty. The Biblical Commission singles out a few of them. For instance, the prophet Daniel tells of his attempt to understand "the counting of the years of which the Lord spoke to the prophet Jeremiah: 'for the ruin of Jerusalem seventy years must pass'" (Dan 9:2). Daniel alludes to the oracles found in Jer 25:11-12 and 29:10[3], undoubtedly uttered shortly before the destruction of Jerusalem in 587 B.C. Centuries later Daniel puzzled over the meaning of the number of those years.

Similarly, when the Ethiopian eunuch of Candace, who was reading about the Servant of Yahweh in Isa 53:7-8, was asked by Philip the evangelist whether he understood what he was reading, he exclaimed, "How can I, unless someone guides me?" (Acts 8:31). Again, early Christians recognized that the Pauline corpus of letters contains "things hard to understand which the uneducated and untrained distort, as they do the other Scriptures, to their own detriment" (2 Pet 3:16). If that were

---

[3] Jer 25:11-12: "This whole land shall become a desert and a ruin; for seventy years shall these nations be enslaved to the king of Babylon. But when the seventy years have passed, I will punish the king of Babylon, the nation and land of the Chaldeans for their guilt". Jer 29:10: "Only after seventy years have passed for Babylon will I visit you and fulfill my promise to bring you back to this place".

the passage of time. Readers today, in order to appropriate the words and deeds of which the Bible speaks, have to project themselves back almost twenty or thirty centuries — a process which always creates difficulty. Furthermore, because of the progress made in the human sciences, questions of interpretation have become more complex in modern times. Scientific methods have been adopted for the study of the texts of the ancient world. To what extent can these methods be considered appropriate for the interpretation of Holy Scripture? For a long period the Church in her

the case in days of old, how much more so in our day, millennia later!

With the passage of centuries new events and new factors have conditioned the understanding of the Bible. It is not that God's revelation contained in it has changed, but the reception of that revelation is conditioned by changes in human life. The progress made in human sciences, e.g. in archaeology, astronomy, biology, history, linguistics, philology, psychology, and sociology, have shed new light on the meaning of the Bible. All of this calls for developing modes of interpretation. As the people of God grows in the comprehension of the divine revelation couched in the Bible, that comprehension is conditioned by all such changes.

During the last century the Roman Catholic Church has on various occasions given guidance to the faithful to help them in the reading, study, and use of the Bible in their spiritual lives[4]. This new document of the Biblical Commission comes, then, on the heels of other important Church writings, some of which are mentioned by the Commission.

The present document, issued on 18 November 1993, commemorates the hundredth anniversary of the encyclical of Pope Leo XIII, *Providentissimus Deus*[5]. That encyclical responded in part to problems that were

---

[4] For a survey of the Church's dealings with Scripture in the last century, see P. Laghi, M. Gilbert, and A. Vanhoye, *Chiesa e Sacra Scrittura: Un secolo di magistero ecclesiastico e studi biblici* (SubBib 17; Rome: Biblical Institute, 1994).

[5] See *ASS* 26 (1893-94) 269-92; *EB* §81-134; *RSS* §81-134. Cf. M. Gilbert, "Cinquant'anni di magistero romano sull'ermeneutica biblica: Leone XIII (1893) - Pio XII (1943)", *Chiesa e Sacra Scrittura* (n. 4 above), 11-33; S. M. Brandi, *La questione biblica e l'Enciclica "Providentissimus Deus" di S. S. Leone XIII* (Rome: Civiltà Cattolica, 1894); F. Spadafora, *Leone XIII e gli studi biblici* (Rovigo: Istituto Padano di Arti Grafiche, 1976); A. C. Cotter, "The Antecedents of the Encyclical *Providentissimus Deus*", *CBQ* 5 (1943) 117-24; R. T. Murphy, "The Teachings of the Encyclical *Providentissimus Deus*", ibid., 125-40; S. Hartdegen, "The Influence of the Encyclical *Providentissimus Deus* on Subsequent Scripture Study", ibid., 141-59. For other commentaries on this encyclical, see M. Claudia Carlen, *A Guide to the Encyclicals of the Roman Pontiffs from Leo XIII to the Present Day (1878-1937)* (New York: Wilson, 1939) 90-91.

pastoral prudence showed herself very reticent in responding to this question, for often the methods, despite their positive elements, have shown themselves to be wedded to positions hostile to the Christian faith. But a more positive attitude has also evolved, signaled by a whole series of pontifical documents, ranging from the encyclical *Providentissimus Deus* of Leo XIII (Nov. 18, 1893) to the encyclical *Divino Afflante Spiritu* of Pius XII (Sept. 30, 1943) and this has been confirmed by the Declaration *Sancta Mater Ecclesia* of the Pontifical Biblical Commission (April 21, 1964) and above all by the Dogmatic Constitution *Dei Verbum* of the Second Vatican Council (Nov. 18, 1965).

That this more constructive attitude has borne fruit cannot be denied. Biblical studies have made great progress in the Catholic Church and the academic value of these studies has been acknowledged more and more in the scholarly world and among the faithful. This has greatly smoothed the path of ecumenical dialogue. The deepening of the Bible's influence upon theology has contributed to theological renewal. Interest in the Bible has

raised by the rationalistic interpretation of the Bible in the nineteenth century and to many historical and archaeological discoveries, scientific advances, progress in textual criticism, and the comparative study of ancient religions. But Leo XIII was also moved in part by a desire "to give an impulse to the noble science of Holy Scripture and to impart to Scripture study a direction suitable to the needs of the present day"[6]. In his allocution of 23 April 1993, Pope John Paul II referred explicitly to this noteworthy encyclical of his predecessor[7].

Fifty years later Pope Pius XII composed another important encyclical on the promotion of biblical studies, *Divino afflante Spiritu*, issued on the feast of St. Jerome, 30 September 1943[8]. That writing of Pius XII was likewise occasioned by the needs of the time, but they were of a different sort. They stemmed mainly from people within the Catholic Church, especially from those who sought to steer the faithful away from the use of a critical-scientific method of interpreting the Bible toward a more

---

[6] *Providentissimus Deus*, prologue (*EB* §82; *RSS* §82).

[7] See *Osservatore Romano*, 24 April 1993, p. 1.

[8] *AAS* 35 (1943) 297-325; *EB* §538-69; *RSS* §538-69. Cf. B. Ahern, "Textual Directives of the Encyclical *Divino afflante Spiritu*", *CBQ* 7 (1945) 340-47; J. Levie, "L'Encyclique sur les études bibliques", *NRT* 68 (1946) 648-70, 766-98; G. J. Hamilton, "Divino afflante Spiritu: Catholic Interpretation of Scripture", *Canadian Catholic Review* (Saskatoon) 6 (1988) 171-76. For other commentaries on the encyclical see, M. Claudia [Carlen], *Guide to the Documents of Pius XII (1939-1949)* (Westminster, MD: Newman, 1951) 82-83 (§530).

grown amongst Catholics, with resultant progress in the Christian life. All those who have acquired a solid formation in this area consider it quite impossible to return to a precritical level of interpretation, a level which they now rightly judge to be quite inadequate.

But the fact is that at the very time when the most prevalent scientific method — the "historical-critical method" — is freely practised in exegesis, including Catholic exegesis, it is itself *brought into question*. To some extent, this has come about in the scholarly world itself, through the rise of alternative methods and approaches. But it has also arisen through the criticisms of many members of the faithful, who judge the method deficient from the point of view of faith. The historical-critical method, as its name suggests, is particularly attentive to the historical development of texts or traditions across the passage of time — that is, to all that is sum-

---

"meditative" or "spiritual" type of exegesis[9]. Pius XII's encyclical was in reality far more significant than that of Leo XIII and was, in fact, revolutionary. It set the Catholic Church on a path of Scripture interpretation that has borne great fruit. It joined the encyclical of Leo XIII in stressing both the human and the divine aspects of the Bible, as Pope John Paul II recognized in his allocution.

It is difficult, however, for us today to realize the dark cloud of reactionism that hung over the Catholic interpretation of the Bible in the first half of the twentieth century. Part of it was occasioned by the Church's general reaction to the rationalism of the nineteenth century, especially to the Modernism that developed within the Church at that time. Part of it was the result of specific Church documents that stemmed from the highest authorities in the Church, from the Pope, Sacred

---

[9] An anonymous pamphlet had been composed and sent to all the Cardinals, Archbishops, Bishops, and Superiors of Religious Congregations in Italy in 1941, entitled *Un gravissimo pericolo per la Chiesa e per le anime: Il sistema critico-scientifico nello studio e nell'interpretazione della Sacra Scrittura, le sue deviazioni funeste et le sue aberrazioni* (A Most Serious Danger for the Church and for Souls: The Critical-scientific System of Studying and Interpreting Holy Scripture, Its Evil Misconceptions and Aberrations). As is well known today, it was composed by an Italian priest, Dolindo Ruotolo, who often used the pen name Dain Cohenel. See R. F. Collins, *Introduction to the New Testament* (Garden City, NY: Doubleday, 1983) 370.

The Biblical Commission replied on 20 August 1941 with "Lettera agli arcivescovi e vescovi d'Italia", *AAS* 33 (1941) 465-72; see *EB* §522-33; *RSS* §522-33. The Commission stressed the need to interpret Scripture according to its literal sense, explained the meaning in which the Latin Vulgate was to be regarded as "authentic", and emphasized the need of textual criticism, the study of oriental languages used in the Bible, and of auxiliary sciences.

med up by the term "*diachronic*". But at the present time in certain quarters it finds itself in competition with methods which insist upon a *synchronic* understanding of texts — that is, one which has to do with their language, composition, narrative structure and capacity for persuasion. Moreover, for many interpreters the diachronic concern to reconstruct the past has given way to a tendency to ask questions of texts by viewing them within a number of contemporary perspectives — philosophical, psychoanalytic, sociological, political, etc. Some value this plurality of methods and approaches as an indication of richness, but to others it gives the impression of much confusion.

---

Congregations, and the Biblical Commission[10].

In contrast, Pius XII's encyclical of 1943 was a liberating document, which was responsible for a remarkable return of Catholics throughout the world to the Bible, to the reading and study of it, to prayer based on it, and to the feeding of their spiritual lives on the written Word of God. It was likewise a return to the Church's original heritage that had become no little neglected in the post-Tridentine Church, partly because of the emphasis put by the sixteenth-century Reformers on Scripture. Unfortunately, Pius XII issued his encyclical in the midst of World War II, when

---

[10] If we are grateful today for the encyclicals of Popes Leo XIII and Pius XII on biblical studies, we have to recall that between them there also appeared the encyclical of Pope Benedict XV, *Spiritus Paraclitus* (*AAS* 12 [1920] 385-422; *EB* §440-95; *RSS* §440-95), commemorating the fifteenth centenary of the death of St. Jerome. In its reaction to the Modernism of the early decades of this century, this encyclical developed a negative approach to Scripture, insisting on its inerrancy and, in effect, denying that one had to interpret the Bible according to its literary forms. The impact of the encyclical of Pope Benedict XV was stifling.

Between the encyclicals of Popes Leo XIII and Pius XII there was also the activity of the watchdog Biblical Commission with its *responsa*, issued over more than thirty years. They created fear and suspicion about everything connected with the Bible so that clergy and faithful alike suspected anyone who tried to interpret it as dangerous and almost unorthodox. The Apostolic Letter by which Pope Leo XIII set up the Biblical Commission was entitled *Vigilantiae* (*ASS* 35 [1902-3] 234-38; *EB* §137-48; *RSS* §137-48), a title which set the tone and summed up the work of that Commission for close to forty years. The *responsa* can be found in *EB* §160-61, 181-84, 187-89, 276-80, 324-39, 383-416, 513-20, 535-37; *RSS* §160-61, 181-84, 187-89, 276-80, 324-39, 383-416, 513-14, 535-37.

To these documents one would have to add others of the same sort that came from Popes or Roman congregations: *EB* §190-256 (*Lamentabili*), 257-67 (*Pascendi*), 268-73 (*Praestantia Scripturae*), 439s (Decree of the Holy Office on the Mosaic Authenticity of the Pentateuch), 497-504 (Decree of the Holy Office condemning a *Manuel biblique*), 512a (Monitum of the Holy Office about an Italian translation of the Bible by G. Luzzi). Cf. D.G. Schultenover, "The Church as Mediterranean Family", *America* 171/10 (8 October 1994) 9-13; P. Grelot, *Combats pour la Bible*, 17-101.

Whether real or apparent, this confusion has brought fresh fuel to the arguments of those opposed to scientific exegesis. The diversity of interpretations only serves to show, they say, that nothing is gained by submitting biblical texts to the demands of scientific method; on the contrary, they allege, much is lost thereby. They insist that the result of scientific exegesis is only to provoke perplexity and doubt upon numerous points which hitherto had been accepted without difficulty. They add that it im-

---

the minds of most people were preoccupied with things other than the Bible and its interpretation. Consequently, it took almost ten years before the impact of that encyclical was felt, and it was only about 1955 that the renewed Catholic biblical movement began to take shape[11].

That encouragement of biblical study did not cease with Pius XII. In 1964 the Biblical Commission, which had in the meantime radically changed its public image, issued a epoch-making *Instructio de historica evangeliorum veritate* (Instruction on the Historical Truth of the

[11] It was just about this time that a semi-official interpretation of the responses of the Biblical Commission was issued. When the fourth edition of the *Enchiridion Biblicum* was published in 1954, the secretary of the Biblical Commission, Athanasius Miller, O.S.B. and the subsecretary, Arduin Kleinhans, O.F.M., both reviewed it. The first-named wrote his review in German in *Benediktinische Monatschrift* 31 (1955) 49-50, and the second-named wrote in Latin in *Antonianum* 30 (1955) 63-65. But apart from the difference in language, the reviews were almost verbatim identical. The burden of the reviews was an important distinction, which the secretaries made between responses of the Biblical Commission that had treated of matters of faith and morals and those that had dealt with merely literary or historical questions. The former were said to be still valid, whereas the latter were time-conditioned and only of passing interest. In the case of the latter category Catholic exegetes were informed that they could conduct their research "with full liberty" (*in aller Freiheit, plena libertate*). Since the vast majority of the responses of the Biblical Commission in the early part of this century had been of the latter category, these reviews thus clarified that the responses were no longer in effect. This double review, then, proved to be an important clarification, which would affect the future work of all Catholic interpreters. See further J. Dupont, "A propos du nouvel Enchiridion Biblicum", *RB* 62 (1955) 414-19; E. F. Siegman, "The Decrees of the Pontifical Biblical Commission: A Recent Clarification", *CBQ* 18 (1956) 23-29. — The reader should beware of the translation of the "excerpts" of the review of Miller given in *RSS* (p. 175), where the obscurantist editor suppressed the all-important phrase "with full liberty". It should read: "As long as these [early Biblical Commission] decrees propose views that are neither immediately nor mediately connected with truths of faith and morals, the interpreter of Sacred Scripture can pursue his scientific research with full liberty and accept the results of these investigations, provided always that he respects the teaching authority of the Church". The suppression of that phrase speaks eloquently of the mentality of the ultra-right wing among American Catholic interpreters of that period, who were afraid to envisage the possibility that the Roman Catholic Church was liberalizing its stand on the interpretation of Scripture.

pels some exegetes to adopt positions contrary to the faith of the Church on matters of great importance, such as the virginal conception of Jesus and his miracles, and even his resurrection and divinity.

Even when it does not end up in such negative positions, scientific exegesis, they claim, is notable for its sterility in what concerns progress in the Christian life. Instead of making for easier and more secure access to the living sources of God's Word, it makes of the Bible a closed book. Interpretation may always have been something of a problem, but now it requires such technical refinements as to render it a domain reserved for a few specialists alone. To the latter some apply the phrase of the gospel: "You have taken away the key of knowledge; you have not entered in yourselves, and you have hindered those who sought to enter" (*Luke* 11:52; cf. *Matt* 23:13).

As a result, in place of the patient toil of scientific exegesis, they think it necessary to substitute simpler approaches, such as one or other of the various forms of synchronic reading which may be considered appropri-

---

Gospels)[12]. That Instruction was noteworthy, not only for its implicit recommendation of the historical-critical method of interpretation and its explicit espousal of form criticism, but also for its distinction of the three stages of the gospel tradition. For one has to reckon with: Stage I, what Jesus of Nazareth actually did and said (roughly corresponding to A.D. 1-33); Stage II, what the disciples and apostles preached about what Jesus did and taught (corresponding to A.D. 33-65); and Stage III, what the evangelists culled from that preaching, explicated, synthesized, and ordered in view of their religious and literary ends (corresponding to A.D. 65-95). Significantly, the Commission did not identify Stage III with Stage I in any naive or fundamentalistic way.

What the Commission spelled out in considerable detail in that Instruction was picked up by the Second Vatican Council. In its dogmatic constitution, *Dei Verbum*, it gave a succinct résumé of the Commission's teaching in paragraph 19[13], which begins with the words "Sancta Mater

---

[12] "Sancta Mater Ecclesia", *AAS* 56 (1964) 712-18; *EB* §644-59. An English translation of the Instruction, distributed by the Commission itself, can be found in *CBQ* 26 (1964) 305-12; *Tablet* (London) 218 (30 May 1964) 617-19; *TBT* 13 (1964) 821-28. My own translation, along with a commentary on the text, is given in an appendix to *A Christological Catechism: New Testament Answers: New Revised and Expanded Edition* (New York/Mahwah, NJ: Paulist, 1991) 119-62.

[13] *AAS* 58 (1966) 826-27; *EB* §698. Cf. W. M. Abbott (ed.), *The Documents of Vatican II* (New York: Herder and Herder/Association Press, 1966) 124; J. A. Fitzmyer, *A Christological Catechism* (n. 12 above), 163-64.

ate. Some even, turning their backs upon all study, advocate a so-called "spiritual" reading of the Bible, by which they understand a reading guided solely by personal inspiration — one that is subjective — and intended only to nourish such inspiration. Some seek above all to find in the Bible the Christ of their own personal vision and, along with it, the satisfaction of their own spontaneous religious feelings. Others claim to find

---

Ecclesia", so that no one could miss the reference to the text of the Commission, which had been officially so entitled.

These are the four Church writings to which the new document of the Biblical Commission explicitly refers: the encyclicals of Leo XIII and Pius XII, the Commission's Instruction of 1964, and the Council's use of it in *Dei Verbum*. They have resulted in the "more constructive attitude" toward the Bible that has prevailed among Catholics in recent decades.

The Introduction also acknowledges "the historical-critical method" to be "the most prevalent scientific method" in use in the Church and among Catholic interpreters today. Later on in the document the Commission will explain this method in some detail, but here in the Introduction it merely mentions it and notes some of the problems that it has evoked: the turning of readers to other approaches to the Bible (literary, narrative, psychological, rhetorical, or sociological), the preference of some for a synchronic understanding of the biblical text[14], a judgment that the method is deficient or sterile from the viewpoint of faith, and the criticism that it even leads some interpreters to adopt positions contrary to the faith of the Church. There have also been calls for a simpler mode of interpretation, for a so-called spiritual reading of the Bible, and even for the recognition of a personal, subjective reading of it, one that would enable people "to find in the Bible the Christ of their own personal vision". Because this situation has at times engendered confusion and conflict[15], the Commission has judged it wise to address itself to the

---

[14] The Commission calls the historical-critical method "diachronic", which means a method that describes features of a text that change or develop *over the course of time* (*dia* + *chronos*). It is contrasted with a method that is "synchronic", which describes the complex of features of a text that exist *at a given time* (like the present) and ignores its historic antecedents (*syn* + *chronos*). "Diachronic" is thus concerned with the past and with historical aspects of a document, whereas "synchronic" deals with the present state of a given document.

[15] See M. Lefébure (ed.), *Conflicting Ways of Interpreting the Bible* (Concilium 138; New York: Seabury; Edinburgh: Clark, 1980), which describes many modes of biblical interpretation. Cf. J. C. O'Neill and W. Baird, "Biblical Criticism", *ABD* 1. 258-62; J. W. Rogerson and W. G. Jeanrond, "Interpretation, History of", *ABD* 3. 424-43.

there immediate answers to all kinds of questions, touching both their own lives and that of the community. There are, moreover, numerous sects which propose as the only way of interpretation one that has been revealed to them alone.

## B. The Purpose of This Document

It is, then, appropriate to give serious consideration to the various aspects of the present situation as regards the interpretation of the Bible — to attend to the criticisms and the complaints, as also to the hopes and aspirations which are being expressed in this matter, to assess the possibilities opened up by the new methods and approaches and, finally, to try to determine more precisely the direction which best corresponds to the mission of exegesis in the Catholic Church.

Such is the purpose of this document. The Pontifical Biblical Commission desires to indicate the paths most appropriate for arriving at an interpretation of the Bible as faithful as possible to its character both human and divine. The Commission does not aim to adopt a position on all the questions which arise with respect to the Bible — such as, for example, the theology of inspiration. What it has in mind is to examine all the methods likely to contribute effectively to the task of making more available the riches contained in the biblical texts. The aim is that the Word of God may become more and more the spiritual nourishment of the members of the People of God, the source for them of a life of faith, of hope and of love — and indeed a light for all humanity (cf. *Dei Verbum*, 21).

To accomplish this goal, the present document:

1. will give a brief description of the various methods and approaches[1], indicating the possibilities they offer and their limitations;

2. will examine certain questions of a hermeneutical nature;

---

[1] By an exegetical "method" we understand a group of scientific procedures employed in order to explain texts. We speak of an "approach" when it is a question of an enquiry proceeding from a particular point of view.

---

proper interpretation of the Bible in the Church.

Section B of the Introduction states the purpose of the document. The Commission does not intend to discuss all aspects of the Bible, but rather "to indicate the paths most appropriate for arriving at an interpretation of the Bible as faithful as possible to its character both human and divine" and "to examine all the methods likely to contribute effectively to the task of making more available the riches" of the written Word of God.

3. will reflect upon the aspects which may be considered characteristic of a Catholic interpretation of the Bible and upon its relationship with other theological disciplines;

4. will consider, finally, the place interpretation of the Bible has in the life of the Church.

---

To achieve this end, the Commission lists the four parts of its document: (I) Methods and Approaches for Interpretation; (II) Hermeneutical Questions; (III) Characteristics of Catholic Interpretation; and (IV) Interpretation of the Bible in the Life of the Church.

# I. METHODS AND APPROACHES FOR INTERPRETATION

## A. The Historical-Critical Method

The historical-critical method is the indispensable method for the scientific study of the meaning of ancient texts. Holy Scripture, inasmuch as it is the "Word of God in human language", has been composed by human authors in all its various parts and in all the sources that lie behind them. Because of this, its proper understanding not only admits the use of this method but actually requires it.

### 1. *History of the Method*

For a correct understanding of this method as currently employed, a glance over its history will be of assistance. Certain elements of this

---

# I. METHODS AND APPROACHES FOR INTERPRETATION

## A. The Historical-Critical Method

The Commission regards the historical-critical method as "indispensable" for ascertaining the meaning of ancient texts. The Bible, being the Word of God set forth in ancient human language, "not only admits the use of this method but requires it". In explanation of this fundamental position, the Commission sketches the history of the method, considers its principles, describes the method, and gives an evaluation of it.

### 1. *History of the Method*

Elements of the historical-critical method were developed by Greek philologians and commentators on the writings of Homer and other Greek

method of interpretation are very ancient. They were used in antiquity by Greek commentators of classical literature and, much later, in the course of the Patristic period, by authors such as Origen, Jerome and Augustine. The method at that time was much less developed. Its modern forms are the result of refinements brought about especially since the time of the Renaissance humanists and their *recursus ad fontes* (return to the sources). The *textual criticism* of the New Testament was able to be developed as a scientific discipline only from about 1800 onwards, after its link with the *Textus receptus* was severed. But the beginnings of *literary criticism* go back to the seventeenth century, to the work of Richard Simon, who drew attention to the doublets, discrepancies in content and differences of style observable in the Pentateuch — discoveries not easy to

---

classics, especially by the scholars of the Alexandrian Library of the Ptolemaic period[16]. They sought to establish the best text of Homer's *Iliad* and *Odyssey*, analyzed their structures, and wrote scholia on their texts.

The methodology of the Alexandrians was adopted by Origen, who applied it to the study of the Hebrew and Greek forms of the Old Testament. In this regard, Origen's *Hexapla* remains a monument to his critical endeavors[17]. This kind of critical study of the Scriptures was continued by

---

[16] See H. I. Marrou, *A History of Education in Antiquity* (London: Sheed and Ward; New York: Mentor, 1956) 160-216, esp. 165-75; R. Pfeiffer, *History of Classical Scholarship from the Beginnings to the End of the Hellenistic Age* (Oxford: Clarendon, 1968) 87-279.

Two directors of the Alexandrian Library were outstanding in this regard: Zenodotus of Ephesus (b. ca. 325 B.C.) and Aristarchus of Samothrace (217-145 B.C.). See H. Browne, *Handbook of Homeric Study* (London/New York: Longmans, Green, 1905) 32-37; J. L. Myres, *Homer and His Critics* (London: Routledge & Kegan Paul, 1958) 13-17. Cf. M. H. van der Valk, *Researches on the Text and Scholia of the Iliad* (2 vols.; Leiden: Brill, 1963-64); T. W. Allen, *The Homeric Scholia* (London: Milford, 1931); H. Erbse, *Scholia graeca in Homeri Iliadem* (Scholia Vetera) (7 vols.; Berlin; de Gruyter, 1969-88); F. Montanari, *Studi di filologia omerica antica* (Pisa: Giardini, 1979); J. Blomqvist, "Alexandrian Science: The Case of Eratosthenes", *Studies in Hellenistic Civilization: Vol. III. Ethnicity in Hellenistic Egypt* (ed. T. E.-P. Per Bilde et al.; Aarhus: Aarhus University, 1992) 53-73.

[17] See F. Field, *Origenis Hexaplorum quae supersunt* (2 vols.; Oxford: Clarendon, 1875). Origen set out the text of the Old Testament in six columns: (1) the Hebrew text in Hebrew characters; (2) the Hebrew text transcribed in Greek characters (to give the proper pronunciation); (3) Aquila's Greek translation; (4) Symmachus's Greek translation; (5) the Septuagint; and (6) Theodotion's Greek translation. Moreover, he marked additions in the fifth column with the *obelus* (÷) and lacunae with the asterisk (✳). Cf. H. B. Swete, *An Introduction to the Old Testament in Greek* (2d ed.; Cambridge: University Press, 1902) 59-86; F. Kenyon, *Our Bible and the Ancient Manuscripts* (4th ed.; London: Eyre & Spottiswoode, 1939; repr. 1951) 57-60.

reconcile with the attribution of the entire text to Moses as single author. In the eighteenth century, Jean Astruc was still satisfied that the matter could be explained on the basis that Moses had made use of various sources (especially two principal ones) to compose the Book of Genesis. But, as time passed, biblical critics contested the Mosaic authorship of the

---

Jerome, who tells of consulting Origen's *Hexapla* in the library of Caesarea[18]. Jerome himself also used the method especially in his commentaries on the Prophets[19], in which he translated the Hebrew (= the Vulgate), supplied variants from the Septuagint, and discussed other Greek readings in the *Hexapla*. To such critical work on the Old Testament Jerome added his commentary and often supplied a spiritual exposition of the passage, relating it to Christ or the Church. At times, Augustine too made use of this method in his commentaries on biblical books, especially in *De Doctrina Christiana* and *De consensu evangelistarum*[20].

In the Western Church, however, the Latin Vulgate was for centuries the form of the Bible that was used by theologians and commentators. It was, however, only in the late Middle Ages and later at the Renaissance, with its emphasis on *recursus ad fontes*, that study of the neglected ancient biblical languages (Hebrew, Greek, Aramaic, and Syriac) came to the fore, and the interpretation of the Bible took on a new dimension. Then it was that the historical-critical method was refined in an important way. The Franciscan Nicholas of Lyra (1270-1340), with his knowledge of Hebrew and familiarity with Jewish commentators (especially Rashi), had contributed greatly to this critical understanding of the Old Testament in its literal sense; for he reacted strongly against the medieval allegorical

---

[18] *Commentarioli in Psalmos*, in Ps 1:4 (CCLat 72. 180).

[19] E.g., *Commentariorum in Esaiam libri I-XI* (CCLat 73 [1963]). Cf. J. N. D. Kelly, *Jerome: His Life, Writings and Controversies* (London: Duckworth, 1975); D. Brown, *Vir Trilinguis: A Study in the Biblical Exegesis of Saint Jerome* (Kampen: Kok Pharos, 1992); A. Kamesar, *Jerome, Greek Scholarship, and the Hebrew Bible: A Study of the Quaestiones Hebraicae in Genesim* (Oxford: Clarendon, 1993).

[20] See R. F. Collins, "Augustine of Hippo Precursor of Modern Biblical Scholarship", *Louvain Studies* 12 (1987) 131-51. Cf. P. Brunner, "Charismatische und methodische Schriftauslegung nach Augustins Prolog zu 'De Doctrina Christiana'", *KD* 1 (1955) 59-69, 85-103. See especially Augustine, *De Doctrina Christiana* 1.1 (CCLat 32. 6). Cf. D. W. Robertson, *On Christian Doctrine* (New York: Liberal Arts, 1958); G. Strauss, *Schriftgebrauch, Schriftauslegung und Schriftbeweis bei Augustin* (BGBH 1; Tübingen: Mohr [Siebeck], 1959).

Pentateuch with ever growing confidence. Literary criticism for a long time came to be identified with the attempt to distinguish in texts different

---

interpretations[21]. The critical work of the Renaissance humanists prepared also for the sixteenth-century Reformers. Both Martin Luther and Jean Calvin likewise reacted against the medieval allegorical interpretations of Scripture, and their efforts to translate and explain the biblical text resulted in the primacy they gave to Scripture over the Church and its traditional interpretations[22].

At the time of the Enlightenment, still further refinements were made to the method, as new modes developed of textual criticism and of what has often been called literary criticism (preferably called today source criticism). It was then that the break was made with the *Textus Receptus* of the Greek New Testament[23]. After the invention of printing by Johann Gutenberg, the Greek New Testament was soon printed, but its text was then based on inferior manuscripts easily consulted in the sixteenth and early seventeenth century. It was only with J. J. Griesbach (1745-1812) that the textual criticism of the New Testament began in earnest, as the effort was made to develop critical editions of the Greek text, based on the valuable ancient manuscripts that were gradually being uncovered[24].

The modern technique of source criticism can be traced back to the

---

[21] See his *Postillae perpetuae in universam S. Scripturam* (5 vols.; first published, Rome, 1471-72). Cf. C. Spicq, *Esquisse d'une histoire de l'exégèse latine au Moyen Age* (Bibliothèque thomiste 26; Paris: Vrin, 1944) 335-42; H. Hailperin, *Rashi and the Christian Scholars* (Pittsburgh, PA: University of Pittsburgh, 1963); E. Shereshevsky, *Rashi, the Man and His World* (New York: Sepher-Hermon, 1982).

[22] Luther especially was greatly influenced by Nicholas of Lyra. "Si Lyra non lyrasset, Lutherus non saltasset" (If Lyra had not played his lyre, Luther would not have danced). Cf. T. Kalita, *The Influence of Nicholas of Lyra on Martin Luther's Commentary on Genesis* (Washington, DC: Dissertation, The Catholic University of America, 1985); H. Bluhm, *Martin Luther: Creative Translator* (St. Louis, MO: Concordia Publishing House, 1965); D. C. Steinmetz, *The Bible in the Sixteenth Century* (Durham, NC: Duke University, 1990).

[23] See B. M. Metzger, *The Text of the New Testament: Its Transmission, Corruption, and Restoration* (3d ed.; New York/Oxford: Oxford University, 1992) 96-118 ("The Pre-Critical Period: The Origins and Dominance of the Textus Receptus"). The term "Textus Receptus" arose from the title put on a 1633 edition of the Greek New Testament published by the Elzevir Brothers of Leiden in Holland, *Textum ergo habes, nunc ab omnibus receptum: in quo nihil immutatum aut corruptum damus* (You have, then, the text received by everyone, in which we give nothing changed or corrupted). This was actually a reproduction of the Greek text published by Théodore de Bèze in 1565.

[24] See B. M. Metzger, *The Text* (n. 23 above), 119-46 ("The Modern Critical Period: From Griesbach to the Present"). The important Codex Sinaiticus was discovered by C. von Tischendorf only in 1844.

sources. Thus it was that there developed in the nineteenth century the "Documentary Hypothesis", which sought to give an explanation of the editing of the Pentateuch. According to this hypothesis, four documents, to some extent parallel with each other, had been woven together: that of

---

seventeenth century. The Commission's document still refers to it with the old, inaccurate title of "literary criticism". This technique was used first in the work of the French Oratorian, Richard Simon (1638-1712). In 1678 he published *Histoire critique du Vieux Testament* and argued from the doublets, discrepancies, and stylistic variants in the Hebrew text that Moses was not the author of the Pentateuch[25]. In the following century Jean Astruc (1684-1766) published anonymously *Conjectures sur les mémoires originaux dont il paroît que Moyse s'est servi pour composer le Livre de la Genèse*[26], in which he explained the doublets by the varying use of "Elohim" (derived from document A) and "Jehovah" (derived from document B)[27]. From these early beginnings there emerged in time the "Documentary Hypothesis", which distinguished the four sources of the Pentateuch as J (Yahwist), E (Elohist), D (Deuteronomy), and P (Priestly Code)[28].

A similar form of source criticism was likewise applied to the Synoptic Gospels in the New Testament. The discordant concord of the first three Gospels (Matthew, Mark, Luke) gave rise to various explanations of their relationship, and gradually there emerged the widely accepted "Two Document Hypothesis", which explained the Matthean and Lucan Gospels as dependent on Mark for the Triple Tradition and on a postulated Greek written source, "Q", for the Double Tradition (i.e. some 230 verses

---

[25] See J. Steinmann, *Richard Simon et les origines de l'exégèse biblique* (Bruges: Desclée de Brouwer, 1960); F. Stummer, *Die Bedeutung Richard Simons für die Pentateuchkritik* (Alttestamentliche Abhandlungen 3/4; Münster in W.: Aschendorff, 1912).

[26] The title continues with *Avec des remarques, qui appuient ou qui éclaircissent ces conjectures* (Brussels [really Paris]: Fricx, 1753; 2d ed., "Bruxelles [Paris]", 1755).

[27] Astruc spoke also of ten other fragmentary sources used in the composition of Genesis. See A. Lods, *Jean Astruc et la critique biblique au xviii<sup>e</sup> siècle...* (Cahiers de *RHPR* 11; Strasbourg: Librairie Istra, 1924); E. O'Doherty, "The *Conjectures* of Jean Astruc, 1753", *CBQ* 15 (1953) 300-304; R. de Vaux, "A propos du second centenaire d'Astruc: Réflexions sur l'état actuel de la critique du Pentateuque", *Congress Volume, Copenhagen 1953* (VTSup 1; Leiden: Brill, 1953) 182-98.

[28] The "Documentary Hypothesis" was preceded by other hypotheses, especially the Fragment Hypothesis and the Supplementary Hypothesis (see O. Eissfeldt, *The Old Testament: An Introduction* (New York/Evanston: Harper and Row, 1965) 162-63. The main contributors to the Documentary Hypothesis were H. Hupfeld, A. Dillmann, and F. Delitzsch (ibid., 164). For a summary discussion of the literary problems that led to this hypothesis, see R. E. Friedman, "Torah (Pentateuch)", *ABD* 6. 605-22, esp. 608-18.

the Yahwist (J), that of the Elohist (E), that of the Deuteronomist (D) and that of the Priestly Author (P); the final editor made use of this latter (Priestly) document to provide a structure for the whole. In similar fashion, to explain both the agreements and disagreements between the three Synoptic gospels, scholars had recourse to the "Two Source" Hypothesis. According to this the gospels of Matthew and Luke were

common to Matthew and Luke and not found in Mark)[29]. A corollary of this hypothesis is that neither Matthew used Luke, nor Luke Matthew; both of these evangelists would have written their Gospels independently of each other.

Both the "Documentary Hypothesis" of the Pentateuch and the "Two Document Hypothesis" of the Synoptic Gospels still dominate the study of these parts of the Bible, even though some scholars continue to challenge both of them[30].

Though this source-critical analysis of the biblical books was an important refinement of the historical-critical method, its preoccupation was too analytical and led to the neglect of the biblical text as it was, i.e. its final form. Then with the development of *Gattungsgeschichte*[31], that situation changed. Hermann Gunkel (1862-1932), who was originally a proponent of the History of Religions approach, became the pioneer in this

[29] The common source for the matter shared by Matthew and Luke was first postulated by J. G. Eichhorn (1752-1827), and the dependence of Matthew and Luke on Mark by C. Lachmann (1793-1851). The work of these pioneers was further developed by C. H. Weisse and C. G. Wilke in 1838, which led to the *Zweiquellentheorie*. The best explanation of this hypothesis is still the book of B. H. Streeter, *The Four Gospels: A Study of Origins, Treating of the Manuscript Tradition, Sources, Authorship, Dates* (New York: Macmillan, 1930) 149-331. Cf. J. A. Fitzmyer, "The Priority of Mark and the 'Q' Source in Luke", *Jesus and Man's Hope* (2 vols.; Pittsburgh, PA: Pittsburgh Theological Seminary, 1970) 1. 131-70; F. Neirynck, "Synoptic Problem", *NJBC*, 587-95 (art. 40); C. M. Tuckett, "Synoptic Problem", *ABD* 6. 263-70.

[30] Reaction against the Documentary Hypothesis has been formulated mainly by W. Möller, B. Jacob, U. Cassuto, J. G. Aalders (see O. Eissfeldt, *The Old Testament: An Introduction* [n. 28 above], 166).

Reaction against the Two Document Hypothesis has been formulated in recent times mainly by W. R. Farmer, who has argued for a form of the Griesbach Hypothesis, that the Marcan Gospel is an abridgement of both Matthew and Luke. See his *The Synoptic Problem: A Critical Analysis* (New York: Macmillan, 1964). For this and other solutions to the Synoptic Problem, see F. Neirynck, "Synoptic Problem", *NJBC* art. 40 (pp. 587-95); C. M. Tuckett, *The Revival of the Griesbach Hypothesis* (SNTSMS 44; Cambridge, UK: Cambridge University, 1983); "Synoptic Problem", *ABD* 6. 263-70; D. L. Dungan, "Two-Gospel Hypothesis", *ABD* 6. 671-79; M.-E. Boismard, "Two-Source Hypothesis", *ABD* 6. 679-82.

[31] I.e. the "history of the genre", a study of the various literary genres of the Bible.

composed out of two principal sources: on the one hand, the Gospel of Mark and, on the other, a collection of the sayings of Jesus (called "Q", from the German word "*Quelle*", meaning "source"). In their essential features, these two hypotheses retain their prominence in scientific exegesis today — though they are also under challenge.

In the desire to establish the chronology of the biblical texts, this kind

---

regard[32]. He realized that we are totally ignorant of the date and authorship of almost all parts of the Old Testament, and so concentrated rather on the literary forms in use in ancient Israel. This led him to distinguish the various forms of Old Testament literature (legends, hymns, laments, dirges, law, prophecy, wisdom) and to assign to them differing *Sitze im Leben*, the vital contexts from which they emerged. This analysis he made use of in his commentaries on Genesis and the Psalms[33]. Thus was born the form-critical refinement of the historical-critical method, i.e. *Formgeschichte*, as it came to be more commonly called, or Form Criticism.

In the twentieth century that refinement was applied to the Synoptic Gospels by Karl Ludwig Schmidt, Martin Dibelius, and Rudolf Bultmann[34]. This was an important advance, because it emphasized the early Christian community's role in the shaping of the Jesus-tradition (the *Sitz im Leben* of the different gospel forms: sayings and parables, miracle stories, pronouncement stories, and stories about Jesus and his disciples). But Bultmann joined to his form criticism a philosophical and demytholo-

---

[32] "Die israelitische Literatur", *Die Kultur der Gegenwart*, I/7 (ed. P. Hinneberg; Berlin: Teubner, 1906) 51-102; 2d ed. (1925) 53-112. Cf. W. Klatt, *Hermann Gunkel: Zu seiner Theologie der Religionsgeschichte und zur Entstehung der formgeschichtlichen Methode* (FRLANT 100; Göttingen: Vandenhoeck & Ruprecht, 1969); A. R. Johnson, "The Psalms", *The Old Testament and Modern Study: A Generation of Discovery and Research* (ed. H. H. Rowley; Oxford: Clarendon, 1951) 162-209.

[33] *Genesis übersetzt und erklärt* (HKAT 1/1; 6th ed.; Göttingen: Vandenhoeck & Ruprecht, 1963); *Die Psalmen* (HKAT 2/2; 4th ed.; Göttingen: Vandenhoeck & Ruprecht, 1926). Cf. his *Einleitung in die Psalmen* (HKAT Ergänzungsband; 4th ed.; Göttingen: Vandenhoeck & Ruprecht, 1933).

[34] See K. L. Schmidt, *Der Rahmen der Geschichte Jesu: Literarkritische Untersuchungen zur ältesten Jesusüberlieferung* (Berlin: Trowitzsch, 1919); M. Dibelius, *Die Formgeschichte des Evangeliums* (Tübingen: Mohr [Siebeck], 1919; 2d ed., 1933; 3d ed., 1959); in English, *From Tradition to Gospel* (London: Nicholson and Watson, 1934; New York, Scribner's Sons, n.d.; repr., London: Clarke, 1971). R. Bultmann, *Die Geschichte der synoptischen Tradition* (FRLANT 29; 2d ed.; Göttingen: Vandenhoeck & Ruprecht, 1931 [with supplement, 1957]); in English, *The History of the Synoptic Tradition* (Oxford: Blackwell, 1963; 2d ed., 1968). For a balanced assessment of the work of the last two scholars, see V. Taylor, *The Formation of the Gospel Tradition* (London: Macmillan, 1949) 1-21.

of literary criticism restricted itself to the task of dissecting and disman-
tling the text in order to identify the various sources. It did not pay sufficient attention to the final form of the biblical text and to the message

---

gizing approach to the Gospels, which tainted this refinement[35]. Today we
recognize the importance of the form-critical work of these scholars, without concurring with the philosophical presuppositions of the Bultmann
approach[36].

A still further refinement of the historical-critical method came in this
century in the form of redaction criticism, "the critical study of the process
of editing" or modifying material inherited from the early Christian community to suit the literary and religious goal that each evangelist had pursued in shaping his story of Jesus and his ministry. The study of the redactional work of each of the evangelists developed out of the early investigations of R. H. Lightfoot and E. Lohmeyer, but was brought to prominence mainly by Willi Marxsen for the Marcan Gospel, Hans Conzelmann
for Luke, and Günther Bornkamm and his colleagues for Matthew[37]. In a
sense it brought to a logical term the critical analysis that had begun with
source criticism, which was mainly atomistic, whereas redaction criticism
was much more interested in explaining the final form of the text.

It was not, however, just the development of such techniques that
significantly modified the historical-critical method, but the extraordinary
historical and archaeological discoveries in the nineteenth and twentieth
centuries have affected the interpretation of the Bible in even more important ways. These discoveries were unexpected, and they have made it
impossible for one to interpret the Bible in a simplistic way and without
consideration of them.

The well-known Rosetta Stone, inscribed in 196 B.C. to honor King
Ptolemy V Epiphanes for many benefactions that he had made to Egyp-

---

[35] The Commission will return to this problem in the section on philosophical
hermeneutics in part II; see pp. 109-31 below.

[36] See the 1964 Instruction of the Biblical Commission (par. V); *A Christological
Catechism* (n. 12 above), 155, 132-33.

[37] See W. Marxsen, *Der Evangelist Markus: Studien zur Redaktionsgeschichte des
Evangeliums* (FRLANT 67; Göttingen: Vandenhoeck & Ruprecht, 1956; 2d ed., 1959); in
English, *Mark the Evangelist: Studies on the Redaction History of the Gospel* (Nashville, TN:
Abingdon, 1969). H. Conzelmann, *Die Mitte der Zeit: Studien zur Theologie des Lukas*
(BHT 17; 2d ed.; Tübingen: Mohr [Siebeck] 1957); in English, *The Theology of St. Luke*
(New York: Harper & Bros., 1960). G. Bornkamm, G. Barth and H. J. Held, *Tradition and
Interpretation in Matthew* (NTL; London: SCM, 1963).

which it conveyed in the state in which it actually exists (the contribution of editors was not held in high regard). This meant that historical-critical exegesis could often seem to be something which simply dissolved and destroyed the text. This was all the more the case when, under the influence of the comparative history of religions, such as it then was, or on the basis of certain philosophical ideas, some exegetes expressed highly negative judgments against the Bible.

It was Hermann Gunkel who brought the method out of the ghetto of

---

tian temples, was written in hieroglypic Egyptian, Demotic, and Greek. It was discovered at Rosetta (Rashid) in the western part of the Nile delta in 1799, but its hieroglyphic text was deciphered only in 1822 by the Frenchman, Jean François Champollion (1790-1832), and the decipherment of Egyptian was only perfected with that of the Decree of Canopus by R. Lepsius in 1866[38]. Then for the first time one began to read the literature of ancient Egyptians, Israel's neighbors to the west[39]. Then, too, for the first time one was able to compare biblical texts with their comparable ancient literary forms. Historical, hymnic, ritual, mythical, and sapiential writings of ancient Egypt provided counterparts for similar passages in the Old Testament.

Likewise for Assyrian and Babylonian literature. The less well-known Bisitun Stone[40] stood for centuries on the caravan-road from Ecbatana to Babylon. It bears a sixth-century B.C. inscription written in three languages, Old Persian, Elamite, and Babylonian (all in different forms of cuneiform) and records the victory of King Darius I over a rebel Gaumata and his other achievements. In 1835 an Englishman, Henry C. Rawlinson, was the first to climb to the site and copy the inscription and make squeezes of it. Finally, it was deciphered in 1839, the result of work done by Rawlinson, a German scholar G. F. Grotefend, an Irishman Edward

---

[38] See E. A. Wallis Budge, *The Rosetta Stone in the British Museum* (London: Religious Tract Society, 1929); *The Decrees of Memphis and Canopus* (New York: Frowde, 1904); R. Lepsius, *Der bilingue Dekret von Kanopus: In der Originalgrösse, mit Übersetzung und Erklärung beider Texte* (Berlin: Hertz, 1866). Cf. H. Hartleben, *Champollion: Sein Leben und sein Werk* (2 vols.; Berlin: Weidmann, 1906); J. Friedrich, *Extinct Languages* (New York: Philosophical Library, 1957) 16-26; C. Andrews, *The British Museum Book of the Rosetta Stone* (New York: Dorset, 1981); C. Lagier, *Autour de la pierre de Rosette* (Brussels: Fondation Egyptologique Reine Elisabeth, 1927); E. Iversen, *The Myth of Egypt and Its Hieroglyphics in European Tradition* (2d ed.; Princeton, NJ: Princeton University, 1993).
[39] See J. Assmann, E. J. Sherman, M. V. Fox, and R. J. Williams, "Egyptian Literature", *ABD*, 2. 378-99. Cf. J. B. Pritchard (ed.), *ANET, ANEP, ANESTP*, passim.
[40] Also called sometimes Behistun or Bisutun.

literary criticism understood in this way. Although he continued to regard the books of the Pentateuch as compilations, he attended to the particular texture of the different elements of the text. He sought to define the genre of each piece (e.g., whether "legend" or "hymn") and its original setting in the life of the community or "*Sitz im Leben*" (e.g., a legal setting, or a liturgical one, etc.). To this kind of research into literary genres was joined the "critical study of forms" ("*Formgeschichte*"), which Martin Dibelius and Rudolf Bultmann introduced into the exegesis of the synoptic gospels. Bultmann combined form-critical studies with a biblical hermeneutic inspired by the existentialist philosophy of Martin Heidegger. As a result, *Formgeschichte* often stirred up serious reservations. But one of the results of this method has been to demonstrate more clearly that the tradition recorded in the New Testament had its origin and found its basic shape within the Christian community, or early Church, passing from the

---

Hincks, and a Frenchman Jules Oppert[41]. That decipherment proved to be the key that unlocked for the first time the secrets of Assyrian and Babylonian literature[42], and it led in time to the decipherment of even older Sumerian literature[43]. Then for the first time Israel's law codes, historical writings, poetry, and didactic and sapiential texts could be studied in comparison with the literature of its neighbors to the east. These discoveries thus opened up areas of information and comparable religious literatures that were unknown to interpreters of the Bible in the patristic, medieval, Renaissance, or Reformation periods. As a result it became clear how important it would be to interpret the Bible according to the ancient literary forms in which it had been composed.

The same would have to be said for similar discoveries in this century: the literature of Ugarit[44], which has proved to be so important for the

---

[41] See H. C. Rawlinson, *The Persian Cuneiform Inscription at Behistun* (London: J. W. Parker, 1846). Cf. E. Hincks, *On the First and Second Kinds of Persepolitan Writing* (Dublin: Gill, 1846); L. W. King and R. C. Thompson, *The Sculptures and Inscription of Darius the Great on the Rock of Behistun in Persia* (London: British Museum, 1907). An Aramaic translation of this inscription was found at Elephantine, Egypt in the early part of this century; see J. C. Greenfield and B. Porten, *The Bisitun Inscription of Darius the Great: Aramaic Version* (Corpus inscriptionum iranicarum I/5; London: Lund Humphries, 1982).

[42] See A. K. Grayson, "Mesopotamia, History of", *ABD* 4. 732-77. Cf. J. B. Pritchard (ed.), *ANET, ANEP, ANESTP*, passim; B. R. Foster, *Before the Muses: An Anthology of Akkadian Literature, Volume 1: Archaic, Classical, Mature; Volume 2: Mature, Late* (Bethesda, MD: CDL Press, 1993).

[43] See W. H. Hallo, "Sumerian Literature", *ABD*, 6. 234-37.

[44] See D. Pardee and P. Bordreuil, "Ugarit: Texts and Literature", *ABD* 6. 682-85.

preaching of Jesus himself to that which proclaimed that Jesus is the Christ. Eventually, Form-Criticism was supplemented by *"Redaktionsge-schichte"* ("Redaction-Criticism"), the "critical study of the process of editing". This sought to shed light upon the personal contribution of each evangelist and to uncover the theological tendencies which shaped his editorial work. When this last method was brought into play, the whole series of different stages characteristic of the historical-critical method became complete: from textual criticism one progresses to literary criticism, with its work of dissection in the quest for sources; then one moves to a critical study of forms and, finally, to an analysis of the editorial process, which aims to be particularly attentive to the text as it has been put together. All this has made it possible to understand far more accurately the intention of the authors and editors of the Bible, as well as the message which they addressed to their first readers. The achievement of these results has lent the historical-critical method an importance of the highest order.

---

study of Hebrew poetry, especially the Psalms; and the Dead Sea Scrolls[45], so important for the study of the text of the Old Testament, the history of ancient pre-Christian Judaism, and the Palestinian Jewish matrix of New Testament writings.

Because of such modern discoveries the interpretation of the Bible according to its ancient historical context cannot be neglected, and for this reason the Commission concludes its account of the history and development of the historical-critical method with the comment:

> All this has made it possible to understand far more accurately the intention of the authors and editors of the Bible, as well as the message which they addressed to their first readers. The achievement of these results has lent the historical-critical method an importance of the highest order.

Consequently, it is impossible for one to return today to a precritical mode of interpreting the Bible.

---

[45] See J. J. Collins, "Dead Sea Scrolls", *ABD*, 2. 85-101; J. A. Fitzmyer, *The Dead Sea Scrolls: Major Publications and Tools for Study, Revised Edition* (SBLRBS 20; Atlanta, GA: Scholars, 1990); *Reponses to 101 Questions on the Dead Sea Scrolls* (New York/Mahwah, NJ: Paulist, 1992); F. García Martínez, *The Dead Sea Scrolls Translated: The Qumran Texts in English* (Leiden: Brill, 1994).

## 2. *Principles*

The fundamental principles of the historical-critical method in its classic form are the following:

It is a *historical* method, not only because it is applied to ancient texts — in this case, those of the Bible — and studies their significance from a historical point of view, but also and above all because it seeks to shed light upon the historical processes which gave rise to biblical texts, diachronic processes that were often complex and involved a long period of time. At the different stages of their production, the texts of the Bible were addressed to various categories of hearers or readers, living in different places and different times.

It is a *critical* method, because in each of its steps (from textual criticism to redaction criticism) it operates with the help of scientific criteria that seek to be as objective as possible. In this way it aims to make accessible to the modern reader the meaning of biblical texts, often very difficult to comprehend.

As an analytical method, it studies the biblical text in the same fashion as it would study any other ancient text and comments upon it as an expression of human discourse. However, above all in the area of redaction criticism, it does allow the exegete to gain a better grasp of the content of divine revelation.

---

## 2. *Principles*

The method is called "historical" because it deals with ancient texts, situates them in the historical context in which they were composed and redacted and sheds light on the process by which the final form of the text came to be. It seeks to tell by whom they were once composed and for whom they were originally written or subsequently redacted. It strives to determine the historical reality reflected in the text. It is called "critical", not because it criticizes the Bible or seeks to discover errors in its text, but because it uses scientific criteria to judge the text as objectively as possible about its historical and literary aspects, employing all available modes of literary criticism (from textual to redactional), and to comment on it as an expression of human discourse. It is analytical in that it strives to enable the reader to grasp the intention that ancient biblical authors expressed in their texts and to "gain a better grasp of the content of divine revelation" that the biblical texts preserve and pass on.

## 3. Description

At the present stage of its development, the historical-critical method moves through the following steps:

Textual criticism, as practised for a very long time, begins the series of scholarly operations. Basing itself on the testimony of the oldest and

---

## 3. Description

The historical-critical method, as employed today, includes a variety of analytical modes of interpreting an ancient text[46].

a. Introductory Questions. The method itself begins with preliminary questions that interpreters have often asked about an ancient text: its authorship, date and place of composition, unity or integrity, occasion and purpose of writing, literary dependence (or background), outline and contents. This mode of analysis is ancient. Its use for the Bible is usually traced to a fifth-century monk named Hadrianos, a member of the Antiochene school, who wrote *Eisagōgē eis tas theias graphas*, "Introduction to the Divine Scriptures" (ca. A.D. 440)[47]. In Latin *Eisagōgē* became *Introductio*, and from it we have inherited the technical name "Introduction"[48]. In German it is usually called *Einleitung*[49]. These introductory questions are not mentioned by the Commission; they are simply taken for granted in its description of the historical-critical method. But they are an important aspect of it, because they condition both the "historical" and the "critical" study of the ancient biblical text.

---

[46] See further E. Krentz, *The Historical-Critical Method* (Guides to Biblical Scholarship; Philadelphia, PA: Fortress, 1975). Cf. H.-J. Kraus, *Geschichte der historisch-kritischen Erforschung des Alten Testaments von der Reformation bis zur Gegenwart* (Neukirchen-Vluyn: Buchhandlung des Erziehungsverein, 1956); E. Zenger, "Von der Unverzichtbarkeit der historisch-kritischen Exegese: Am Beispiel des 46. Psalms", *BLit* 62 (1989) 10-20; M. Hengel, "Historische Methode und theologische Auslegung des Neuen Testaments", *KD* 19 (1973) 86-90.

[47] See PG 98. 1273-1312. Cf. G. Mercati, "Pro Adriano", *RB* 11 (1914) 246-55; E. Schweizer, *ZNW* 40 (1941) 73-74.

[48] For example, O. Eissfeldt, *Einleitung in das Alte Testament* (3d ed.; Tübingen: Mohr [Siebeck], 1964); in English, *The Old Testament: An Introduction* (n. 28 above); W. G. Kümmel, *Einleitung in das Neue Testament* (Heidelberg: Quelle & Meyer, 1973); in English, *Introduction to the New Testament* (London: SCM; Nashville, TN: Abingdon, 1975); A. Wikenhauser and J. Schmid, *Einleitung in das Neue Testament* (6th ed.; Freiburg im B.: Herder, 1973).

[49] That term was apparently first used by J. D. Michaelis (1717-1791), *Einleitung in die göttlichen Schriften des Neuen Bundes* (Göttingen: Vandenhoeck, 1750).

best manuscripts, as well as of papyri, certain ancient versions and patristic texts, textual-criticism seeks to establish, according to fixed rules, a biblical text as close as possible to the original.

---

b. Textual Criticism. This mode of criticism is traced to the scholars of the Alexandrian Library. It seeks to determine what are the oldest and best manuscripts of the different biblical books, to what text-families or text-traditions they belong, and how they are to be evaluated. Modern critical editions of the Hebrew Old Testament, such as the *Biblia hebraica stuttgartensia*, or of the Greek New Testament, such as the twenty-seventh edition of Nestle-Aland, *Novum Testamentum graece*, or the fourth edition of the United Bible Societies, *The Greek New Testament*, are the results of this mode of biblical criticism and offer a modern form of the texts that is as close as possible to the original[50]. Joined to this study of the Hebrew or Greek manuscripts is that of the ancient versions of the Bible: the Septuagint for the Old Testament[51], the Latin Vulgate[52] and the Syriac

---

[50] See K. Elliger and W. Rudolph (eds.), *Biblia Hebraica Stuttgartensia* (Stuttgart: Deutsche Bibelstiftung, 1967-77); B. and K. Aland et al. (eds.), *The Greek New Testament* (4th ed.; Stuttgart: Deutsche Bibelgesellschaft; New York et alibi: United Bible Societies, 1993); *Novum Testamentum graece* (27th ed.; Stuttgart: Deutsche Bibelgesellschaft, 1993).

Cf. B. J. Roberts, *The Old Testament Text and Versions: The Hebrew Text in Transmission and the History of the Ancient Versions* (Cardiff: University of Wales, 1951); E. Würthwein, *The Text of the Old Testament: An Introduction to the Biblia Hebraica* (tr. E. F. Rhodes from the 4th German ed.; Grand Rapids, MI: Eerdmans, 1979); L. H. Brockington, *The Hebrew Text of the Old Testament: The Readings Adopted by the Translators of the New English Bible* (Oxford and Cambridge: University Presses, 1973); E. Tov, *Textual Criticism of the Hebrew Bible* (Minneapolis, MN: Augsburg Fortress, 1992).

K. and B. Aland, *The Text of the New Testament: An Introduction to the Critical Editions and to the Theory and Practice of Modern Textual Criticism* (Grand Rapids, MI: Eerdmans, 1987); B. M. Metzger, *The Text of the New Testament: Its Transmission, Corruption, and Restoration* (3d ed.; New York/Oxford: Oxford University, 1992); J. H. Greenlee, *Introduction to New Testament Textual Criticism* (Grand Rapids, MI: Eerdmans, 1964); E. J. Epp, "Textual Criticism (NT)", *ABD* 6.412-35.

[51] See A. Rahlfs et al. (eds.), *Septuaginta: Vetus Testamentum graecum auctoritate Societatis Litterarum Gottingensis editum* (many vols.; Göttingen: Vandenhoeck & Ruprecht, 1931-); A. E. Brooke, N. McLean, and H. St. J. Thackeray, *The Old Testament in Greek* (3 vols. in several parts; Cambridge, UK: Cambridge University, 1906-).

S. Jellicoe, *The Septuagint and Modern Study* (Ann Arbor, MI: Eisenbrauns, 1978); E. Tov, "Textual Criticism (OT)", *ABD* 6. 393-412; P. Walters, *The Text of the Septuagint: Its Corruptions and Their Emendations* (ed. D. W. Gooding; Cambridge, UK: Cambridge University, 1973); E. Tov, *The Text-Critical Use of the Septuagint in Biblical Research* (Jerusalem Biblical Studies; Jerusalem: Simor Ltd., 1981).

[52] See Benedictines of San Girolamo, *Biblia sacra juxta latinam Vulgatam versionem ad*

The text is then submitted to a linguistic (morphology and syntax) and semantic analysis, using the knowledge derived from historical philol-

---

Peshitta[53] for both Testaments, and occasionally other ancient versions. The study of these versions is important in textual criticism because they sometimes reflect a more original Hebrew or Greek reading than may be preserved in any of the known Hebrew or Greek manuscripts themselves[54]. Also important for this mode of criticism are the quotations of biblical texts in patristic writers, since some of them may antedate even important Greek, Latin, or Syriac manuscripts of the Old or New Testament[55]. The study of these quotations presupposes, however, that one has access to critical texts of the patristic writers[56], because one cannot simply depend in this matter on the readings in J. Migne, *Patrologia graeca* or *Patrologia latina*.

c. Philological Analysis. The Commission now speaks of "linguistic" analysis, but this is preferably called "philological", because "linguistic" has another connotation today. The philological analysis consists in the grammatical and semantic aspects of the biblical text, which studies its morphology and syntax in order to discover the meaning of the words and phrases in their sentences. Such study yields the textual meaning, but it has also to be joined to their contextual meaning, as well as their relational meaning. The textual meaning is the sense of words and phrases in themselves, such as one might find in a dictionary; the contextual mean-

---

*codicum fidem... edita* (to date, 14 vols.; Rome: Vatican Polyglot Press, 1926-). Cf. R. Weber (ed.), *Biblia sacra juxta Vulgatam versionem* (2 vols.; Stuttgart: Württembergische Bibelanstalt, 1969; 2d ed., 1975); J. Wordsworth and H. J. White (eds.), *Nouum Testamentum domini nostri Jesu Christi latine secundum editionem S. Hieronymi ad codicum manuscriptorum fidem* (3 vols.; Oxford: Clarendon, 1889-1954).

[53] See the Peshitta Institute of the University of Leiden, *The Old Testament in Syriac according to the Peshitta Version* (to date, 12 vols.; Leiden: Brill, 1972-); P. E. Pusey and G. H. Gwilliam, *Tetraeuangelium sanctum juxta simplicem Syrorum versionem ad fidem codicum, massorae, editionum denuo recognitum* (Oxford: Clarendon, 1901). For the rest of the New Testament there is no critical text of the Syriac version.

[54] See B. M. Metzger, *The Early Versions of the New Testament: Their Origin, Transmission, and Limitations* (Oxford: Clarendon, 1977).

[55] A very useful tool for the study of such citations can be found in J. Allenbach et al. (eds.), *Biblia patristica: Index des citations et allusions bibliques dans la littérature patristique* (to date, 5 vols.; Paris: Centre National de Recherche Scientifique, 1975-).

[56] Such critical editions can be found in the following series: Griechische christliche Schriftsteller (Leipzig); Corpus Scriptorum Ecclesiasticorum Latinorum (Vienna); Corpus Christianorum, Series Latina (Turnhout, Belgium); Corpus Christianorum, Series Graeca (Turnhout); Sources Chrétiennes (Paris); Corpus Scriptorum Christianorum Orientalium (Paris).

ogy. It is the role of literary criticism to determine the beginning and end of textual units, large and small, and to establish the internal coherence of

---

ing, the sense of the words and phrases derived from the context in which they are found, e.g., in a paragraph or a unit of text; and the relational meaning, their sense in the work as a whole or in a corpus of writings of the same author. For a word or a phrase yields its sense not just from its own morphology and syntax, but also from its function in the paragraph or work, and from its relation to other uses of such words or phrases in the work or corpus as a whole. All of this, the textual, contextual, and relational aspects, belong to the semantic analysis of a biblical text.

Another part of the philological analysis is what the Commission calls "literary criticism[57]", which in reality is "source criticism". It involves the determination of "the beginning and end of textual units, large and small", and of their "internal coherence". This would entail the study of doublets, irreconcilable differences, and other indicators that reveal the composite character of a textual unit, and perhaps even the sources on which the unit depends or the separate documents from which it has been put together[58].

Still another part of this analysis is "genre criticism", which seeks to identify the literary form of a textual unit, its features, and its *Sitz im Leben*, or social context from which it emerged. In some cases one can even trace the history of the shapes that the form or genre has taken, and this would involve what is technically called *Formgeschichte*[59]. Closely re-

---

[57] In the past, it was often also called "higher criticism", to distinguish it from "lower criticism", by which was meant textual criticism.

[58] See N. C. Habel, *Literary Criticism of the Old Testament* (Guides to Biblical Scholarship, Old Testament Series; Philadelphia, PA: Fortress, 1971). Cf. J. Barton, *Reading the Old Testament: Method in Biblical Study* (Philadelphia, PA: Westminster, 1984) 20-29; "Source Criticism (OT)", *ABD* 6. 162-65; R. E. Clements, *A Century of Old Testament Study* (rev. ed.; Guildford, UK: Lutterworth, 1982) 7-30; D.-A. Koch, "Source Criticism (NT)", *ABD* 165-71.

[59] See E. V. McKnight, *What Is Form Criticism?* (Guides to Biblical Scholarship, New Testament Series; Philadelphia, PA: Fortress, 1973); E. B. Redlich, *Form Criticism: Its Value and Limitations* (London: Duckworth, 1939, repr. 1956); J. Barton and V. K. Robbins, "Form Criticism", *ABD* 2. 838-44; R. Knierim, *Old Testament Form Criticism Reconsidered* (Institute for Antiquity and Christianity, Occasional Papers 6; Claremont, CA: Institute for Antiquity and Christianity, 1973); G. M. Tucker, *Form Criticism of the Old Testament* (Guides to Biblical Scholarship, Old Testament Series; Philadelphia, PA: Fortress, 1971); J. H. Hayes (ed.), *Old Testament Form Criticism* (Trinity University Monograph Series in Religion 2; San Antonio, TX: Trinity University, 1974).

For the New Testament, see W. E. Barnes, *Gospel Criticism and Form Criticism*

the text. The existence of doublets, of irreconcilable differences and of other indicators is a clue to the composite character of certain texts. These can then be divided into small units, the next step being to see whether these in turn can be assigned to different sources. Genre criticism seeks to

---

lated to this endeavor is what is sometimes called "tradition criticism", which attempts to describe the development involved in the history of the form[60].

A further feature of philological analysis is "redaction criticism", which concentrates on the modifications that traditional texts have undergone as they have been edited or redacted by a biblical author for the sake of his literary or religious purpose in composing the work[61]. This is an important feature because it concentrates on the final form of the biblical text and its analysis ceases to be diachronic and becomes synchronic, i.e. it is not interested solely in the pre-history of the text, but in its final shape, which has to be analyzed by "literary criticism" in its more modern sense[62]. It is especially this final analysis that is concerned with the relation of a textual unit to the work as a whole or to the corpus to which it belongs. It is thus particularly concerned with the message that the biblical author sought to communicate to his contemporaries, and indirectly to the readers of all ages. When such textual units are related to events of history, then "historical criticism" in the proper sense enters the picture, "so as to determine the historical significance of the text", because in this way "one accounts for the various stages that lie behind the biblical revelation in its concrete historical development".

It is important to realize that the goal of the interpreter who uses this

---

(Edinburgh: Clark, 1936); K. Berger, *Formgeschichte des Neuen Testaments* (Heidelberg: Quelle & Meyer, 1984); F. C. Grant, *Form Criticism: A New Method of New Testament Research.* (Chicago, IL: Willett Clarke & Co., 1934); repr. as R. Bultmann and K. Kundsin, *Form Criticism: Two Essays on New Testament Research* (Harper Torchbooks; New York: Harper & Bros., 1962); W. A. Maier, *Form Criticism Reexamined* (Contemporary Theology Series; St. Louis, MO: Concordia, 1973).

[60] See R. S. Barbour, *Traditio-Historical Criticism of the Gospels: Some Comments on Current Methods* (Studies in Creative Criticism 4; London: SPCK, 1972); W. E. Rast, *Tradition History of the Old Testament* (Guides to Biblical Scholarship, Old Testament Series; Philadelphia, PA: Fortress, 1972); D. A. Knight, "Tradition History", *ABD* 6. 633-38.

[61] See N. Perrin, *What Is Redaction Criticism?* (Guides to Biblical Scholarship, New Testament Series; Philadelphia, PA: Fortress, 1969); J. Barton, *Reading the Old Testament* (n. 58 above), 45-60.

[62] See W. A. Beardslee, *Literary Criticism of the New Testament* (Guides to Biblical Scholarship, New Testament Series; Philadelphia, PA: Fortress, 1970).

identify literary genres, the social milieu that give rise to them, their particular features and the history of their development. Tradition criticism situates texts in the stream of tradition and attempts to describe the development of this tradition over the course of time. Finally, redaction criticism studies the modifications that these texts have undergone before being fixed in their final state; it also analyzes this final stage, trying as far as possible to identify the tendencies particularly characteristic of this concluding process. While the preceding steps have sought to explain the text by tracing its origin and development within in a diachronic perspective, this last step concludes with a study that is synchronic: at this point the text is explained as it stands, on the basis of the mutual relationships between its diverse elements, and with an eye to its character as a message com-

---

philological, grammatical, and semantic analysis or the historical-critical method is to ascertain what Pius XII did not hesitate to call the "literal sense" of the biblical text.

> Let the Catholic interpreter undertake the task, of all those imposed on him the greatest, that, namely, of ascertaining and expounding the genuine meaning of the Sacred Books. In the performance of this task let interpreters bear in mind that their foremost and greatest endeavor should be to discern and define clearly that sense of the biblical words that is called literal. Aided by the context and by comparison with similar passages, let them therefore by means of their knowledge of languages, search out with all diligence the literal meaning of the words... so that the mind of the author may be made abundantly clear, ... What is the literal sense of a passage is not always as obvious in the speeches and writings of ancient authors of the East, as it is in the works of our own day. For what they wanted to express is not to be determined by rules of grammar and philology alone, or solely by the context; the interpreter must, as it were, go back wholly in spirit to those distant centuries of the East and with the aid of history, archaeology, ethnology, and other sciences, determine accurately what modes of writing, so to speak, the authors of that ancient period were likely to use, and in fact did use[63].

Another way of speaking of this kind of interpretation of the Bible is

---

[63] *Divino afflante Spiritu* §23, 35 (*EB* §550, 558; *RSS*, pp. 92, 97). The emphasis that Pius XII put here on the inspired author's intention in writing was echoed by Vatican Council II in its dogmatic constitution *Dei Verbum* §12. Cf. N. Lohfink, "Der weisse Fleck in *Dei Verbum*, Artikel 12", *Trierer theologische Zeitschrift* 101 (1992) 20-35.

municated by the author to his contemporaries. At this point one is in a position to consider the demands of the text from the point of view of action and life (*fonction pragmatique*).

When the texts studied belong to a historical literary genre or are related to events of history, historical criticism completes literary criticism, so as to determine the historical significance of the text, in the modern sense of this expression.

It is in this way that one accounts for the various stages that lie behind the biblical revelation in its concrete historical development.

### 4. *Evaluation*

What value should we accord to the historical-critical method, especially at this present stage of its development?

It is a method which, when used in an objective manner, implies of itself no *a priori*. If its use is accompanied by a priori principles, that is not something pertaining to the method itself, but to certain hermeneutical choices which govern the interpretation and can be tendentious.

---

"exegesis". Many modern languages have a form of this word, which is used specifically for what *Webster's Third New International Dictionary* calls "a critical interpretation of a text or portion of Scripture". The reason for the special word is that this kind of interpretation makes use of the tools and criteria of classical philology, but it is not merely philology. It is "philology plus", and the plus implies the presupposition of faith with which this mode of interpretation is conducted. More will be said about this form of presupposition below, but first the method has to be evaluated in the light of other presuppositions with which it has been used.

### 4. *Evaluation*

The Commission recognizes that the historical-critical method, "when used in an objective manner, implies of itself no *a priori*. If its use is accompanied by *a priori* principles, that is not something pertaining to the method itself, but to certain hermeneutical choices which govern the interpretation and can be tendentious". What underlies this judgment is the fact that the method is borrowed from classical philology and is *per se* neutral. It is a method of analyzing works of literature, which has been used for literatures of all sorts, times, and places. Given a specific type of literature, one might have to make adjustments in the use of some fea-

Oriented, in its origins, towards source criticism and the history of religions, the method has managed to provide fresh access to the Bible. It

---

tures of the method. It is, however, particularly apt for the analysis of ancient literatures because of its "historical" concern[64].

This method can, however, be joined with "hermeneutical choices which... can be tendentious". Unfortunately, the Commission has given no examples of such choices. Yet the fact is that the historical-critical method was tainted at crucial points in its history with presuppositions or hermeneutical prejudices that were not really part of it. For this very reason, it still remains suspect in the eyes of some people today[65].

For instance, the rationalist presuppositions of the *Leben-Jesu-Forschung* of the eighteenth and nineteenth centuries contaminated the method, as it was practised by such writers as H. S. Reimarus[66], F. C. Baur, H. E. G. Paulus, D. F. Strauss, B. Bauer, and E. Renan. In their attempt to reconstruct the life of the historical Jesus, using the Gospels merely as ancient human records, these endeavors often stemmed from deist attacks on traditional Christianity or from historical studies that

---

[64] See further J. A. Fitzmyer, "Historical Criticism: Its Role in Biblical Interpretation and Church Life", *TS* 50 (1989) 244-59; T. R. Curtin, *Historical Criticism and the Theological Interpretation of Scripture: The Catholic Discussion of a Biblical Hermeneutic: 1958-1983* (Rome: Dissertation, Gregorian University, 1987); P. Stuhlmacher, *Historical Criticism and Theological Interpretation of Scripture: Toward a Hermeneutics of Consent* (Philadelphia, PA: Fortress, 1977). Cf. R. B. Robinson, *Roman Catholic Exegesis since Divino afflante Spiritu: Hermeneutical Implications* (SBLDS 111; Atlanta, GA: Scholars, 1988).

[65] See the *Report of the Commission on Theology and Church Relations: A Lutheran Stance Toward Contemporary Biblical Studies* (St. Louis, MO: The Lutheran Church - Missouri Synod, n.d.). Cf. G. Maier, *The End of the Historical-Critical Method* (tr. E. W. Leverenz and R. F. Norden; St. Louis, MO: Concordia, 1974); E. Linnemann, *Wissenschaft oder Meinung? Anfragen und Alternativen* (Neuhausen: F. Hünssler, 1986); in English, *Historical Criticism of the Bible: Methodology or Ideology?* (Grand Rapids, MI: Baker, 1990).

[66] See *Von dem Zweck Jesu und seiner Jünger: Noch ein Fragment des Wolfenbüttelschen Ungenannten* (Berlin: Wever, 1784); *Fragmente des Wolfenbüttelschen Ungenannten: Ein Anhang zu dem Fragment Vom Zweck Jesu und seiner Jünger* (Berlin, 1788; 5th ed., Berlin: Reimer, 1895). The eighteenth-century Deist, H. S. Reimarus (1694-1768), never published his work in his lifetime, out of fear of consequences. After his death seven parts of an early draft of his work were published by the philosopher G. E. Lessing, who identified the author only as "the Wolfenbüttel Unnamed One". Reimarus's son disclosed the identity of the unnamed author in 1814. The complete manuscript was only published in 1972: *Apologie: Oder Schützschrift für die vernünftigen Verehrer Gottes* (2 vols.; Frankfurt: Insel Verlag). Cf. *Reimarus Fragments* (ed. C. H. Talbert; Lives of Jesus Series; Philadelphia, PA: Fortress, 1970; H. S. Reimarus, *The Goal of Jesus and His Disciples* (ed. G. W. Buchanan; Leiden: Brill, 1970).

has shown the Bible to be a collection of writings, which most often, especially in the case of the Old Testament, are not the creation of a single

---

sought to be free of all influence of dogmatic theology. A. Schweitzer finally unmasked this mode of research in *The Quest of the Historical Jesus*. He showed that such investigation of the life of Jesus had sprung not from a purely historical interest in him, but from a "struggle against the tyranny of dogma", and that the greatest of such "lives" had been "written with hate" — "not so much hate of the Person of Jesus as of the supernatural nimbus with which it was so easy to surround him"[67]. Thus deist and rationalist presuppositions were associated with the historical-critical method as it was being developed about the time of the Enlightenment. Yet what was at fault was not the method, but the anti-dogmatic presuppositions. And for this reason the method is still sometimes thought to be basically rationalistic[68].

Again, at the beginning of this century, when K. L. Schmidt, M. Dibelius, and R. Bultmann were applying form criticism to the Synoptic Gospels, Bultmann associated with this refinement of the method a *Vorverständnis* or presupposition of a different nature. He used a form of kerygmatic theology, which depended heavily on Lutheran justification *sola fide*, Strauss's radical and skeptical reading of the Gospels, an understanding of New Testament theology that nothing to do with what Jesus of Nazareth did or said, but that only began with the kerygma, and not before it, a form of existentialist philosophy borrowed from the young Heidegger, and an emphasis on the preached Word. Thus despite the laudable pastoral concern of Bultmann to make the New Testament message a challenge for people in the twentieth century, his use of the method was tainted with philosophical and demythologizing presuppositions that are not necessarily part of it[69]. These, then, are two examples of the tenden-

---

[67] *The Quest of the Historical Jesus: A Critical Study of Its Progress from Reimarus to Wrede* (London: Black, 1910; repr., 1948) 4-5.

[68] See S. Scherrer, "The Lord of History and Historical Criticism", *SJP News* (Maryknoll, NY: St. Jerome Publications) 1/2 (1992) 1-6, esp. 2 ("basing its key exegetical decisions on *reason alone*"). Contrast the teaching of Pope Leo XIII, who acknowledged that the use of human reason had a place in biblical interpretation, quoting Augustine, *De Gen. ad litt.* 8.7.13: *nisi qua eum vel ratio tenere prohibeat vel necessitas cogat dimittere* (except only where reason makes it untenable or necessity requires), *Providentissimus Deus* §112. Cf. P. Patterson and R. James, "The Historical-Critical Study of the Bible: Dangerous or Helpful?" *Theological Educator* 37 (1988) 45-74.

[69] See his *Theology of the New Testament* (2 vols.; London: *SCM*, 1952) 1. 3, 35; *Jesus* (Tübingen: Mohr [Siebeck], 1926); in English, *Jesus and the Word* (New York: Scribner's

author, but which have had a long prehistory, inextricably tied either to
the history of Israel or to that of the early Church. Previously, the Jewish

---

tious hermeneutics with which the historical-critical method has been
used.

The Commission recognizes that "for a long time" scholars have
ceased combining the method with such philosophical presuppositions.
This is true, but, as R. Bultmann himself pointed out decades ago, there is
no presuppositionless interpretation of the Bible[70]. Every exegete brings
to his or her interpretation certain presuppositions or hermeneutical
choices. With such presuppositions a believing Jew, a believing Protestant, or a believing Catholic would work in interpreting the Bible. This is
likewise recognized in the Commission's document, in effect, by the emphasis put in its later sections on the way the Bible must be interpreted in
the Church. For one thing, that emphasis involves a major presupposition
of Christian faith[71].

Such a presupposition would include the belief that the book being
critically interpreted is the Word of God couched in human language of
long ago; that the Bible is an inspired text, having authority for people of
the Jewish-Christian heritage[72]; that it represents a restricted canon of
authoritative writings; that it has been given by God to his people for their
edification and salvation; that the Spirit who inspired its human authors is

---

Sons, 1958); "The New Testament and Mythology", *Kerygma and Myth: A Theological
Debate* (ed. H. W. Bartsch; London: SPCK, 1953) 1-44; *Jesus Christ and Mythology* (New
York: Scribner's Sons, 1958). Cf. D. E. Nineham, "Demythologization", *A Dictionary of
Biblical Interpretation* (Ed. R. J. Coggins and J. L. Houlden; London: SCM; Philadelphia,
PA: Trinity Press International, 1990) 171-74; M. M. Bourke, "Rudolf Bultmann's Demy-
thologizing of the New Testament", *The Catholic Theological Society of America, Procee-
dings* 12 (1957) 103-32.

[70] See "Ist voraussetzungslose Exegese möglich?" *TZ* 13 (1957) 409-17; "Is Exegesis
without Presuppositions Possible?" *Existence and Faith: Shorter Writings of Rudolf Bultmann* (ed. S. M. Ogden; New York: Meridian Books, Inc., 1960) 289-96.

[71] This is a matter of no little debate today. See J.-M. Sevrin, "L'Exégèse critique com-
me discipline théologique", *RTL* 21 (1990) 146-62; B. S. Childs, "Interpretation in Faith",
*Interpretation* 18 (1964) 432-49. Cf. A. Vanhoye, "Dopo la Divino afflante Spiritu: Progressi
e problemi dell'esegesi cattolica", *Chiesa e Sacra Scrittura* (n. 4 above), 35-51, esp. 44-47.

The misunderstanding of the position espoused in the Commission's document has given
rise to misguided discussion: F. Dreyfus, "Exégèse en Sorbonne, exégèse en église", *RB* 82
(1975) 321-59; "L'Actualisation à l'intérieur de la Bible", *RB* 83 (1976) 161-202; "L'Actualisation de l'Ecriture", *RB* 86 (1979) 321-84; Anon., "Nessuna speranza per l'esegesi cattolica?" *Si si No no* 15/8 (30 April 1989) 1-3.

[72] See "Scriptural Authority", *ABD* 5. 1017-56.

or Christian interpretation of the Bible had no clear awareness of the concrete and diverse historical conditions in which the Word of God took root among the people; of all this it had only a general and remote awareness. The early confrontation between traditional exegesis and the scientific approach, which initially consciously separated itself from faith and at times even opposed it, was assuredly painful; later however it proved to be salutary: once the method was freed from external prejudices, it led to a more precise understanding of the truth of Sacred Scripture (cf. *Dei Verbum*, 12). According to *Divino Afflante Spiritu*, the search for the *literal sense* of Scripture is an essential task of exegesis and, in order to fulfill this task, it is necessary to determine the literary genre of texts (cf. *EB*, 560), something which the historical-critical method helps to achieve.

To be sure, the classic use of the historical-critical method reveals its limitations. It restricts itself to a search for the meaning of the biblical text within the historical circumstances that gave rise to it and is not concerned with other possibilities of meaning which have been revealed at later stages of the biblical revelation and history of the Church. Nonetheless, this method has contributed to the production of works of exegesis and of biblical theology which are of great value.

---

the same Spirit that guides the community of interpreters and believers (the Church) to understand its text; that through the Bible God continues to speak to readers of every generation; and that it is properly expounded only in relation to the Tradition that has grown out of it. These are tenets that a Christian believes about the Bible, tenets that systematic theology explains more in detail.

In its evaluation of the historical-critical method, apart from the question of presuppositions, the Commission singles out four advantages of the method in the interpretation of the Bible: (1) It has revealed the Bible to be "a collection of writings", which are not the creation of an inspired single human author. (2) It has shown that these writings often have a long pre-history, tied to the history of Israel or of the early Church. These concrete and diverse historical conditions had long been neglected in the interpretation of the Bible in bygone centuries. (3) It has distinguished the various literary forms or genres in which biblical books have been composed, a distinction that is absolutely necessary in the "search for the literal sense of Scripture"[73]. (4) It has contributed to the produc-

---

[73] The Commission refers to the encyclical *Divino afflante Spiritu* §38 (*EB* §560), quoted in part on p. 43 above.

For a long time now scholars have ceased combining the method with a philosophical system. More recently, there has been a tendency amongst exegetes to move the method in the direction of a greater insistence upon the form of a text, with less attention paid to its content. But this tendency has been corrected through the application of a more diversified semantics (the semantics of words, phrases, text) and through the study of the demands of the text from the point of view of action and life (*aspect pragmatique*).

With respect to the inclusion, in the method, of a synchronic analysis of texts, we must recognize that we are dealing here with a legitimate operation, for it is the text in its final stage, rather than in its earlier editions, which is the expression of the Word of God. But diachronic study remains indispensable for making known the historical dynamism which animates Sacred Scripture and for shedding light upon its rich complexity: for example, the Covenant Code (*Exodus* 21–23) reflects a political, social and religious situation of Israelite society different from that reflected in the other law codes preserved in Deuteronomy (chapters 12–26) and in Leviticus (the Holiness Code, chapters 17–26). We must take care not to

---

tion of exegetical commentaries and works of biblical theology of great value. For these reasons the method cannot be dismissed or neglected.

The Commission, however, singles out limitations of the historical-critical method and, significantly, mentions only one: its concentration on "a search for the meaning of the biblical text within the historical circumstances that gave rise to it" and a consequent neglect of concern for "other possibilities of meaning which have been revealed at later stages of the biblical revelation and history of the Church". A more balanced concentration on the historical circumstances as well as of the form of the text, especially in its final shape, would call for more of a synchronic approach in interpretation than has been customary in the use of the historical-critical method even in fairly recent times. Having admitted this limitation, however, the Commission still notes the need of diachronic analysis. That "remains indispensable" and is needed to bring to light the historical dynamism that gives light to Scripture. It illustrates this by comparing the diverse historical contexts (political, social, and religious) that are reflected in and give rise to the different law codes found in the Pentateuch: the Covenant Code of Exod 20:22–23:33[74], the Holiness Code of

---

[74] The name is derived from Exod 24:7. See H. Cazelles, *Etudes sur le Code de l'Alliance* (Paris: Letouzey et Ané, 1946) 6.

replace the historicizing tendency, for which the older historical-critical exegesis is open to criticism, with the opposite excess, that of neglecting history in favor of an exegesis which would be exclusively synchronic.

To sum up, the goal of the historical-critical method is to determine, particularly in a diachronic manner, the meaning expressed by the biblical authors and editors. Along with other methods and approaches, the historical-critical method opens up to the modern reader a path to the meaning of the biblical text, such as we have it today.

## B. New Methods of Literary Analysis

No scientific method for the study of the Bible is fully adequate to

---

Leviticus 17–26[75], and the laws in Deuteronomy 12–26[76].

The concluding paragraph stresses the openness of the historical-critical method to be refined by other approaches to the Bible.

## B. New Methods of Literary Analysis

The Commission, for all its insistence on the value of the historical-critical method, nevertheless admits that no scientific method can bring out or exhaust all the riches of the biblical text. Despite the remarkable results that that method has produced since it was restored to a rightful place in Catholic interpretation, it has not yet been brought to perfection. Consequently, other modes of literary analysis and other approaches to the Bible can be used to supplement it or refine it.

The Commission speaks now of various modes of literary analysis. Before one comes to the specific forms that the document discusses in some detail, one might recall that there have been numerous appeals for a more "literary" approach to the Bible. Yet a certain kind of literary analysis of the biblical texts — in the proper sense of "literary"[77] — has always formed part of the historical-critical method itself. That method is called

---

[75] The name for this section of Leviticus was first proposed by A. Klostermann (1877). See L. E. Elliott-Binns, "Some Problems of the Holiness Code", *ZAW* 67 (1955) 26-40; A. Cholewiński, *Heiligkeitsgesetz und Deuteronomium: Eine vergleichende Studie* (AnBib 66; Rome: Biblical Institute, 1976); W. Kornfeld, *Studien zum Heiligkeitsgesetz* (*Lev 17–26*) (Vienna: Herder, 1952); H. T. C. Sun, "Holiness Code", *ABD* 3. 254-57.

[76] See M. Weinfeld, *Deuteronomy and the Deuteronomic School* (Oxford: Clarendon, 1972).

[77] And not in the sense of source criticism.

comprehend the biblical texts in all their richness. For all its overall validity, the historical-critical method cannot claim to be totally sufficient in

---

"critical", precisely because it utilizes criteria peculiar to a literary analysis
of texts.

In recent decades, however, the literary criticism of the Bible has
sought to borrow skills and insights developed in the criticism of other
kinds of literature, and especially from what has been called "New
Criticism[78]". This mode of criticism not only studies the literary genres of
epic and lyric poetry, prophecy, wisdom, and drama, but concentrates on
the images, symbols, and poetical or rhetorical language in an effort to
understand how texts create a world of their own and communicate their
meanings. Such criticism treats the literary text as an artefact, as *poiēma*,
the product of a literary carpenter or craftsman. As a result, the work is
not so much a window open on the author's mind, emotion, or world as a
sublime expression produced by the craft of words. This criticism is little
interested in the author's intention in writing, or his intended meaning, for
that could be an "intentional fallacy". Rather, what is said (or written) is
of the greatest importance, the sense that the words bear. Often too the
text has to be considered as to its place in a literary canon, in the tradition
of which the literary work forms a part. This mode of literary analysis is
not one; there are numerous forms of it, but its emphasis on "the text
itself" is the one important element[79].

---

[78] For some of the proponents of this criticism, see T. S. Eliot, "Tradition and Individual Talent", *Selected Essays: New Edition* (New York: Harcourt, Brace and World, Inc.,
1950; repr. 1964) 3-11; "The Function of Criticism", ibid., 12-22; "The Frontiers of Criti-
cism", *On Poetry and Poets* (New York: Farrar, Straus and Giroux, 1957) 113-31. I. A.
Richards, *Science and Poetry* (New Science Series 2; New York: Norton, 1926); *Principles of
Literary Criticism* (5th ed.; London: Kegan Paul, Trench, Trubner; New York: Harcourt,
Brace, 1934; repr., 1947); *Practical Criticism: A Study of Literary Judgment* (New York:
Harcourt, Brace; London: Routledge & Kegan Paul, 1929, repr. 1952, 1956). W. Empson,
*Seven Types of Ambiguity* (Norfolk, CT: New Directions, 1930; 3d ed., 1953; repr., Cleve-
land, OH: World Publ., 1955). Cf. J. C. Ransom, *The New Criticism* (Westport, CT: Green-
wood, 1968, repr., 1979); S. Doubrovsky, *The New Criticism in France* (Chicago, IL: Uni-
versity of Chicago, 1973); W. K. Wimsatt, Jr. and C. Brooks, *Literary Criticism: A Short
History* (New York: Knopf, 1966); R. Wellek, *Theory of Literature* (3d ed.; New York:
Harcourt, Brace and World, Inc., 1956).

[79] This mode of biblical literary criticism is not really new, for R. G. Moulton in *The
Literary Study of the Bible: An Account of the Leading Forms of Literature Represented in the
Sacred Writings: Intended for English Readers* (Boston: Heath, 1895; rev. ed., 1899) had
already practised a form of it. Cf. D. Norton, *A History of the Bible as Literature* (2 vols.;
Cambridge, UK/New York: Cambridge University, 1993).

this respect. It necessarily has to leave aside many aspects of the writings which it studies. It is not surprising, then, that at the present time, other

Yet one must note how much even this literary approach to the Bible borrows from the historical-critical method itself. Among the literary ap-

For the application of new literary criticism to the Bible, see L. Alonso Schökel, *La palabra inspirada: La Biblia a la luz de la ciencia del lenguaje* (Barcelona: Editorial Herder, 1967); in English, *The Inspired Word: Scripture in the Light of Language and Literature* (New York: Herder and Herder, 1965; repr., 1972); "Hermeneutics in the Light of Language and Literature", *CBQ* 25 (1963) 371-86; R. Alter, *The Art of Biblical Poetry* (New York: Basic Books, 1985); *The World of Biblical Literature* (London: SPCK, 1992); R. Alter and F. Kermode (eds.), *The Literary Guide to the Bible* (Cambridge, MA: Belknap Press of Harvard University, 1987); E. Auerbach, *Mimesis: The Representation of Reality in Western Literature* (Princeton, NJ: Princeton University; New York: Doubleday, 1953); C. A. Dinsmore, *The English Bible as Literature* (Boston/New York: Houghton Mifflin, 1931); J. C. Exum, *Signs and Wonders: Biblical Texts in Literary Focus* (Semeia Studies; Atlanta, GA: Society of Biblical Literature, 1989); N. Frye, *The Great Code: The Bible and Literature* (New York: Harcourt Brace Jovanovich; London: Routledge & Kegan Paul, 1982); *Words with Power: Being a Second Study of "The Bible and Literature"* (San Diego, CA: Harcourt Brace Jovanovich, 1990); J. B. Gabel and C. B. Wheeler, *The Bible as Literature: An Introduction* (New York: Oxford University, 1986; 2d ed., 1990); J. H. Gottcent, *The Bible: A Literary Study* (Boston: Twayne Publishers, 1986); *The Bible as Literature: A Selective Bibliography* (Boston: G. K. Hall, 1979); T. R. Henn, *The Bible as Literature* (London: Lutterworth; New York: Oxford University, 1970); A. Loades and M. McLain (eds.), *Hermeneutics, the Bible, and Literary Criticism* (London: Macmillan; New York: St. Martin's Press, 1992); T. Longman III, *Literary Approaches to Biblical Interpretation* (Foundations of Contemporary Interpretation 3; Grand Rapids, MI: Academie, Zondervan; Leicester, UK: Apollos, 1987); E. V. McKnight, *The Bible and the Reader: An Introduction to Literary Criticism* (Philadelphia, PA: Fortress, 1985); J. Maier and V. L. Tollers (eds.), *Literary Approaches to the Hebrew Bible* (Lewisburg: Bucknell University, 1990); L. M. Poland, *Literary Criticism and Biblical Hermeneutics: A Critique of Formalist Approaches* (AAR Academy Series 48; Chico, CA: Scholars, 1985); M. A. Powell et al., *The Bible and Modern Literary Criticism: A Critical Assessment and Annotated Bibliography* (New York: Greenwood, 1992); S. Prickett (ed.), *Reading the Text: Biblical Criticism and Literary Theory* (Oxford: Blackwell, 1991); D. A. Robertson, *The Old Testament and the Literary Critic* (Guides to Biblical Scholarship, Old Testament Series; Philadelphia, PA: Fortress, 1977); L. Ryken, *How to Read the Bible as Literature* (Grand Rapids, MI: Academie, Zondervan, 1984); P. C. Sands, *Literary Genius of the Old Testament* (Oxford: Clarendon; Folcroft, PA: Folcroft Editions, 1924); R. M. Schwartz (ed.), *The Book and the Text: The Bible and Literary Theory* (Oxford: Blackwell, 1990); J.-L. Ska, "La 'nouvelle critique' et l'exégèse anglo-saxonne", *RSR* 80 (1992) 29-53; J. Stalker, *The Beauty of the Bible: A Study of Its Poets and Poetry* (Humanism of the Bible; London: J. Clark & Co., 1918); V. L. Tollers and J. Maier (eds.), *The Bible in Its Literary Milieu: Contemporary Essays* (Grand Rapids, MI: Eerdmans, 1979); M. Weinfeld, "The Bible as Literature", *"Sha'arei Talmon": Studies in the Bible, Qumran and the Ancient Near East Presented to Shemaryahu Talmon* (ed. M. Fishbane and E. Tov; Winona Lake, IN: Eisenbrauns, 1992) 25*-30* (in Hebrew);

methods and approaches are proposed which serve to explore more profoundly other aspects worthy of attention.

In this section B, we will present certain methods of literary analysis which have been developed recently. In the following sections (C, D, E), we will examine briefly different approaches, some of which relate to the study of the tradition, others to the "human sciences", others still to particular situations of the present time. Finally (F) we will consider the fundamentalist reading of the Bible, a reading which does not accept any systematic approach to interpretation.

Taking advantage of the progress made in our day by linguistic and literary studies, biblical exegesis makes use more and more of new methods of literary analysis, in particular rhetorical analysis, narrative analysis and semiotic analysis.

## 1. *Rhetorical Analysis*

Rhetorical anaylsis in itself is not, in fact, a new method. What is new is the use of it in a systematic way for the interpretation of the Bible and also the start and development of a "new rhetoric".

---

proaches that have developed in recent decades the Commission singles out and comments on three specific modes.

## 1. *Rhetorical Analysis*

The Commission defines rhetoric as "the art of composing discourse aimed at persuasion". Given the generic purpose of the Bible to bring

N. Watson, "Authorial Intention — Suspect Concept for Biblical Scholarship", *Australian Biblical Review* 35 (1987) 6-13.

For the New Testament, see W. Beardslee, *Literary Criticism of the New Testament* (Philadelphia, PA: Fortress, 1970); C. Focant, "The Synoptic Gospels: Source Criticism and the New Literary Criticism: Colloquium Biblicum Lovaniense XLI (1992)", *ETL* 68 (1992) 494-99; P. Grant, *Reading the New Testament* (Basingstoke, UK: Macmillan; Grand Rapids, MI: Eerdmans, 1989); D. Jasper, *The New Testament and the Literary Imagination* (Atlantic Highlands, NJ: Humanities Press International; Basingstoke, UK: Macmillan, 1987); S. D. Moore, *Literary Criticism and the Gospels: The Theoretical Challenge* (New Haven, CT: Yale University, 1989); N. R. Petersen, *Literary Criticism for New Testament Critics* (Guides to Biblical Scholarship, New Testament Series; Philadelphia, PA: Fortress, 1978); L. Ryken, *The New Testament in Literary Criticism* (New York: Ungar, 1984). Cf. H. L. Gardner, *The Limits of Literary Criticism: Reflections on the Interpretation of Poetry and Scripture* (Oxford: Oxford University, 1956; repr. as Riddell Memorial Lectures 28; Philadelphia, PA: R. West, 1978).

*Rhetoric* is the art of composing discourse aimed at persuasion. The fact that all biblical texts are in some measure persuasive in character

---

human beings closer to God and to communion with him, its persuasive character is obviously important. Hence the rhetorical analysis of it is clearly "worthy of high regard". Some aspects of the rhetorical character of the Bible have always been part of the literary criticism that developed within the basic historical-critical method itself, for it is "an approach of eminent lineage" (J. Muilenburg). Yet new emphasis has been put on its rhetorical aspects in recent decades, and new techniques of rhetorical analysis have been developed. The Commission distinguishes three kinds of rhetoric: (a) classical rhetoric, derived from ancient Greco-Roman oratory; (b) Semitic rhetoric, derived from modes of composition in Semitic languages; and (c) the "New Rhetoric".

Public speaking involves three elements: speaker, discourse, and audience. Because ancient speeches and other similar compositions, such as one finds in the Bible, have become texts, one can analogously distinguish the author, the text, and readers.

Classical rhetoric emphasized the authority of the speaker, the force or quality of the discourse, and the emotional effects aroused in the audience addressed. It also distinguished modes of argumentation: judicial or forensic (proper to law courts), deliberative (proper to political assemblies), and demonstrative or epideictic (proper to celebrations)[80].

---

[80] This distinction is traced to Aristotle, *Ars rhetorica* 1.3 (§1358b). In this writing, Aristotle sought to analyze classical oratory as it was practised in mid-fourth century Athens. He called the three forms, respectively, *dikanikon, symbouleutikon*, and *epideiktikon*. His analysis was continued in *Rhetorica ad Alexandrum* (often attributed to him) 1.1 (§1421b) and by Plato in *Phaedrus* (261A-262B); and later by the Latin rhetorical handbook called *Rhetorica ad Herennium*, once (erroneously) ascribed to Cicero, possibly authored *ca.* 86-82 B.C. by an unknown Cornificius. Cicero himself included rhetorical analysis in various of his writings, especially in his youthful *De Inventione*, but also in his more mature *De oratore* and *De partitione oratoria*. But the most famous ancient rhetorician was Marcus Fabius Quintilianus, who wrote *Institutio oratoria* sometime about A.D. 92-95, which describes the training of the ideal orator from babyhood to adult life and describes all manner of rhetorical devices. See M. Winterbottom, *M. Fabi Quintiliani Institutionis Oratoriae libri duodecim* (OCT; Oxford: Clarendon, 1970); H. E. Butler, *The Institutio Oratoria of Quintilian with an English Translation* (LCL; 4 vols.; Cambridge, MA: Harvard University, 1920-22); J. Cousin, *Etudes sur Quintilien* (2 vols.; Paris: Boivin & Cie., 1936).

See R. E. Volkmann, *Die Rhetorik der Griechen und Römer* (Handbuch der klassischen Altertums-Wissenschaft 2; 2d ed.; Munich: Beck, 1885; repr., Hildesheim: Olms, 1963); H. Lausberg, *Handbuch der literarischen Rhetorik: Eine Grundlegung der Literaturwissenschaft* (2 vols.; Munich: Hueber, 1960); C. Neumeister, *Grundsätze der forensischen Rhetorik*

means that some knowledge of rhetoric should be part of the normal scholarly equipment of all exegetes. Rhetorical analysis must be carried out in a critical way, since scientific exegesis is an undertaking which necessarily submits itself to the demands of the critical mind.

A considerable number of recent studies in the biblical area have devoted considerable attention to the presence of rhetorical features in Scripture. Three different approaches can be distinguished. The first is based upon classical Greco-Roman rhetoric; the second devotes itself to Semitic procedures of composition; the third takes its inspiration from more recent studies — namely, from what is called the "New Rhetoric".

Every situation of discourse involves the presence of three elements: the speaker (or author), the discourse (or text) and the audience (or the addressees). *Classical rhetoric* distinguished, accordingly, three factors which contribute to the quality of a discourse as an instrument of persuasion: the authority of the speaker, the force of the argument and the feelings aroused in the audience. The diversity of situation and of audience largely determines the way of speaking adopted. Classical rhetoric, since Aristotle, distinguishes three modes of public speaking: the judicial mode

---

Biblical passages can be isolated that follow the rules for each of these modes of argumentation. Elements of judicial rhetoric are found in Paul's Second Letter to the Corinthians[81], elements of deliberative rhetoric, in Jesus' Sermon on the Mount/Plain[82], and elements of epideictic rhetoric,

---

*gezeigt an Gerichtsreden* (Munich: Hueber, 1964). Cf. M. Platnauer, *Fifty Years (and Twelve) of Classical Scholarship* (2d ed.; Oxford: Blackwell; New York: Barnes & Noble, 1968) 416-64; G. A. Kennedy, *Classical Rhetoric and Its Christian and Secular Tradition from Ancient to Modern Times* (Chapel Hill, NC: University of North Carolina; London: Croom Helm, 1980).

[81] See G. A. Kennedy, *New Testament Interpretation through Rhetorical Criticism* (Chapel Hill, NC/London: University of North Carolina, 1984) 86-96; R. Majercik, T. B. Dozeman, and B. Fiore, "Rhetoric and Rhetorical Criticism", *ABD* 5. 710-19. Cf. F. Young and D. F. Ford, *Meaning and Truth in 2 Corinthians* (London: SPCK, 1987). For other Pauline writings, see E. Schüssler Fiorenza, "Rhetorical Situation and Historical Reconstruction in I Corinthians", *NTS* 33 (1987) 386-403; H. D. Betz, "The Literary Composition and Function of Paul's Letter to the Galatians", *NTS* 21 (1974-75) 353-79; *Galatians: A Commentary on Paul's Letter to the Churches in Galatia* (Hermeneia; Philadelphia, PA: Fortress, 1979).

[82] G. A. Kennedy, *New Testament Interpretation* (n. 81 above), 39-72. Cf. A. N. Wilder, *The Language of the Gospel: Early Christian Rhetoric* (Cambridge, MA: Harvard University, 1964; 2d ed., 1971); *The Bible and the Literary Critic* (Minneapolis, MN: Fortress, 1991); J. Lambrecht, "Rhetorical Criticism and the New Testament", *Bijdragen* 50 (1989) 239-53.

(adopted in a court of law); the deliberative mode (for the political assembly) and the demonstrative mode (for celebratory occasions).

Recognizing the immense influence of rhetoric in Hellenistic culture, a growing number of exegetes make use of treatises on classical rhetoric as an aid towards analysing certain aspects of biblical texts, especially those of the New Testament.

Other exegetes concentrate upon the characteristic features of the *biblical literary tradition*. Rooted in Semitic culture, this displays a distinct preference for symmetrical compositions, through which one can detect relationships between different elements in the text. The study of the multiple forms of parallelism and other procedures characteristic of the Semitic mode of composition allows for a better discernment of the literary structure of texts, which can only lead to a more adequate understanding of their message.

The *"New Rhetoric"* adopts a more general point of view. It aims to be something more than a simple catalogue of stylistic figures, oratorical

---

in Jesus' discourses at the Last Supper in John 13–17[83].

Rhetorical aspects of Old Testament writings, especially of the late postexilic period, may share at times some elements of these classical rhetorical forms, which were developed in Hellenistic areas, but in most Old Testament writings one has rather to reckon with modes of Semitic rhetoric, i.e., techniques such as symmetrical composition, parallelism (frequent in the Psalms), and other procedures, such as *inclusio* (as in Jer 3:1–4:4), repetitive tricola (as in Judg 5:19-21), or anaphora (as in Psalm 150)[84].

The so-called New Rhetoric is not interested so much in a catalogue of stylistic figures, oratorical devices, and kinds of argument or discourse as it is to determine what makes a particular use of language effective and convincing and how it affects an audience or arouses its emotions. To this end it often borrows techniques from linguistics, semiotics, anthropology, and sociology.

When applied to biblical texts, it seeks to penetrate to the core of the

---

[83] G. A. Kennedy, *New Testament Interpretation* (n. 81 above), 73-85. Cf. M. Davies, *Rhetoric and Reference in the Fourth Gospel* (JSNTSup 69; Sheffield, UK: JSOT, 1992).

[84] See further J. Muilenburg, "Form Criticism and Beyond", *JBL* 88 (1969) 1-18, esp. 8-18. Cf. L. Alonso Schökel, *Estudios de poetica hebrea* (Barcelona: J. Flors, 1963); E. König, *Stilistik, Rhetorik und Poetik in Bezug auf die biblische Litteratur* (Leipzig: Dieterich, 1900).

stratagems and various kinds of discourse. It investigates what makes a particular use of language effective and successful in the communication of conviction. It seeks to be "realistic" in the sense of not wanting to limit itself to an analysis that is purely formal. It takes due account of the actual situation of debate or discussion. It studies style and composition as means of acting upon an audience. To this end, it benefits from contributions made of late in other areas of knowledge, such as linguistics, semiotics, anthropology and sociology.

Applied to the Bible, the "New Rhetoric" aims to penetrate to the very core of the language of revelation precisely as persuasive religious discourse and to measure the impact of such discourse in the social context of the communication thus begun.

Because of the enrichment it brings to the critical study of texts, such rhetorical analysis is worthy of high regard, above all in view of the greater depth achieved in more recent work. It makes up for a negligence of long standing and can lead to the rediscovery or clarification of original perspectives that had been lost or obscured.

The "New Rhetoric" is surely right in its drawing attention to the capacity of language to persuade and convince. The Bible is not simply a statement of truths. It is a message that carries within itself a function of communication within a particular context, a message which carries with it a certain power of argument and a rhetorical strategy.

Rhetorical analysis does have, however, its limitations. When it remains simply on the level of description, its results often reflect a concern for style only. Basically synchronic in nature, it cannot claim to be an independent method which would be sufficient by itself. Its application to biblical texts raises several questions. Did the authors of these texts belong to the more educated levels of society? To what extent did they follow the rules of rhetoric in their work of composition? What kind of rhetoric is relevant for the analysis of any given text: Greco-Roman or Semitic? Is there sometimes the risk of attributing to certain biblical texts a rhetorical structure that is really too sophisticated? These questions —

---

language of revelation precisely as persuasive religious discourse and to measure its impact. For the Bible is not just a message or a statement of truths, but carries "within itself a function of communication within a particular context, a message which carries with it a certain power of argument and a rhetorical strategy".

For all its positive qualities, however, rhetorical analysis has its limitations. The Commission singles out mainly three: (1) It can become a

and there are others — ought not in any way cast doubt upon the use of this kind of analysis; they simply suggest that it is not something to which recourse ought be had without some measure of discernment.

## 2. *Narrative Analysis*

Narrative exegesis offers a method of understanding and communicating the biblical message which corresponds to the form of story and personal testimony, something characteristic of Holy Scripture and, of course, a fundamental modality of communication between human persons. The Old Testament in fact presents a story of salvation, the powerful recital of which provides the substance of the profession of faith, liturgy and catechesis (cf. *Ps* 78:3-4; *Exod* 12:24-27; *Deut* 6:20-25; 26:5-11). For its own part, the proclamation of the Christian kerygma amounts in essentials to a sequence telling the story of the life, death and resurrection of Jesus

---

merely superficial description of the text's style; (2) being a synchronic approach to the Bible, it cannot claim an independence or autonomy as a substitute for the basic (diachronic) method; and (3) it can be eisegetical, attributing to the biblical text a degree of sophistication of either Greco-Roman or Semitic rhetoric that it really may not have. Hence, rhetorical analysis has to be used with discernment[85].

Rhetorical analysis, however, remains an important refinement of the historical-critical method and cannot be neglected.

## 2. *Narrative Analysis*

A great deal of the Bible is per se narrative, because it tells the story of God's salvific plan and how it unfolded for centuries in the history of Israel and for the better part of a century in the early Christian community. It also recounts the personal testimony of individual human beings chosen by God to carry on his work. Thus the Old Testament provides a powerful *recital* of Israel's profession of faith, liturgy, and catechesis through that story of God's activity at work on behalf of the

---

[85] R. Meynet, *L'Analyse rhétorique: Une nouvelle méthode pour comprendre la Bible: Textes fondateurs et exposé systématique* (Paris: Editions du Cerf, 1989); *Initiation à la rhétorique biblique: "Qui donc est le plus grand?"* (Initiations; Paris: Cerf, 1982). M. Warner (ed.), *The Bible as Rhetoric: Studies in Biblical Persuasion and Credibility* (Warwick Studies in Philosophy and Literature; London/New York: Routledge, 1990); W. Wuellner, "Where Is Rhetorical Criticism Taking Us?" *CBQ* 49 (1987) 448-63.

Christ, events of which the gospels offer us a detailed account. Catechesis itself also appears in narrative form (cf. *1 Cor* 11:23-25).,

With respect to the narrative approach, it helps to distinguish methods of analysis, on the one hand, and theological reflection, on the other.

Many *analytic methods* are in fact proposed today. Some start from

---

Chosen People and the account of individuals raised up to accomplish it. The Commission appeals explicitly to Ps 78:3-4 ("We have heard them [the lessons from of old], we know them; our ancestors have recited them to us. We do not keep them from our children; we recite them to the next generation"); to Exod 12:24-27 (the story of the origin of Passover); to Deut 6:20-25 (the instruction of Jewish children about how God brought Israel out of Egypt); 26:5-11 (the story of how Israel left Egypt and entered Canaan). Similarly, in the New Testament, the recorded Christian kerygma tells the story of the life, ministry, death, and resurrection of Jesus Christ, and its catechesis even narrates the institution of the Eucharist at the Last Supper (1 Cor 11:23-25)[86].

---

[86] See further R. Alter, *The Art of Biblical Narrative* (New York: Basic Books; London: Allen & Unwin, 1981); A. Berlin, *Poetics and Interpretation of Biblical Narrative* (Sheffield, UK: Almond, 1983; repr. Winona Lake, IN: Eisenbrauns, 1994); D. Damrosch, *The Narrative Covenant: Transformations of Genre in the Growth of Biblical Literature* (San Francisco, CA: Harper & Row, 1987); J. C. Exum, *Tragedy and Biblical Narrative: Arrows of the Almighty* (Cambridge, UK: Cambridge University, 1992); K. R. R. Gros Louis et al., *Literary Interpretations of Biblical Narratives* (2 vols.; Bible in Literature Courses; Nashville, TN: Abingdon, 1974, 1982); D. M. Gunn and D. N. Fewell, *Narrative in the Hebrew Bible* (Oxford Bible Series; Oxford: Oxford University, 1993); F. Kermode, *The Genesis of Secrecy: On the Interpretation of Narrative* (Cambridge, MA: Harvard University, 1979); W. A. Kort, *Story, Text, and Scripture: Literary Interests in Biblical Narrative* (University Park, PA: Pennsylvania State University, 1988); J. Licht, *Storytelling in the Bible* (Jerusalem: Magnes, 1978); B. O. Long (ed.), *Images of Man and God: Old Testament Short Stories in Literary Focus* (Bible and Literature Series 1; Sheffield, UK: Almond, 1981); F. McConnell (ed.), *The Bible and the Narrative Tradition* (New York: Oxford University, 1986); M. J. Oosthuizen, "Narrative Analysis of the Old Testament — Some Challenges and Prospects", *JNSL* 18 (1992) 145-61; M. A. Powell, *What Is Narrative Criticism? A New Approach to the Bible* (London: SPCK, 1993); J. P. Rosenblatt and J. C. Sitterson, Jr. (eds.), *"Not in Heaven": Coherence and Complexity in Biblical Narrative* (Indiana Studies in Biblical Literature; Bloomington, IN: Indiana University, 1991); U. E. Simon, *Story and Faith in the Biblical Narrative* (London: SPCK, 1975); J.-L. Ska, *"Our Fathers Have Told Us": Introduction to the Analysis of Hebrew Narratives* (SubBib 13; Rome: Biblical Institute, 1990); M. Sternberg, *The Poetics of Biblical Narrative: Ideological Literature and the Drama of Reading* (Indiana Literary Biblical Series; Bloomington, IN: Indiana University, 1985; repr., 1987).

the study of ancient models of narrative. Others base themselves upon present day "narratology" in one or other of its forms, in which case there can often be points of contact with semiotics. Particularly attentive to elements in the text which have to do with plot, characterization and the point of view taken by a narrator, narrative analysis studies how a text tells a story in such a way as to engage the reader in its "narrative world" and the system of values contained therein.

Several methods introduce a distinction between "real author" and "implied author", "real reader" and "implied reader". The "real author" is the person who actually composed the story. By "implied author" one means the image of the author which the text progressively creates in the course of the reading (with his or her own culture, character, inclinations, faith, etc.). The "real reader" is any person who has access to the text — from those who first read it or heard it read, right down to those who read or hear it today. By "implied reader" one means the reader which the text presupposes and in effect creates, the one who is capable of performing the mental and affective operations necessary for entering into the narrative world of the text and responding to it in the way envisaged by the real author through the instrumentality of the implied author.

A text will continue to have an influence in the degree to which real readers (e.g., ourselves in the late 20th century) can identify with the implied reader. One of the major tasks of exegesis is to facilitate this process of identification.

---

The Commission distinguishes two aspects of narrative analysis as important: analytic modes that are profitably used and a mode of theological reflection.

*Analytic Methods.* Since these are many and diverse, the Commission singles out two for comment. There is the study of "ancient models" of narration, by which is meant apparently a rather unsophisticated mode of storytelling. There is also present-day "narratology", which concentrates on a text's plot, characterization, and the way the story is developed so as to bring the reader into its "narrative world" and into contact with the system of values contained in the account[87]. The Commission explains the distinctions made in such narrative analysis between the "real author" and

---

[87] See P. Bühler and J.-F. Habermacher (eds.), *La narration: Quand le récit devient communication* (Publications de la Faculté de Théologie de l'Université de Neuchâtel, Lieux théologiques 12; Geneva: Labor et Fides, 1988). Cf. M. W. G. Stibbe, *John as Storyteller: Narrative Criticism and the Fourth Gospel* (SNTSMS 73; Cambridge, UK: Cambridge University, 1992).

Narrative analysis involves a new way of understanding how a text works. While the historical-critical method considers the text as a "window" giving access to one or other period (not only to the situation which the story relates but also to that of the community for whom the tale is told), narrative analysis insists that the text also functions as a "mirror", in the sense that it projects a certain image — a "narrative world" — which exercises an influence upon readers' perceptions in such a way as to bring them to adopt certain values rather than others.

Connected with this kind of study, primarily literary in character, is a certain mode of *theological reflection*, as one considers the implications the "story" (and also the "witness") character of Scripture has with respect to the consent of faith and as one derives from this a hermeneutic of a more practical and pastoral nature. There is here a reaction against the reduction of the inspired text to a series of theological theses, often formulated in non-scriptural categories and language. What is asked of narrative exegesis is that it rehabilitate in new historical contexts the modes of communicating and conveying meaning proper to the biblical account, in order to open up more effectively its saving power. Narrative analysis insists upon the need both to tell the story of salvation (the "informative"

the "implied author" and between the "real reader" and the "implied reader" and shows that the goal of such analysis it to facilitate the process whereby real readers of today can identify themselves with the implied reader, which the text seeks to create. Hence the biblical text, instead of being a "window", through which the diachronic historical-critical method enables readers to view the period about which the story tells, functions as a "mirror" projecting a narrative world that can influence readers to adopt certain values rather than others.

*Theological Reflection*. This reflection seeks to study the implications of the biblical "story" or "testimony" so analyzed for the reaction and consent of faith that it can elicit. As a result, it has a hermeneutic of a more practical and pastoral nature, because it seeks not to formulate theological theses, but rather allows the biblical story to communicate more effectively its own saving power. Narrative analysis not only recounts the story of salvation (in an "informative" way), but also tells it (in a "performative" way) in order to accost readers to get them to reflect existentially on the narrative's salvific power for them. The usefulness of such a narrative analysis of the Bible is evident, because it helps in the transit from what the text meant (ascertained by the historical-critical method) to what it means for the readers of today.

aspect) and to tell the story in view of salvation (the "performative" aspect). The biblical account, in effect, whether explicitly or implicitly as the case may be, contains an existential appeal addressed to the reader.

The usefulness of narrative analysis for the exegesis of the Bible is clear. It is well suited to the narrative character which so many biblical texts display. It can facilitate the transition, often so difficult, from the meaning of the text in its historical context (the proper object of the historical-critical method) to its significance for the reader of today. On the other hand, the distinction between the "real author" and the "implied author" does tend to make problems of interpretation somewhat more complex.

When applied to texts of the Bible, narrative analysis cannot rest content with imposing upon them certain pre-established models. It must strive to adapt itself to their own proper character. The synchronic approach which it brings to texts needs to be supplemented by diachronic studies as well. It must, moreover, beware of a tendency that can arise to exclude any kind of doctrinal elaboration in the content of biblical narratives. In such a case it would find itself out of step with the biblical tradition itself, which practises precisely this kind of elaboration, and also with the tradition of the Church, which has continued further along the same way. Finally, it is worth noting that the existential subjective effectiveness of the impact of the Word of God in its narrative transmission cannot be

---

This mode of analysis of the Bible, however, can be more complicated than need be, especially in the distinction between "real" and "implied" authors and readers and in forcing the biblical text into a "pre-established model". Whereas its synchronic analysis of the Bible may have merit as a "mirror" in which readers may see themselves reflected and challenged, it cannot wholly dispense with the diachronic aspect, the "window" looking on the past, because the biblical story and its tradition have a doctrinal value important in the history of the Church. The elaboration of a story and its historical tradition have indeed contributed to the development of dogma within the Church, and this aspect of the story cannot be neglected or overlooked.

The Commission concludes by noting that "the existential subjective effectiveness of the impact of the Word of God in its narrative transmission cannot be considered to be in itself a sufficient indication that its full truth has been adequately grasped". The reason for this conclusion is that the Bible, though it is the Word of God that still accosts human beings in its narrative account, is also the record of a faith-community, the Christian

considered to be in itself a sufficient indication that its full truth has been adequately grasped.

## 3. *Semiotic Analysis*

Ranged amongst the methods identified as synchronic, those, namely, which concentrate on the study of the biblical text as it comes before the reader in its final state, is semiotic analysis. This has experienced a notable development in certain quarters over the last twenty years. Originally known by the more general term "Structuralism", this method can claim as forefather the Swiss linguist Ferdinand de Saussure, who at the beginning of the present century worked out the theory according to which all language is a system of relationships obeying fixed laws. Several linguists and literary critics have had a notable influence in the development of the method. The majority of biblical scholars who make use of semiotics in the study of the Bible take as their authority Algirdas J. Greimas and the School of Paris which he founded. Similar approaches and methods, based upon modern linguistics, have developed elsewhere. But it is Greimas' method which we intend to present and analyse briefly here.

Semiotics is based upon three main principles or presuppositions:

The *principle of immanence*: each text forms a unit of meaning com-

---

Church, and it has to be understood along with the tradition that has grown historically out of it within that community. Its full truth may well involve more than its narrative character[88].

## 3. *Semiotic Analysis*

"Semiotics" is derived from the Greek word *sēmeiōtikos*, "observant of signs", or one who is an "observer of signs". It is a philosophical system that has implications for more than merely the literary structure of a text or document. This mode of synchronic analysis, however, is concerned with the final form of the biblical text and has often been called "structuralist", because it strives to analyze the basic structure or system of fixed relationships (signs) found in all language. But, in reality, semiotics has become a very specific form of structuralism, focusing on the

---

[88] See further P. Perkins, "Crisis in Jerusalem? Narrative Criticism in New Testament Studies", *TS* 50 (1989) 296-313.

plete in itself; the analysis considers the entire text but only the text; it does not look to any date "external" to the text, such as the author, the audience, any events it describes or what might have been its process of composition.

The *principle of the structure of meaning*: there is no meaning given except in and through relationship, in particular the relationship of "difference"; the analysis of the text consists then in establishing the network of relationships (of opposition, confirmation, etc.) between the various elements; out of this the meaning of the text is constructed.

The *principle of the grammar of the text*: each text follows a *"grammar"*, that is to say, a certain number of rules or structures; in the collection of sentences that we call discourse there are various levels, each of which has its own distinct grammar.

---

signs or conventions by which a literary work produces its meaning[89].

As applied to the Bible, the mode of semiotic analysis of A. J. Greimas has been most widely used[90]. It works with three principles: immanence (considering the text as a unit in itself, apart from external

---

[89] See D. S. Clarke, *Principles of Semiotic* (New York: Routledge & Kegan Paul, 1987); U. Eco, *A Theory of Semiotics* (Bloomington, IN/London: Indiana University, 1976); E. Güttgemanns, *Studia linguistica neotestamentica: Gesammelte Aufsätze zur linguistischen Grundlage einer neutestamentlichen Theologie* (Munich: Kaiser, 1971); *Fragmenta semiotico-hermeneutica: Eine Texthermeneutik für den Umgang mit der Hl. Schrift* (Bonn: Linguistica Biblica, 1983); Iu. M. Lotman, *Analysis of the Poetic Text* (Ann Arbor, MI: Ardis, 1976); *The Structure of the Artistic Text* (Ann Arbor, MI: [Department of Slavic Languages and Literature], 1977); J. C. Giroud et L. Panier (eds.), *Analyse sémiotique des textes: Introduction, théorie, pratique* (Lyon: Presses Universitaires de Lyon, 1979); R. E. Scholes, *Semiotics and Interpretation* (New Haven, CT: Yale University, 1982).

On structuralism, see R. Barthes (ed.), *Analyse structurale et exégèse biblique: Essais d'interprétation* (Bibliothèque théologique; Neuchâtel: Delachaux et Niestlé, 1972); A. Fossion, *Lire les Ecritures: Théorie et pratique de la lecture structurale* (Collection "Ecritures" 2; Brussels: Lumen Vitae, 1980); A. M. Johnson, Jr. (ed.), *Structuralism and Biblical Hermeneutics: A Collection of Essays* (Pittsburgh Theological Monograph Series 22; Pittsburgh, PA: Pickwick, 1979).

[90] See A. J. Greimas, *Du sens: Essais sémiotiques* (2 vols.; Paris: Editions du Seuil, 1970); *Narrative Semiotics and Cognitive Discourses* (London: Pinter, 1990). Cf. R. Schleifer, *A. J. Greimas and the Nature of Meaning: Linguistics, Semiotics and Discourse Theory* (London: Croom Helm, 1987); L. Orr, *Semiotic and Structuralist Analyses of Fiction: An Introduction and a Survey of Applications* (Troy, NY: Whitston Pub. Co., 1987); D. Patte, *The Religious Dimensions of Biblical Texts: Greimas's Structural Semiotics and Biblical Exegesis* (Semeia Studies; Atlanta, GA: Scholars, 1990); J.-N. Aletti, "Exégèse biblique et sémiotique: Quels enjeux?" *RSR* 80 (1992) 9-28.

The overall content of a text can be analyzed at three different levels.

*The narrative level.* Here one studies in the story the transformations which move the action from the initial to the final state. Within the course of the narrative, the analysis seeks to retrace the different phases, logically bound to each other, which mark the transformation from one state to another. In each of these phases it establishes the relationships between the "roles" played by the "actants" which determine the various stages of development and bring about transformation.

*The level of discourse.* The analysis here consists of three operations: (a) the fixing and classification of figures, that is to say, the elements of meaning in a text (actors, times, places); (b) the tracking of the course of each figure in the text in order to determine just how the text uses each one; (c) enquiry into the thematic value of the figures. This last operation consists in discerning "in the name of what" (= what value) the figures such a path in the text determined in this way.

*The logico-semantic level.* This is the so-called deep level. It is also the most abstract. It proceeds from the assumption that certain forms of logic and meaning underlie the narrative and discursive organization of all discourse. The analysis at this level consists in identifying the logic which governs the basic articulations of the narrative and figurative flow of a text. To achieve this recourse is often had to an instrument called the "semiotic square" (*carré sémiotique*), a figure which makes use of the relationships between two "contrary" terms and two "contradictory" terms (for example, black and white; white and not-white; black and not-black).

The exponents of the theory behind the semiotic method continue to produce new developments. Present research centers most particularly upon enunciation and intertextuality. Applied in the first instance to the narrative texts of Scripture, to which it is most readily applicable, the use of the method has been more and more extended to other kinds of biblical discourse as well.

The description of semiotics that has been given and above all the formulation of its presuppositions should have already served to make clear the *advantages* and the *limitations* of this method. By directing great-

---

aspects, either author or reader); structure of meaning (establishing the network of relationships of elements of the text, opposition, confirmation, etc.); and grammar of the text (the rules in the collection of sentences that make up the text). Using these principles, one can analyze the text on different levels: narrative level, which traces the transformation of an action from the initial to a final stage and the relations between the roles

er attention to the fact that each biblical text is a coherent whole, obedient to a precise linguistic mechanic of operation, semiotics contributes to our understanding of the Bible as Word of God expressed in human language.

Semiotics can be usefully employed in the study of the Bible only in so far as the method is separated from certain assumptions developed in structuralist philosophy, namely the refusal to accept individual personal identity within the text and extra-textual reference beyond it. The Bible is a Word that bears upon reality, a Word which God has spoken in a historical context and which God addresses to us today through the mediation of human authors. The semiotic approach must be open to history: first of all to the history of those who play a part in the texts; then to that of the authors and readers. The great risk run by those who employ semiotic analysis is that of remaining at the level of a formal study of the content of texts, failing to draw out the message.

When it does not become lost in remote and complex language and when its principal elements are taught in simple terms, semiotic analysis can give Christians a taste for studying the biblical text and discovering certain of its dimensions, without their first having to acquire a great deal of instruction in historical matters relating to the production of the text

---

played by the "actants" that determine the various stages of development and bring about the transformation; the level of discourse, which fixes and classifies figures (actors, times, places), tracks the course of each figure to determine how it is used; and inquires into the thematic value of the figures to determine "in the name of what" value the figure acts; the logico-semantic level, the so-called deep level, which seeks to determine the logic and meaning underlying the narrative and discursive organization of all discourse. To achieve this, recourse is had to the "semiotic square" which explains the relationships as contrary or contradictory.

This mode of analysis of the biblical text is very complicated, as the description of it given by the Commission makes clear. Significantly, the Commission does not say what the advantages of this mode of analysis really are. That semiotics discovers something about the underlying structure of language or certain dimensions of discourse in a biblical text may be conceded. That it contributes to one's understanding of the Bible as the Word of God expressed in human language is another matter. The Commission finally admits that the method entails a certain structuralist philosophy that may not be universally acceptable. There is also the risk "of remaining at the level of a formal study of the content of texts, failing

and its socio-cultural world. It can thus prove useful in pastoral practice itself, providing a certain appropriation of Scripture amongst those who are not specialized in the area.

## C. Approaches Based on Tradition

The literary methods which we have just reviewed, although they differ from the historical-critical method in that they pay greater attention to the internal unity of the texts studied, remain nonetheless insufficient for the interpretation of the Bible, because they consider each of its writings in isolation. But the Bible is not a compilation of texts unrelated to each other; rather, it is a gathering together of a whole array of witnesses from one great Tradition. To be fully adequate to the object of its study, biblical exegesis must keep this truth firmly in mind. Such in fact is the perspective adopted by a number of approaches which are being developed at present.

---

to draw out the message" itself[91]. For it can get lost in remote and complex language, often far more abstruse than any instruction in the historical aspects of a biblical text.

## C. Approaches Based on Tradition

The foregoing synchronic methods, which pay due attention to the internal unity of biblical texts, actually remain "insufficient for the interpretation of the Bible, because they consider each of its writings in isolation". Other modern approaches to the Bible, however, consider it in its variety as witnesses from one great Tradition. So under this heading the Commission takes up three approaches derived from the canon, Jewish traditions of interpretation, and the history of the biblical text's influence (its *Wirkungsgeschichte*).

---

[91] The semiotician might object to the way the Commission has formulated this judgment, because "the message" is not something that exists in the text prior to a reading (like a rabbit that a magician pulls out of a hat); the sense emerges in the process of reading and is not really separate from the reader. Every text would really be a dialogue between an implied author and an implied reader, and the rules of meaning in that dialogue are governed by an intention. In reading and in giving life to the text, the reader perceives that an appeal is being made and that this is not a creation of the reader, but a meeting of two minds.

## 1. *The Canonical Approach*

The "canonical" approach, which originated in the United States some twenty years ago, proceeds from the perception that the historical-critical method experiences at times considerable difficulty in arriving, in its conclusions, at a truly theological level. It aims to carry out the theological task of interpretation more successfully by beginning from within an explicit framework of faith: the Bible as a whole.

To achieve this, it interprets each biblical text in the light of the Canon of Scriptures, that is to say, of the Bible as received as the norm of faith by a community of believers. It seeks to situate each text within the

---

## 1. *The Canonical Approach*

This approach strives to interpret a biblical text in the light of the canon of Scripture, i.e. the collection of sacred writings accepted as the norm of faith by a community of believers. The canon or collection of sacred writings is seen as a witness to "the single plan of God", and individual texts are interpreted in their relation to the whole testimony that the entire canon gives of that plan. This approach thus seeks to come to an understanding of the text that is truly valid for today. This approach is not a substitute for the historical-critical method, but a complement to it, which enables one to come more easily to a fully theological understanding of a biblical text in its relation to the Bible as a whole.

The Commission briefly summarizes two slightly different canonical approaches: that of B. S. Childs, which concentrates on the final form of the text accepted by the community as an authoritative expression of its faith and rule of life[92]; and that of J. A. Sanders, which devotes more attention to the "canonical process" (its progressive development) by

---

[92] See B. S. Childs, *Introduction to the Old Testament as Scripture* (Philadelphia, PA: Fortress, 1979); *The New Testament as Canon: An Introduction* (Philadelphia, PA: Fortress, 1984); *Old Testament Theology in a Canonical Context* (Philadelphia, PA: Fortress, 1986); "Die theologische Bedeutung der Endform eines Textes", *TQ* 167 (1987) 242-51.

Cf. R. P. Carroll, "Childs and Canon", *IBS* 2 (1980) 211-36; J. Barr, "Childs' Introduction to the Old Testament as Scripture", *JSOT* 16 (1980) 12-23; *Holy Scripture: Canon, Authority, Criticism* (Philadelphia, PA: Westminster, 1983); R. R. Topping, "The Canon and the Truth: Brevard Childs and James Barr on the Canon and the Historical-Critical Method", *TJT* 8 (1992) 239-60; G. T. Sheppard, "Canonical Criticism", *ABD* 1. 861-88.

Though Childs is reluctant to admit it, there is a certain affinity with his canonical interpretation and some of the tenets of New Criticism. See J. Barton, *Reading the Old Testament* (n. 58 above), 141-54.

single plan of God, the goal being to arrive at a presentation of Scripture truly valid for our time. The method does not claim to be a substitute for the historical-critical method; the hope is, rather, to complete it.

---

which the faith-community came to accept a text as normative[93]. Sanders studies the way in which older traditions have been used again in new contexts as they gradually shape the whole in which the community finds its identity. The use of older traditions can be midrashic, serving to make the biblical text relevant for a later time.

The canonical approach refuses to be content with a meaning alleged to be original and early, as if it alone were authentic. Inspired Scripture means that it has been accepted by the Church as the rule of faith, and the final form of each book becomes "biblical" only in its relation to the canon as a whole. "It is the believing community that provides a truly adequate context for interpreting canonical texts". Thus both faith and the guidance of the community by Holy Spirit enrich the interpretation, and these are part of the presuppositions with which the historical-critical method becomes properly oriented[94].

The Commission notes some of the problems that this canonical approach can encounter, especially in the quest to determine the canonical process. When does a text become canonical? That might mean that a text would become such from the time that it was recognized as normative or authoritative by the community, even if that were to be before it reached its final and definitive form. That raises a further question: Should the interpretive process which led to the formation of the Canon be recognized as the guiding principle for the interpretation of Scripture today? That cannot be answered easily, because, whereas the final and definitive

---

[93] See J. A. Sanders, *Torah and Canon* (Philadelphia, PA: Fortress, 1972); *Canon and Community: A Guide to Canonical Criticism* (Philadelphia, PA: Fortress, 1984); *From Sacred Story to Sacred Text: Canon as Paradigm* (Philadelphia, PA.: Fortress, 1987).

Cf. E. Zenger, "Unser Erstes Testament: Von der Bedeutung des Alten Testaments für die Christen", *BLit* 63 (1990) 129-41; C. J. Scalise, *Hermeneutics as Theological Prolegomena: A Canonical Approach* (Studies in American Hermeneutics 8; Macon, GA: Mercer University, 1993).

[94] The Commission adds a significant comment about the role of the Church's teaching authority (or *magisterium*): "Church authority, exercised as a service of the community, must see to it that this interpretation remains faithful to the great Tradition which has produced the texts". It refers to *Dei Verbum* §10: "This teaching office is not above the word of God, but serves it, teaching only what has been handed on, listening to it devoutly, guarding it scrupulously, and explaining it faithfully by divine commission, and with the help of the Holy Spirit" (*The Documents of Vatican II*, 118).

Two different points of view have been proposed:

Brevard S. Childs centers his interest on the final canonical form of the text (whether book or collection), the form accepted by the community as an authoritative expression of its faith and rule of life.

James A. Sanders, rather than looking to the final and fixed form of the text, devotes his attention to the "canonical process" or progressive development of the Scripture which the believing community has accepted as a normative authority. The critical study of this process examines the way in which older traditions have been used again and again in new contexts, before finally coming to constitute a whole that is at once stable and

---

form is certainly canonical and authoritative, it is far from certain that earlier forms in the process would have been so recognized by the entire community of faith or that the earlier forms are valid criteria of interpretation, despite the light that they may shed on the genesis or development of the text concerned.

There are other problems too. Prominent among them is the diversity of canons that exist. There is the Jewish canon, consisting of what is often called the Hebrew Scriptures. For Christians these Scriptures have become the "Old Testament", a term derived from a New Testament way of referring to it, "the old covenant (that) is read" (2 Cor 3:14).

Unfortunately, the Commission speaks merely of "the Christian Church" and does not discuss the difference of canons used by various Christians. Most Protestant Christians limit their Old Testament to the Hebrew Scriptures, the corpus of sacred writings used by Palestinian Jews, or the so-called Palestinian canon. Yet there are Protestants who would at least accord some recognition to the so-called deuterocanonical writings of the Old Testament as used by Catholics[95]. Initially, the Christian Church accepted as the Old Testament writings that were authoritative in the Hellenistic Jewish community, i.e. part of the so-called Alexandrian canon, whereas the Protestant canon dates from the sixteenth-century Reformation[96]. In other words, Catholics recognize as deuterocanonical

---

[95] The name "deuterocanonical" is traced to Sixtus of Siena, O.P. (1520-1569): "Canonici secundi ordinis (qui olim Ecclesiastici vocabantur & nunc a nobis Deuterocanonici dicuntur), *Bibliotheca sancta...* (rev. ed. J. Hay; Lyons: Landry, 1592) 10. It refers to the seven texts and additions mentioned below.

[96] See A. C. Sundberg, Jr., *The Old Testament of the Early Church* (HTS 20; Cambridge, MA: Harvard University, 1964; repr. New York: Kraus Reprint Co., 1969). Cf. R. E. Murphy, A. C. Sundberg, Jr., and S. Sandmel, "A Symposium on the Canon of Scripture", *CBQ* 28 (1966) 189-207.

yet adaptable, coherent while holding together matter that is diverse — in short, a complete whole, in which the faith community can find its identity. In the course of this process various hermeneutic procedures have been at work and this continues to be the case even after the fixing of the canon. These procedures are often midrashic in nature, serving to make the biblical text relevant for a later time. They encourage a constant interaction between the community and the Scriptures, calling for an interpretation which ever seeks to bring the tradition up to date.

The canonical approach rightly reacts against placing an exaggerated value upon what is supposed to be original and early, as if this alone were authentic. Inspired Scripture is precisely Scripture in that it has been recognized by the Church as the rule of faith. Hence the significance, in this light, of both the final form in which each of the books of the Bible

---

seven books beyond the Palestinian canon, seven books which are found in the Greek Septuagint (Tobit, Judith, Wisdom, Sirach [or Ecclesiasticus], Baruch, and 1–2 Maccabees) and the additions to Daniel (Song of the Three Young Men, Susanna, and Bel and the Dragon) and to Esther also found there. These writings are often called "Apocrypha" by Protestant Christians, a term that Catholics also use for the other writings in the Septuagint that are not part of the Catholic canon (1 Esdras [= Greek Esdras A and Latin 3 Esdras, found in the appendix of the Sixto-Clementine Vulgate], 3–4 Maccabees, Psalm 151, the Prayer of Manasseh [also found in the appendix of the Sixto-Clementine Vulgate], Psalms of Solomon)[97]. To these one would have to add 2 Esdras, not found in the Septuagint, but known in the Latin tradition as 4 Esdras (found in the appendix of the Sixto-Clementine Vulgate)[98]. Because of this situation the

---

[97] The Christian canon is still more complicated if one considers the shape that it takes in the eastern Orthodox Churches, which recognize as canonical further Greek writings of the Septuagint: 1 Esdras, Prayer of Manasseh, Psalm 151, 3 Maccabees. (4 Maccabees, though never recognized as canonical, has been used by the Greek Orthodox almost as if it were [actually in an appendix of the Orthodox Greek Bible].) In the Slavonic Bible is also included 3 Esdras (= 2 Esdras in the *NRSV with the Apocrypha*; 4 Esdras in the appendix of the Sixto-Clementine Latin Vulgate). On these matters, see B. M. Metzger, "To the Reader", *The New Oxford Annotated Bible with the Apocryphal/Deuterocanonical Books: New Revised Standard Version* (ed. B. M. Metzger and R. E. Murphy; New York: Oxford University, 1991) ix-xiv and xxi-xxiii. Cf. A. Rahlfs, *Septuaginta: Id est Vetus Testamentum, graece iuxta LXX interpretes* (8th ed.; Stuttgart: Württembergische Bibelanstalt, 1935; repr. 1965).

[98] Part of 2 Esdras (the seven apocalyptic visions of chapters 3-14) is also known as 4 Ezra. See R. Weber (ed.), *Biblia sacra iuxta Vulgatam versionem* (n. 52 above) 2. 1907-75.

appears and of the complete whole which all together make up as Canon. Each individual book only becomes biblical in the light of the Canon as a whole.

It is the believing community that provides a truly adequate context for interpreting canonical texts. In this context faith and the Holy Spirit enrich exegesis; Church authority, exercised as a service of the community, must see to it that this interpretation remains faithful to the great Tradition which has produced the texts (cf. *Dei Verbum*, 10).

The canonical approach finds itself grappling with more than one problem when it seeks to define the "canonical process". At what point in time precisely does a text become canonical? It seems reasonable to describe it as such from the time that the community attributes to it a normative authority, even if this should be before it has reached its final, definitive form. One can speak of a "canonical" hermeneutic once the repetition

canonical interpretation of the Bible will differ for Jews, Catholics, Orthodox, and Protestants.

Moreover, the Christian Church has always read "the Old Testament in the light of the paschal mystery — the death and resurrection of Jesus Christ — who brings a radical newness and, with sovereign authority, gives a meaning to the Scriptures that is decisive and definitive"[99]. This christological dimension of the Bible as a whole is supremely authoritative for Christians, for the second part of it, the New Testament, has given a meaning to the whole that has become normative in a new way. For as a whole the Bible contains the fullness of God's revelation for Christians.

The Commission, however, carefully recognizes that the christological dimension does not imply the doing away with the "earlier canonical interpretation which preceded the Christian Passover". What the Hebrew Scriptures meant to the people of Israel of old can still have meaning for Christians. "One must respect each stage of the history of salvation. To empty out of the Old Testament its own proper meaning would be to

---

[99] In support of this the Commission appeals to *Dei Verbum* §4: "Jesus perfected revelation by fulfilling it through His whole work of making Himself present and manifesting Himself: through His words and deeds, His signs and wonders, but especially through His death and glorious resurrection from the dead and final sending of the Spirit of truth. Moreover, He confirmed with divine testimony what revelation proclaimed: that God is with us to free us from the darkness of sin and death, and to raise us up to life eternal. The Christian dispensation, therefore, as the new and definitive covenant, will never pass away, and we now await no further new public revelation before the glorious manifestation of our Lord Jesus Christ (cf. 1 Tim. 6:14 and Tit. 2:13)" (*The Documents of Vatican II*, 113).

of the traditions, which comes about through the taking into account of new aspects of the situation (be they religious, cultural or theological), begins to preserve the identity of the message. But a question arises: should the interpretive process which led to the formation of the Canon be recognized as the guiding principle for the interpretation of Scripture today?

On the other hand, the complex relationships that exist between the Jewish and Christian Canons of Scripture raise many problems of interpretation. The Christian Church has received as "Old Testament" the writings which had authority in the Hellenistic Jewish community, but some of these are either lacking in the Hebrew Bible or appear there in somewhat different form. The *corpus* is therefore different. From this it follows that the canonical interpretation cannot be identical in each case, granted that each text must be read in relation to the whole *corpus*. But, above all, the Church reads the Old Testament in the light of the paschal mystery — the death and resurrection of Jesus Christ — who brings a radical newness and, with sovereign authority, gives a meaning to the

---

deprive the New of its roots in history". That is why the Christian must beware of reading the Old Testament simply as *praeparatio evangelica*. The way that God revealed himself in speaking through Moses and the Prophets is still part of God's revelation to Christians as well, and Christians have to learn to listen better to God's Word in that form.

The explanation that the Commission thus offers has another consequence that is not expressed. For it should, then, be possible for Jewish and Christian interpreters to agree on the basic meaning of Old Testament texts. Using properly the historical-critical method to ascertain the textual, contextual, and relational meaning of, say, the Book of Jeremiah, they should be able to agree on its religious and spiritual meaning for Jewish and Christian readers alike. For the latter there may also be a christological meaning or a plus value that the New Testament has added by a *relecture* of Jeremiah passages[100]. But since the basic religious and spiritual meaning of the Old Testament was intended to feed the religious life of the Jewish people, what they found there as their spiritual sustenance is something that can and must nourish Christian spirituality as well — even apart from any christological consideration or added nuance from New Testament teaching. In other words, the Jewish canonical meaning of

---

[100] E.g., as Jer 31:31-34 is used in Heb 8:8-12; or as Jer 22:23 is used in 1 Cor 1:31.

Scriptures that is decisive and definitive (cf. *Dei Verbum*, 4). This new determination of meaning has become an integral element of Christian faith. It ought not, however, mean doing away with all attempt to be consistent with that earlier canonical interpretation which preceded the Christian Passover. One must respect each stage of the history of salvation. To empty out of the Old Testament its own proper meaning would be to deprive the New of its roots in history.

### 2. *Approach through Recourse to Jewish Traditions of Interpretation*

The Old Testament reached its final form in the Jewish world of the four or five centuries preceding the Christian era. Judaism of this time also provided the matrix for the origin of the New Testament and the infant

---

the Old Testament is not without relevance for Christian readers of the first part of God's written Word[101].

### 2. *Approach through Recourse to Jewish Traditions of Interpretation*

If the Jewish canonical meaning of Scripture can have significance for Christian readers of the Bible, then one would have to consider as well Jewish traditions of biblical interpretation[102], for they represent the beginnings of biblical interpretation. Most of the Old Testament itself reached its definitive form during the last four pre-Christian centuries. Ancient

---

[101] See further R. E. Murphy, "Christian Understanding of the Old Testament", *TD* 18 (1970) 321-32; "The Old Testament as Word of God", *A Light unto My Path: Old Testament Studies in Honor of Jacob M. Myers* (ed. H. N. Bream et al.; Philadelphia, PA: Temple University, 1974) 363-74; "Old Testament/Tanakh-Canon and Interpretation", *Hebrew Bible or Old Testament? Studying the Bible in Judaism and Christianity* (Christianity and Judaism in Antiquity 5; ed. R. Brooks and J. J. Collins; Notre Dame, IN: University of Notre Dame, 1990) 11-29; "The Fear of the Lord: A Fear to End All Fears", *Overcoming Fear between Jews and Christians* (ed. J. H. Charlesworth et al.; The American Interfaith Institute; New York: Crossroad, 1992) 172-80, esp. 174-75; J. D. Levenson, *The Hebrew Bible, the Old Testament, and Historical Criticism: Jews and Christians in Biblical Studies* (Louisville, KY: Westminster/John Knox, 1993); A. Graeme Auls, "Can a Biblical Theology Also Be Academic or Ecumenical?" *Text and Pretext: Essays in Honour of Robert Davidson* (JSOTSup 138; Sheffield, UK: JSOT, 1992) 13-27.

[102] See M. A. Fishbane, *Biblical Interpretation in Ancient Israel* (Oxford: Clarendon, 1985); L. Jacobs, *Jewish Biblical Exegesis* (New York: Behrman House, 1973); F. E. Greenspahn, *Scripture in the Jewish and Christian Traditions: Authority, Interpretation, Relevance* (Nashville, TN: Abingdon, 1982); S. Garfinkel, "Applied Peshat: Historical-Critical Method and Religious Meaning", *JANES* 22 (1993) 19-28.

Church. Numerous studies of the history of ancient Judaism and notably the manifold research stimulated by the discoveries at Qumran have highlighted the complexity of the Jewish world, both in the land of Israel and in the Diaspora, throughout this period.

---

Judaism of that period, as it is now known to us from discoveries in Israel and in the Diaspora during the nineteenth and twentieth centuries (especially from the discovery of the Dead Sea Scrolls[103]), developed various modes of biblical interpretation. During this time the Hebrew Scriptures were translated into Greek in the Septuagint and into Aramaic in targums[104]. Such translations were already an interpretation of Scripture, because they were a mode of presenting the biblical texts to readers of other language backgrounds. None of them was so literal that it did not nuance the biblical text and at times make intelligible what was obscure in the original Hebrew. The Greek form of the Jewish Bible became the first part of the Christian Church's Bible and remained so for four centuries in the West (until the Latin Vulgate began to dominate the scene) and continues to do so today in the East.

Varieties of Jewish exegetical procedures are also found in the Old Testament itself, as postexilic writers rewrote the stories of Samuel and Kings in 1–2 Chronicles. Modes of *relecture* likewise developed, as the Exodus-theme was utilized in Deutero-Isaiah for the consolation of Jews returning from Babylonian Captivity.

In this pre-Christian period, too, there emerged extracanonical Jewish literature, often misnamed (by Christians) as "intertestamental literature". As it has recently become known, it displays an abundance and variety of interpretations of the Scriptures themselves[105]. Much of that literature (e.g., *Jubilees, 1 Enoch,* the *Genesis Apocryphon* from Qumran Cave 1) is actually parabiblical, a paraphrastic development or an

---

[103] See J. A. Fitzmyer, *The Dead Sea Scrolls: Major Publications and Tools for Study* (rev. ed.; Atlanta, GA: Scholars, 1990).

[104] Three fragmentary targums have come to light in the Qumran caves (4QtgLev, 4QtgJob, 11QtgJob), which show that the translation of parts of the Old Testament into Aramaic was already in writing in pre-Christian times. See further J. A. Fitzmyer, *Dead Sea Scrolls* (n. 103 above), 45, 70; J. W. Bowker, *The Targums and Rabbinic Literature: An Introduction to Jewish Interpretations of Scripture* (London: Cambridge University, 1969); R. Le Déaut, *Introduction à la littérature targumique: Première partie* (Rome: Biblical Institute, 1966); P. S. Alexander, "Targum, Targumim", *ABD* 6. 320-31.

[105] See J. H. Charlesworth, *The Pseudepigrapha and Modern Research, With a Supplement* (SBLSCS 7S; [Atlanta, GA]: Scholars, 1981). Cf. G. J. Brooke, *Exegesis at Qumran: 4QFlorilegium in Its Jewish Context* (JSOTSup 29; Sheffield, UK: JSOT Press, 1985).

It is in this world that the interpretation of Scripture had its beginning. One of the most ancient witnesses to the Jewish interpretation of the Bible is the Greek translation known as the Septuagint. The Aramaic Targums represent a further witness to the same activity, which has carried on down to the present, giving rise in the process to an immense mass of

---

embellishment of the biblical stories themselves. From such literature we have come to learn of Jewish anthological writing, *florilegia, pesharim*, new hymnic forms, apocalyptic dreams and visions, and sapiential compositions. In this period too developed the first forms of *midrash*, commentaries on biblical books[106].

As time passed, early Christian interpreters learned from the Jewish interpreters who preceded them ways of understanding better the Old Testament itself. Thus Origen and Jerome consulted Jewish interpreters[107]. Later on, medieval Christian interpreters learned to use Jewish commentaries, grammars, and lexica[108].

Jewish modes of interpretation have also stimulated writers of the New Testament[109]. The study of isolated Old Testament quotations in the Qumran literature reveals that New Testament writers often quoted the Old Testament in very similar fashion[110]. Certain passages in the New Testament have been recognized as midrashic in character, e.g., Pauline passages such as 1 Cor 10:1-5; 2 Cor 3:7–4:6; and Heb 7:1-11. Jewish allegory is imitated in Gal 4:21-31 (allegory of Sarah and Hagar). A *pesher*-like comment is found in Eph 5:32 (interpreting Gen 2:24)[111]. A collection of macarisms, similar to 4QBeatitudes, is now recognized in

---

[106] See R. Bloch, "Midrash", *DBSup* 5. 1263-81; in English, "Midrash", *Approaches to Ancient Judaism* (ed. W. S. Green; Missoula, MT: Scholars, 1978) 29-50; J. Neusner, *Midrash in Context: Exegesis in Formative Judaism* (Philadelphia, PA: Fortress, 1983), with bibliography on pp. 197-207; G. G. Porton, "Midrash", *ABD* 4. 818-22.

[107] See Origen, *Ep. ad Iulium Africanum* 11 (7), SC 302. 538; 12 (8), SC 302.540; *Comm. in ev. Joann.* 6.13.76, SC 157. 184. Cf. N. R. M. de Lange, *Origen and the Jews: Studies in Jewish-Christian Relations in Third-Century Palestine* (Cambridge, UK/New York: Cambridge University, 1976) 20-21. See Jerome, *Tobias*, prologue, *Biblia sacra iuxta latinam Vulgatam versionem...* (Vatican City: Vatican Polyglott Press) 8 (1950) 156.

[108] See p. 77 below.

[109] See F. F. Bruce, *The New Testament Development of Old Testament Themes* (Grand Rapids, MI: Eerdmans, 1969).

[110] See J. A. Fitzmyer, "The Use of Explicit Old Testament Quotations in Qumran Literature and in the New Testament", *ESBNT*, 3-58.

[111] See J. A. Fitzmyer, *ESBNT*, 257.

learned procedures for the preservation of the text of the Old Testament and for the explanation of the meaning of biblical texts. At all stages, the more astute Christian exegetes, from Origen and Jerome onwards, have sought to draw profit from the Jewish biblical learning in order to acquire a better understanding of Scripture. Many modern exegetes follow this example.

The ancient Jewish traditions allow for a better understanding particularly of the Septuagint, the Jewish Bible which eventually became the first part of the Christian Bible for at least the first four centuries of the Church and has remained so in the East down to the present day. The extra-canonical Jewish literature, called apocryphal or intertestamental, in its great abundance and variety, is an important source for the interpretation of the New Testament. The variety of exegetical procedures practised by the different strains of Judaism can actually be found within the Old Testament itself, for example, in Chronicles with reference to the Books of Samuel and Kings, and also within the New Testament, as for example in certain ways Paul goes about argument from Scripture. A great variety of forms — parables, allegories, anthologies and *florilegia*, re-readings (*relectures*), *pesher* technique, methods of associating otherwise unrelated texts, psalms and hymns, vision, revelation and dream sequences, wisdom compositions — all are common to both the Old and the New Testaments, as well as in Jewish circles before and after the time of Jesus. The Targums and the Midrashic literature illustrate the homiletic tradition and mode of biblical interpretation practised by wide sectors of Judaism in the first centuries.

Many Christian exegetes of the Old Testament look, besides, to the Jewish commentators, grammarians and lexicographers of the mediaeval and more recent period as a resource for understanding difficult passages or expressions that are either rare or unique. References to such Jewish

Jesus' beatitudes in Matt 5:3-11 and Luke 6:20-22[112].

Yet despite such similarities of interpretive techniques there is a radical difference, in that Christian writers who used them centered their teaching on faith in Christ Jesus, who ministered to people in Judea, was

[112] See E. Puech, "4Q525 et les péricopes des Béatitudes en Ben Sira et Matthieu", *RB* 98 (1991) 80-106; J. A. Fitzmyer, "A Palestinian Collection of Beatitudes", *The Four Gospels 1992: Festschrift Frans Neirynck* (BETL 100; 3 vols.; ed. F. van Segbroeck et al.; Louvain: Leuven University/Peeters, 1992) 1. 509-15.

works appear in current exegetical discussion much more frequently than was formerly the case.

Jewish biblical scholarship in all its richness, from its origins in antiquity down to the present day, is an asset of the highest value for the exegesis of both Testaments, provided that it be used with discretion. Ancient Judaism took many diverse forms. The Pharisaic form which eventually came to be the most prevalent, in the shape of rabbinic Judaism, was by no means the only one. The range of ancient Jewish texts extends across several centuries; it is important to rank them in chronological order before proceeding to make comparisons. Above all, the overall pattern of the Jewish and Christian communities is very different: on the Jewish side, in very varied ways, it is a question of a religion which defines a people and a way of life based upon written revelation and an oral tradition; whereas, on the Christian side, it is faith in the Lord Jesus — the one who died, was raised and lives still, Messiah and Son of God; it is around faith in his person that the community is gathered. These two diverse starting points create, as regards the interpretation of the Scriptures, two separate contexts, which for all their points of contact and similarity, are in fact radically diverse.

---

put to death, and eventually was raised by the Father to glory. This emphasis on the role of Jesus makes the traditions, which developed and are recorded in the New Testament, radically different from the interpretive traditions borrowed from ancient Judaism. Moreover, one has to date carefully the Jewish interpretive traditions, since they do not all come from a time prior to or contemporary with the composition of the Christian New Testament. In particular, the Commission singles out the Pharisaic-rabbinic tradition, which, though at first oral, was eventually put into writing in the Mishnah. It was first codified in written form by Rabbi Judah the Prince only at the beginning of the third century A.D.[113]. The extent, then, to which that later rabbinic written tradition can be used for the interpretation of the New Testament always remains problematic. It becomes even more problematic when that rabbinic tradition is found in the fifth-century Jerusalem Talmud or the sixth-century Babylonian Talmud or the even later Midrash Rabbah.

---

[113] See H. L. Strack and G. Stemberger, *Introduction to the Talmud and Midrash* (Edinburgh: Clark, 1991) 1-16, 119-66; H. Danby, *The Mishnah* (Oxford: Oxford University, 1933).

3. *Approach by the History of the Influence of the Text* (Wirkungsgeschichte)

This approach rests upon two principles: *a*) a text only becomes a literary work in so far as it encounters readers who give life to it by appropriating it to themselves; *b*) this appropriation of the text, which can occur either on the individual or community level and can take shape in various spheres (literary, artistic, theological, ascetical and mystical), contributes to a better understanding of the text itself.

---

3. *Approach by the History of the Influence of the Text* (Wirkungsgeschichte)

This approach to the Bible is a relatively recent development, which seeks to trace the effect that a biblical writing, which has become a literary and normative work for certain people, has had on them, and to see how such an effect influences the interpretation of the text. It thus evaluates the role that the tradition which has grown out of the text plays in its interpretation. It also considers the mutual relationship between the text and its readers. Two principles are at work in this approach: (a) a text becomes a literary work when readers appropriate it as part of their literature; and (b) this appropriation (by individuals or a community) takes shape in various spheres, literary, artistic, theological, ascetical, or mystical. The mutual relationship brings about a distinctive interpretation of the text in question.

For instance, the Song of Songs, which is a magnificent lyric poem about human love, the love of a man and a woman, was appropriated by the Jewish people of old not only as part of their literature, but as part of their sacred writings. Once so appropriated, it was understood as an allegorical description of the mutual love of Yahweh and the people Israel, and it was so interpreted. That appropriation brought it about that the Song became part of Israel's canon, part of the Hebrew Scriptures[114].

---

[114] See M. Simon (tr.), *Song of Songs* (Midrash Rabbah 9/2; London: Soncino, 1951). Cf. J. Neusner, *Israel's Love Affair with God: Song of Songs* (Valley Forge, PA: Trinity Press International, 1993); *Song of Songs Rabbah: An Analytical Translation* (Brown Judaic Studies 197-98; Atlanta, GA: Scholars, 1989). Cf. W. Riedl, *Die Auslegung des Hohenliedes in der jüdischen Gemeinde und der griechischen Kirche* (Leipzig: Deichert, 1898). Cf. J. Gnilka, "Die Wirkungsgeschichte als Zugang zum Verständnis der Bibel", *MTZ* 40 (1989) 51-62.

Without being entirely unknown in antiquity, this approach was developed in literary studies between 1960 and 1970, a time when criticism became interested in the relation between a text and its readers. Biblical studies can only draw profit from research of this kind, all the more so since the philosophy of hermeneutics for its own part stresses the necessary distance between a work and its author, as well as between a work and its readers. Within this perspective, the history of the effect produced by a book or a passage of Scripture (*"Wirkungsgeschichte"*) begins to enter into the work of interpretation. Such an enquiry seeks to assess the development of interpretation over the course of time under the influence of the concerns readers have brought to the text. It also attempts to evaluate the importance of the role played by tradition in finding meaning in biblical texts.

The mutual presence to each other of text and readers creates its own dynamic, for the text exercises an influence and provokes reactions. It

---

When these Scriptures became part of the Old Testament in the Christian Bible, the Song of Songs was in turn appropriated by followers of Jesus of Nazareth. So it became a canticle about the love of Christ for his Church, triggered, no doubt, by what is said about that love in Eph 5:25b and 29c. This appropriation was picked up and exploited in the patristic and medieval interpretations of the Song, especially by St. John of the Cross[115].

---

[115] See Origen, *In Canticum Canticorum*, commentary and homilies; GCS 33. 26-60 (homilies), 61-241 (commentary); *Origen: The Song of Songs* (ACW 26; Westminster, MD: Newman, 1957). Cf. R. E. Murphy, "The Song of Songs: Critical Biblical Scholarship vis-à-vis Exegetical Traditions", *Understanding the Word: Essays in Honor of Bernhard W. Anderson* (JSOTSup 37; ed. J. T. Butler et al.; Sheffield, UK: JSOT, 1985) 53-69; "Recent Literature on the Canticle of Canticles", *CBQ* 16 (1954) 1-11; "Patristic and Medieval Exegesis-Help or Hindrance?" *CBQ* 43 (1981) 505-16; J. de Monléon, *Le Cantique des Cantiques: Commentaire mystique d'après les Pères de l'église* (Paris: Nouvelles Editions Latines, 1969); J. Marti Ballester, *San Juan de la Cruz: Cántico espiritual leido hoy* (5th ed.; Madrid: Ediciones Paulinas, 1982); J. L. Morales, *El cántico espiritual de San Juan de la Cruz: Su relación con el Cantar de los Cantares y otras fuentes escriturísticas y literarias* (Madrid, 1971); R. J. Tournay, *Quand Dieu parle aux hommes le langage de l'amour: Etudes sur le Cantique des Cantiques* (Cahiers de la *RB* 21; Paris: Gabalda, 1982); *Word of God, Song of Love: A Commentary on the Song of Songs* (New York: Paulist, 1988); H. Riedlinger, *Die Makellosigkeit der Kirche in den lateinischen Hoheliedkommentaren des Mittelalters* (BGPTM 38/3; Münster in W.: Aschendorff, 1958); A. W. Astell, *The Song of Songs in the Middle Ages* (Ithaca, NY: Cornell University, 1990).

makes a resonant claim that is heard by readers, whether as individuals or as members of a group. The reader is in any case never an isolated subject. He or she belongs to a social context and lives within a tradition. Readers come to the text with their own questions, exercise a certain selectivity, propose an interpretation and, in the end, are able either to create a further work or else take initiatives inspired directly from their reading of Scripture.

Numerous examples of such an approach are already evident. The history of the reading of the Song of Songs offers an excellent illustration: it would show how this book was received in the Patristic period, in monastic circles of the mediaeval Church and then again how it was taken up by a mystical writer such as St. John of the Cross. The approach thus offers a better chance of uncovering all the dimensions of meaning contained in such a writing. Similarly, in the New Testament, it is both possible and useful to throw light upon the meaning of a passage (for example, that of the Rich Young Man in *Matt* 19:16-26) by pointing out how fruitful its influence has been throughout the history of the Church.

At the same time, history also illustrates the prevalence from time to time of interpretations that are tendentious and false, baneful in their effect — such as, for example, those that have promoted antisemitism or other forms of racial discrimination or, yet again, various kinds of millenarian delusions. This serves to show that this approach cannot constitute a discipline that would be purely autonomous. Discernment is required. Care must be exercised not to privilege one or other stage of the history of the text's influence to such an extent that it becomes the sole norm of its interpretation for all time.

---

The Commission also cites the episode of the Rich Young Man (Matt 19:16-26) as an example from the New Testament, which has also had a notable *Wirkungsgeschichte*[116].

The Commission, however, is aware of the dangers of such later interpretation since some of it has been "tendentious and false, baneful in its effect". The later interpretation of some texts has, in fact, promoted anti-semitism[117], racial discrimination[118], and millenarian delusions[119].

---

[116] An interpretation of that passage is found in Clement of Alexandria, *Quis dives salvetur* 11.2; GCS 17 (2d ed., 1970). 166. But the real effect of Matt 19:21 is seen in such later documents as Athanasius, *Vita S. Antonii* 2; PG 26. 841C; and in the Bull of Pope Honorius III approving the rule of the Fratres Minores (29 November 1223).

[117] An example of the *Wirkungsgeschichte* that contributed to anti-semitism would be

## D. Approaches That Use the Human Sciences

In order to communicate itself, the Word of God has taken root in the life of human communities (cf. *Sir* 24:12) and it has been through the psychological dispositions of the various persons who composed the biblical writings that it has pursued its path. It follows, then, that the human sciences — in particular, sociology, anthropology and psychology — can contri-

---

## D. Approaches That Use the Human Sciences

Under this heading the Commission singles out three approaches to the Bible that have received much attention in recent times, the sociological, the anthropological, and the psychological. These approaches are being considered because God's written Word has been composed in the midst of human communities affected by varying cultures and with the

---

the patristic and medieval interpretations of Matt 27:25 ("All the people answered, 'His blood be upon us and upon our children'"): "Propterea sanguis Iesu non solum super eos factus est, qui tunc fuerunt, verum etiam super omnes generationes Iudaeorum post sequentes usque ad consummationem" (Origen, *Hom. in Matt.* 17:25; GCS 38. 260); cf. *Contra Celsum* 4.22; GCS 1. 292. "Et ideo Iudaei peccaverunt, non solum tamquam hominis Christi sed etiam tamquam Dei crucifixores" (Thomas Aquinas, *S.T.* III. 47. 5 [ed. Blackfriars 54 (1963) 70]).

See also Justin Martyr, *Dialogue with Trypho* 16.4 ("You slew the Just One and his prophets before him. Now you reject and, as far as it is possible for you, dishonor those who have put their hope in him, and God the Almighty and Maker of all things who sent him, as you curse in your synagogues those who believe in Christ..." (and Justin then quotes Isa 57:1-4 to support his contention). Tertullian, *Adversus Iudaeos* 8.18; CCLat 2. 1363-64.

Recall the patristic use of Old Testament *testimonia* (see A. Lukyn Williams, *Adversus Judaeos* (Cambridge, UK: Cambridge University, 1935), chap. 1. Cf. E. H. Flannery, *The Anguish of the Jews: Twenty-three Centuries of Antisemitism* (2d ed.; New York/Mahwah, NJ: Paulist, 1985) 34-65.

Cf. D. A. Rausch, *Fundamentalist-Evangelicals and Anti-Semitism* (Valley Forge, PA: Trinity Press International, 1993).

[118] See J. N. Gerstner, *The Thousand Generation Covenant: Dutch Reformed Covenant Theology and Group Identity in Colonial South Africa, 1652-1814* (Studies in the History of Christian Thought 44; Leiden: Brill, 1991) esp. 107-11, 258-62; J. W. de Gruchy and C. Villa-Vicencio, *Apartheid Is a Heresy* (CapeTown: D. Philip; Guildford, UK: Lutterworth; Grand Rapids, MI: Eerdmans, 1983); G. D. Kelsey, *Racism and the Christian Understanding of Man* (New York: Scribner's Sons, 1965); I. J. Mosala, *Biblical Hermeneutics and Black Theology in South Africa* (Grand Rapids, MI: Eerdmans, 1989).

[119] See W. H. Oliver, *Prophets and Millennialists: The Uses of Biblical Prophecy in England from the 1790s to the 1840s* (Auckland: Auckland University; Oxford: Oxford University, 1978).

bute towards a better understanding of certain aspects of biblical texts. It should be noted, however, that in this area there are several schools of thought, with notable disagreement among them upon the very nature of these sciences. That said, a good number of exegetes have drawn considerable profit in recent years from research of this kind.

### 1. *The Sociological Approach*

Religious texts are bound in reciprocal relationship to the societies in which they originate. This is clearly the case as regards biblical texts. Con-

---

psychological dispositions of many persons inspired to pass on God's Word. These approaches help the reader to understand certain aspects of biblical texts that might otherwise be passed over. Though the human sciences selected for consideration are important, none of them represents a one-school approach. Each of these disciplines is shaped by different modes of thought that sometimes disagree notably among themselves.

### 1. *The Sociological Approach*

Because the Bible came into being over a long period of time, it reflects various human societies, different milieux, and their diverse social conditions. Thus the biblical text bears traces of the social complex in which it was born and requires accurate sociological analysis.

Form Criticism, in its effort to assign a *Sitz im Leben* or vital context to different forms, had already begun to analyze the socio-cultural milieu in which a given form arose and was transmitted. Independent of this effort, however, was the outright empirical study of the socio-historical situation of early Christianity by members of the so-called Chicago School of Theology in the early part of this century[120]. In the last twenty-five

---

[120] The main proponents of this school were E. D. Burton, Shirley J. Case, Shailer Mathews, and Frederick C. Grant. See S. J. Case, *The Evolution of Early Christianity: A Genetic Study of First-Century Christianity in Relation to Its Religious Environment* (Chicago, IL: University of Chicago, 1914). S. Mathews, *Jesus on Social Institutions* (New York: Macmillan, 1928; repr. in Lives of Jesus Series; ed. K. Cauthen; Philadelphia, PA: Fortress, 1971). F. C. Grant, *The Economic Background of the Gospels* (London: Oxford University, 1926). Cf. W. Dean, *American Religious Empiricism* (Albany, NY: State University of New York, 1986); W. J. Hynes, *Shirley Jackson Case and the Chicago School: The Socio-Historical Method* (Chico, CA: Scholars, 1981); B. E. Meland, "Introduction: The Empirical Tradition in Theology at Chicago", *The Future of Empirical Theology* (Essays in Divinity 7; ed. B. E. Meland; Chicago/London: University of Chicago, 1969) 1-62.

sequently, the scientific study of the Bible requires as exact a knowledge as is possible of the social conditions distinctive of the various milieus in which the traditions recorded in the Bible took shape. This kind of socio-historical information needs then to be completed by an accurate sociological explanation, which will provide a scientific interpretation of the implications for each case of the prevailing social conditions.

The sociological point of view has had a role in the history of exegesis for quite some time. The attention which Form-Criticism devoted to the social circumstances in which various texts arose (*Sitz im Leben*) is already an indication of this: it recognized that biblical traditions bore the mark of the socio-cultural milieu which transmitted them. In the first third of the 20th century, the Chicago School studied the socio-historical situation of early Christianity, thereby giving historical criticism a notable impulse in this direction. In the course of the last twenty years (1970-1990), the

years, however, the sociological approach to the Bible has enjoyed renewed interest, and its contribution has been an important refinement of the historical-critical method[121]. This approach has broadened the exegetical enterprise in many positive aspects.

---

[121] See further R. R. Wilson, *Sociological Approaches to the Old Testament* (Guides to Biblical Scholarship, Old Testament Series; Philadelphia, PA: Fortress, 1984); N. K. Gottwald, *The Tribes of Yahweh: A Sociology of the Religion of Liberated Israel, 1250-1050 B.C.E.* (London: SCM; Maryknoll, NY: Orbis, 1979); *The Hebrew Bible in Its Social World and in Ours* (Semeia Studies; Atlanta, GA: Scholars, 1993); R. E. Clements (ed.), *The World of Ancient Israel: Sociological, Anthropological, and Political Perspectives: Essays by Members of the Society for Old Testament Study* (Cambridge, UK/New York: Cambridge University, 1989).

B. Holmberg, *Sociology and the New Testament: An Appraisal* (Minneapolis, MN: Fortress, 1990); S. R. Garrett, "Sociology of Early Christianity", *ABD* 6. 89-99; C. A. Osiek, *What Are They Saying about the Social Setting of the New Testament?* (New York: Paulist, 1984); H. C. Kee, *Knowing the Truth: A Sociological Approach to New Testament Interpretation* (Minneapolis, MN: Fortress, 1989); G. Theissen, *Sociology of Early Palestinian Christianity* (Philadelphia, PA: Fortress; London: SCM, 1978); R. A. Horsley, *Sociology and the Jesus Movement* (New York: Crossroad, 1989; 2d ed., 1994); P. F. Esler, *Community and Gospel in Luke-Acts: The Social and Political Motivations of Lucan Theology* (Cambridge, UK/New York: Cambridge University, 1987); J. H. Neyrey, *The Social World of Luke-Acts: Models for Interpretation* (Peabody, MA: Henrickson, 1991); R. J. Cassidy, *Society and Politics in the Acts of the Apostles* (Maryknoll, NY: Orbis, 1987); J. H. Elliott, *A Home for the Homeless: A Sociological Exegesis of 1 Peter, Its Situation and Strategy* (Philadelphia, PA: Fortress, 1981); R. Bauckham, *The Bible in Politics: How to Read the Bible Politically* (London: SPCK; Louisville, KY: Westminster/John Knox, 1989).

sociological approach to biblical texts has become an integral part of exegesis.

The questions which arise in this area for the exegesis of the Old Testament are manifold. One should ask, for example, concerning the various forms of social and religious organisation which Israel has known in the course of its history. For the period before the formation of a nation-state, does the ethnological model of a society which is segmentary and lacking a unifying head (acephalous) provide a satisfactory base from which to work? What has been the process whereby a loosely organised tribal league became, first of all, an organised monarchical state and, after that, a community held together simply by bonds of religion and common descent? What economic, military and other transformations were brought about by the movement towards political and religious centralisation that led to the monarchy? Does not the study of the laws regulating social behaviour in the Ancient Near East and in Israel make a more useful contribution to the understanding of the Decalogue than purely literary attempts to reconstruct the earliest form of the text?

For the exegesis of the New Testament, the questions will clearly be somewhat different. Let us mention some: to account for the way of life adopted by Jesus and his disciples before Easter, what value can be accorded to the theory of a movement of itinerant charismatic figures, living without fixed home, without family, without money and other goods? In the matter of the call to follow in the steps of Jesus, can we speak of a genuine relationship of continuity between the radical detachment involved in following Jesus in his earthly life and what was asked of members of the Christian movement after Easter in the very different social conditions of early Christianity? What do we know of the social structure of the Pauline communities, taking account in each case, of the relevant urban culture?

In general, the sociological approach broadens the exegetical enterprise and brings to it many positive aspects. Knowledge of sociological

---

For the interpretation of the Old Testament the Commission mentions the kinds of sociological questions that are important and need due investigation: the social and religious organization of the tribes of Israel in the pre-monarchic period; the economic, military, and other political factors that led to the organization of the centralized monarchy; the bonds of religion and common descent that bonded the Jewish community; the cultural and legal background of the ancient Near East and of Israel in

data which help us understand the economic, cultural and religious func-
tioning of the biblical world is indispensable for historical criticism. The
task incumbent upon the exegete, to gain a better understanding of the
early Church's witness to faith, cannot be achieved in a fully rigorous way
without the scientific research which studies the strict relationship that
exists between the texts of the New Testament and life as actually lived by
the early Church. The employment of models provided by sociological
science offers historical studies into the biblical period a notable potential
for renewal — though it is necessary, of course, that the models employed
be modified in accordance with the reality under study.

Here let us signal some of the risks involved in applying the sociological approach to exegesis. It is surely the case that, if the work of sociology consists in the study of currently existing societies, one can expect difficulty when seeking to apply its methods to historical societies belonging to
a very distant past. Biblical and extra-biblical texts do not necessarily provide the sort of documentation adequate to give a comprehensive picture

---

particular that helped fashion the Mosaic Law and its Decalogue. To these
questions one could add others: the economic and social conditions that
gave rise to the prophetic movement in Israel; the social factors reflected
in Israel's wisdom literature and its psalms and hymns.

For the interpretation of the New Testament a different set of
questions is raised: the way of life adopted by Jesus and his disciples as
itinerant preachers; the call that he made to followers to come after him;
and the social structure of early Christian communities, at first in
Jerusalem, and then elsewhere, especially in urban centers like Corinth or
Ephesus.

There are, however, risks that the sociological approach to the Bible
can run. Some risk comes from the sociological criteria, derived mainly
from contemporary modern societies, when the attempt is made to apply
them to historical societies known only from ancient texts that scarcely
give a complete picture of the complex communities that they were. Some
risk also stems from the attention given to institutional, economic, and
political aspects of human life rather than to personal and religious
dimensions, which are of greater importance in the biblical texts.

The sociological approach is really more interested in reading between the lines of the biblical text to dig out the positive historical factors
that shaped human and community life in biblical times than it is in determining the religious meaning of God's Word itself. In other words, for all
the important contribution that the sociological approach has recently

of the society of the time. Moreover, the sociological method does tend to pay rather more attention to the economic and institutional aspects of human life than to its personal and religious dimensions.

## 2. *The Approach through Cultural Anthropology*

The approach to biblical texts which makes use of the study of cultural anthropology stands in close relationship with the sociological approach. The distinction between the two approaches exists, at one and the same time, on the level of perception, on that of method and on that of the aspect of reality under consideration. While the sociological approach — as we have just mentioned — studies economic and institutional aspects above all, the anthropological approach is interested in a wide assortment of other aspects, reflected in language, art, religion, but also in dress, ornament, celebration, dance, myth, legend and all that concerns ethnography.

In general, cultural anthropology seeks to define the characteristics of different kinds of human beings in their social context — as, for example, the "Mediterranean person" — with all that this involves by way of studying the rural or urban context and with attention paid to the values recognized by the society in question (honor and dishonor, secrecy, keeping faith, tradition, kinds of education and schooling), to the manner in which social control is exercised, to the ideas which people have of family, house, kin, to the situation of women, to institutionalized dualities (pa-

---

made in the study of the Bible, it rarely contributes much to the meaning of the written Word of God itself.

## 2. *The Approach through Cultural Anthropology*

This approach is closely related to the sociological, but is interested in a wider range of factors in human and community life: language, art, religion, costumes, folk customs (celebrations, dances, festivals), myths and legends. The anthropological approach inquires into the differences of urban and rural life and of the values cultivated in various kinds of society. It also studies such factors of human existence as honor and shame, secrecy and privacy, taboos and magic, fidelity and infidelity, tradition and innovation, education and schooling, family and home; the relations between men, women, children, between patrons and clients, between owners and tenants, between free persons and slaves, between benefactors and

tron-client, owner-tenant, benefactor-beneficiary, free person-slave), taking into account also the prevailing conception of the sacred and the profane, taboos, rites of passage from one state to another, magic, the source of wealth, of power, of information, etc. On the basis of these diverse elements, typologies and "models" are constructed, which are claimed to be common to a number of cultures.

Clearly this kind of study can be useful for the interpretation of biblical texts. It has been effectively applied to the study of the ideas of kinship in the Old Testament, of the position of women in Israelite society, of the influence of agrarian rituals, etc. In the texts which report the teaching of Jesus, for example the parables, many details can be explained thanks to this approach. This is also the case with regard to fundamental ideas, such as that of the Reign of God or of the way of conceiving time with respect to the history of salvation, as well as of the processes by which the first Christians came to gather in communities. This approach allows one to distinguish more clearly those elements of the biblical message that are permanent, as having their foundation in human nature, and those which are more contingent, being due to the particular features of certain cultures. Nevertheless, no more than is the case with respect to other particularized approaches, this approach is not qualified simply by itself to

---

beneficiaries[122]. This approach to the Bible has brought out important aspects in the stories of the Old Testament, especially regarding kinship, women, agrarian and cultic rites. In the study of the New Testament it has helped in the understanding of Jesus' parables, or the numerous cultural factors and the process by which the early Christian communities were shaped.

This approach, however, as in the case of others derived from human sciences, is not qualified of itself to determine what is specifically the content of revelation. As with the sociological approach, this one tends to read between the lines of the biblical text and not the lines themselves. In

---

[122] See further H. W. Wolff, *Anthropology of the Old Testament* (Philadelphia, PA: Fortress; London: SCM, 1974); B. Lang (ed.), *Anthropological Approaches to the Old Testament* (Issues in Religion and Theology 8; Philadelphia, PA: Fortress; London: SPCK, 1985); B. J. Malina, *Christian Origins and Cultural Anthropology: Practical Models for Biblical Interpretation* (Atlanta, GA: John Knox, 1986); J. W. Rogerson, *Anthropology and the Old Testament* (Oxford: Blackwell, 1978; Atlanta, GA: John Knox, 1979); "Anthropology and the OT", *ABD* 1. 258-62.

determine what is specifically the content of Revelation. It is important to keep this in mind when appreciating the valuable results it has brought.

### 3. *Psychological and Psychoanalytical Approaches*

Psychology and theology continue their mutual dialogue. The modern extension of psychological research to the study of the dynamic structures of the subconscious has given rise to fresh attempts at interpreting ancient texts, including the Bible. Whole works have been devoted to the psychoanalytic interpretation of biblical texts, which has led to vigorous discussion: in what measure and under what conditions can psychological

---

other words, the anthropological aspects of Bible do not necessarily bring the reader closer to the religious or spiritual meaning of God's Word.

### 3. *Psychological and Psychoanalytical Approaches*

The psychological and psychoanalytical approaches to the Bible strive to understand it in terms of the experience of human life and conduct. As a document that has emerged from a religious setting, the Bible naturally reflects the human psyche and the subconscious aspects of human life[123].

---

[123] See Y. Spiegel (ed.), *Psychoanalytische Interpretationen biblischer Texte* (Munich: Kaiser, 1972); C. Karakash, "La psychanalyse au secours de la Bible", *RTP* 124 (1992) 177-88.

The psychoanalytical approach to the Bible has enjoyed great vogue in Germany, especially in the writings of E. Drewermann, only a few of which have been translated into English. See, e.g., *Tiefenpsychologie und Exegese: Traum, Mythos, Märchen, Sage und Legende* (Munich: Deutscher Taschenbuch Verlag, 1984; 2d ed., 1991); *Tiefenpsychologie und Exegese* (2d ed.; Freiburg im B.: Walter-Verlag, 1989); *Strukturen des Bösen: Die jahwistische Urgeschichte in exegetischer, psychoanalytischer und philosophischer Sicht* (4 vols.; Paderborn: Schöningh, 1977-80); *Das Matthäusevangelium* (Olten: Walter-Verlag, 1992); *Dein Name ist wie der Geschmack des Lebens: Tiefpsychologische Deutung der Kindheitsgeschichte nach dem Lukasevangelium* (Freiburg im B.: Herder, 1986). Cf. G. Fehrenbacher, *Drewermann verstehen: Eine kritische Einführung* (Freiburg: Walter, 1991); C. Marcheselli-Casale, *Il caso Drewermann: Psicologia del profondo: Un nuovo metodo per leggere la Bibbia* (Casale Monferrato: Piemme, 1991); H. R. Seeliger, "Historische Kritik oder psychologisches Verstehen? Zu einer falschen Alternative im Denken Eugen Drewermanns", *TP* 67 (1992) 402-12.

See also W. G. Rollins, *Jung and the Bible* (Atlanta, GA: John Knox, 1983); D. Cox, *Jung and St. Paul: A Study of the Doctrine of Justification by Faith and Its Relation to the Concept of Individuation* (London/New York: Longmans, Green, 1959); I. N. Rashkow, *The Phallacy of Genesis: A Feminist-Psychoanalytic Approach* (Louisville, KY: Westminster/John Knox, 1993).

and psychoanalytical research contribute to a deeper understanding of Sacred Scripture?

Psychological and psychoanalytical studies do bring a certain enrichment to biblical exegesis in that, because of them, the texts of the Bible can be better understood in terms of experience of life and norms of behavior. As is well known, religion is always in a relationship of conflict or debate with the unconscious. It plays a significant role in the proper orientation of human drives. The stages through which historical criticism passes in its methodical study of texts need to be complemented by study of the different levels of reality they display. Psychology and psychoanalysis attempt to show the way in this respect. They lead to a multidimensional understanding of Scripture and help decode the human language of Revelation.

Psychology and, in a somewhat different way, psychoanalysis have led, in particular, to a new understanding of symbol. The language of symbol makes provision for the expression of areas of religious experience that are not accessible to purely conceptual reasoning but which have a genuine value for the expression of truth. For this reason, interdisciplinary study conducted in common by exegetes and psychologists or psychoanalysts offers particular advantages, especially when objectively grounded and confirmed by pastoral experience.

Numerous examples could be cited showing the necessity of a collaborative effort on the part of exegetes and psychologists: to ascertain the meaning of cultic ritual, of sacrifice, of bans, to explain the use of imagery in biblical language, the metaphorical significance of miracle stories, the wellsprings of apocalyptic visual and auditory experiences. It is not simply a matter of describing the symbolic language of the Bible but of grasping how it functions with respect to the revelation of mystery and the issuing of challenge — where the "numinous" reality of God enters into contact with the human person.

The dialogue between exegesis and psychology or psychoanalysis, begun with a view to a better understanding of the Bible, should clearly be

---

The Commission recognizes this when it admits that psychology and psychoanalysis, in their probing of the subconscious drives, impulses, and structures of human life, can lead to a multidimensional understanding of Scripture and help decode the human language of revelation. This approach can, then, be a useful complement to the historical-critical method, and psychological analyses of biblical books can be profitable. Moreover, since the biblical message is often cast in symbols or symbolic language, the interpretation of them is greatly aided by the psychological

conducted in a critical manner, respecting the boundaries of each discipline. Whatever the circumstances, a psychology or psychoanalysis of an atheistic nature disqualifies itself from giving proper consideration to the data of faith. Useful as they may be to determine more exactly the extent of human responsibility, psychology and psychoanalysis should not serve to eliminate the reality of sin and of salvation. One should, moreover, take care not to confuse spontaneous religiosity and biblical revelation or impugn the historical character of the Bible's message, which bestows upon it the value of a unique event.

Let us note moreover that one cannot speak of "psychoanalytical exegesis" as though it existed in one single form. In fact, proceeding from the different fields of psychology and from the various schools of thought, there exists a whole range of approaches capable of shedding helpful light upon the human and theological interpretation of the Bible. To absolutize one or other of the approaches taken by the various schools of psychology and psychoanalysis would not serve to make collaborative effort in this area more fruitful but rather render it harmful.

The human sciences are not confined to sociology, cultural anthropology and psychology. Other disciplines can also be very useful for the interpretation of the Bible. In all these areas, it is necessary to take good account of competence in the particular field and to recognize that only

---

approach. They also help in analyzing cultic rituals, sacrifice, bans, miracle stories, and apocalytic visual and auditory descriptions.

Yet in this sensitive area there can also be problems, since neither psychology nor psychoanalysis is the same thing as biblical interpretation. Even if both techniques deal with the realities of responsibility, guilt, sin, and salvation, they deal with them in different ways, and the differences have to be respected.

Moreover, a psychology or psychoanalysis of atheistic inspiration would be incapable of aiding in the interpretation of the Bible and dealing with the realm of faith that the Bible evokes. The revelation in the Bible cannot be reduced to some spontaneous, natural religiosity, since the historical character of the Bible's message has conferred on it the value of a unique event, with which one cannot dispense for some psychological reason. Again, one has to cope with different schools of psychology and not absolutize one or other of them.

In general, then, in all the approaches to the Bible that use the human sciences one has to recognize that only rarely will one and the same person be qualified in both exegesis and one or other of these disciplines so that his or her competence can be trusted. All of which is to say that these

rarely will one and the same person be fully qualified in both exegesis and one or other of the human sciences.

## E. Contextual Approaches

The interpretation of a text is always dependent on the mindset and concerns of its readers. Readers give privileged attention to certain aspects and, without even being aware of it, neglect others. Thus it is inevitable that some exegetes bring to their work points of view that are new and responsive to contemporary currents of thought which have not up till now been taken sufficiently into consideration. It is important that they do so with critical discernment. The movements in this regard which claim particular attention today are those of liberation theology and feminism.

### 1. *The Liberationist Approach*

The theology of liberation is a complex phenomenon, which ought not be oversimplified. It began to establish itself as a theological move-

---

approaches are not sufficient in themselves for the interpretation of the Bible and hence do not replace the basic historical-critical method, even if they prove to be valuable complements to it.

## E. Contextual Approaches

Readers of the Bible often bring to it concerns that derive from contemporary life and its problems or from the context in which they live. In recent decades there have developed approaches to the Bible that stem from such contexts, and the Commission books under this heading two prominent examples, liberationism and feminism. Both of them have emerged from political contexts in modern society and even church life. This approach to the Bible has sometimes been called "advocacy exegesis", because it is an interpretation of the Bible used to support change in existing social or religious conditions; it is interpretation in support of a modern ideology.

### 1. *The Liberationist Approach*

The origins of the complex phenomenon that is called "liberation theology" are traced not only to Latin American economic, social, and

ment in the early 1970s. Over and beyond the economic, social and political circumstances of Latin America, its starting point is to be found in two great events in the recent life of the Church: the Second Vatican Council, with its declared intention of *aggiornamento* and of orienting the pastoral work of the Church towards the needs of the contemporary world, and the Second General Conference of the Episcopate of Latin America held at Medellin in 1968, which applied the teachings of the Council to the needs of Latin America. The movement has since spread also to other parts of the world (Africa, Asia, the black population of the United States).

It is not all that easy to discern if there truly exists "one" theology of liberation and to define what its methodology might be. It is equally difficult to determine adequately its manner of reading the Bible, in a way which would lead to an accurate assessment of advantages and limitations. One can say that liberation theology adopts no particular methodology. But, starting from its own socio-cultural and political point of view, it practises a reading of the Bible which is oriented to the needs of the people, who seek in the Scriptures nourishment for their faith and their life.

Liberation theology is not content with an objectifying interpretation which concentrates on what the text said in its original context. It seeks a reading drawn from the situation of people as it is lived here and now. If a

---

political circumstances, but also to the *aggiornamento* of the Church in the Second Vatican Council and the consequent efforts of the bishops of Latin America at their second episcopal conference meeting at Medellin, Colombia in 1968 to implement that updating.

Moreover, diverse are the ways of reading the Bible associated with this so-called theology; in fact, it adopts no particular methodology. It approaches the Bible from its own socio-cultural and political situation and engages in a type of reading oriented to the needs of people who seek in the Scriptures nourishment for their faith, their life, and their social problems. It is thus not interested in an interpretation of the biblical text itself, but in a reading of it drawn from the situation of people here and now. When people are oppressed, they turn to the Bible with a vision of faith, looking for something to sustain them in their struggle and hopes. The reality that they presently face has to be allowed to shed light on the Word of God, from which they draw courage to transform society with justice and love. For the God of the Bible is the one who brings salvation to his people, the God of the poor and the oppressed. Hence the interpretation of the Bible cannot be neutral; it must allow that understanding to emerge that can be discovered only when its text is read in solidarity with

people lives in circumstances of oppression, one must go to the Bible to find there nourishment capable of sustaining the people in its struggles and its hopes. The reality of the present time should not be ignored but, on the contrary, met head on, with a view to shedding upon it the light of the Word. From this light will come authentic Christian praxis, leading to the transformation of society through works of justice and love. Within the vision of faith, Scripture is transformed into a dynamic impulse for full liberation.

The main *principles* guiding this approach are the following:

God is present in the history of his people, bringing them salvation. He is the God of the poor and cannot tolerate oppression or injustice.

It follows that exegesis cannot be neutral, but must, in imitation of God, take sides on behalf of the poor and be engaged in the struggle to liberate the oppressed.

It is precisely participation in this struggle that allows those interpretations to surface which are discovered only when the biblical texts are read in a context of solidarity with the oppressed.

Because the liberation of the oppressed is a communal process, the community of the poor is the privileged addressee of the Bible as word of liberation. Moreover, since the biblical texts were written for communities, it is to communities in the first place that the reading of the Bible has been entrusted. The Word of God is fully relevant — above all because of the capacity inherent in the "foundational events" (the Exodus from

the community of the poor and the oppressed[124].

The Commission acknowledges that the liberationist approach includes elements of undoubted value: an awareness of the presence of the

---

[124] See further C. Rowland and M. Corner, *Liberating Exegesis: The Challenge of Liberation Theology to Biblical Studies* (Louisville, KY: Westminster/John Knox; London: SPCK, 1989); E. Tamez, *Bible of the Oppressed* (Maryknoll, NY: Orbis, 1982); N. K. Gottwald, *The Bible and Liberation: Political and Social Hermeneutics* (Maryknoll, NY: Orbis, 1983; rev. ed., 1993); A. R. Ceresko, *Introduction to the Old Testament: A Liberation Perspective* (Maryknoll, NY; London: Chapman, 1992); N. Lohfink, *Option for the Poor: The Basic Principle of Liberation Theology in the Light of the Bible* (Berkeley, CA: Bibal Press, 1987); P. L. Schrieber, "Liberation Theology and the Old Testament", *ConcJ* 13 (1987) 27-46; C. Bussmann, *Who Do You Say? Jesus Christ in Latin American Theology*" (Maryknoll, NY: Orbis, 1985); T. P. Hanks, *God So Loved the Third World: The Biblical Vocabulary of Oppression* (Maryknoll, NY: Orbis, 1983); R. G. Musto, *Liberation Theologies: A Research Guide* (New York: Garland, 1991); A. T. Hennelly, *Liberation Theology: A Documentary History, Edited with Introductions, Commentary, and Translations* (Maryknoll, NY: Orbis, 1990).

Egypt, the passion and resurrection of Jesus) for finding fresh realisation again and again in the course of history.

Liberation theology includes elements of undoubted value: the deep awareness of the presence of God who saves; the insistence on the communal dimension of faith; the pressing sense of need for a liberating praxis rooted in justice and love; a fresh reading of the Bible which seeks to make of the Word of God the light and the nourishment of the People of God in the midst of its struggles and hopes. In all these ways it underlines the capacity of the inspired text to speak to the world of today.

But a reading of the Bible from a stance of such commitment also involves some risks. Since liberation theology is tied to a movement that is still in a process of development, the remarks which follow can only be provisional.

This kind of reading is centered on narrative and prophetic texts which highlight situations of oppression and which inspire a praxis leading to social change. At times, such a reading can be limited, not giving enough attention to other texts of the Bible. It is true that exegesis cannot be neutral, but it must also take care not to become one-sided. Moreover, social and political action is not the direct task of the exegete.

---

saving God to his people, an insistence on the communal dimension of faith, a pressing need of love and justice in modern society, and a fresh reading of the Bible itself as a source of inspiration for praxis and social change.

Yet it also recognizes that this way of reading the Bible is problematic. Five risks are pointed out: (1) The liberationist approach centers on narrative and prophetic passages of the Bible that highlight situations of oppression and call for social change. The risk here is that, though there is no presuppositionless exegesis, this mode of reading the Bible is selective, limited, and becomes one-sided; it does not give enough attention to biblical texts that may bear other messages[125]. (2) The direct task of the interpreter of the Bible is not social and political action. Such action springs from an ideology, which may invoke biblical teachings for motivation, but which cannot be equated with or supplant the function of the biblical exegete. (3) Some liberation ideologists have brought to their interpretation of the Bible an analysis inspired by materialist doctrines, and espe-

---

[125] Contrast Isa 2:4 and Mic 4:3, which speak of beating "swords into ploughshares, and spears into pruning hooks", with Joel 4:10, which recommends beating "your ploughshares into swords and your pruning hooks into spears"!

In their desire to insert the biblical message into a socio-political context, some theologians and exegetes have made use of various instruments for the analysis of social reality. Within this perspective certain streams of liberation theology have conducted an analysis inspired by materialist doctrines and it is within such frame of reference that they have also read the Bible, a practice which is very questionable, especially when it involves the Marxist principle of the class struggle.

Under the pressure of enormous social problems, there has understandably been more emphasis on an earthly eschatology. Sometimes this has been to the detriment of the more transcendent dimensions of scriptural eschatology.

More recent social and political changes have led this approach to ask itself new questions and to seek new directions. For its further development and fruitfulness within the Church, a decisive factor will be the clarification of its hermeneutical presuppositions, its methods and its coherence with the faith and the Tradition of the Church as a whole.

## 2. *The Feminist Approach*

The feminist biblical hermeneutic had its origin in the United States toward the end of the 19th century. In the socio-cultural context of the

---

cially by the Marxist principle of class struggle[126]. (4) The liberationist mode of reading the Bible emphasizes what may be answers in it for modern social problems on this earth but plays down the transcendent dimensions of biblical eschatology[127]. (5) Recent social and political changes are calling upon liberation ideology to redefine its directions, and this in turn demands a clarification of its hermeneutical presuppositions.

## 2. *The Feminist Approach*

This approach to the Bible is traced to the nineteenth-century struggle in the United States for the rights of women, and specifically to *The*

---

[126] See J. Miranda, *Communism in the Bible* (Maryknoll, NY: Orbis, 1982); *Marx and the Bible: A Critique of the Philosophy of Oppression* (Maryknoll, NY: Orbis, 1974).

[127] See J. D. Levenson, "Exodus and Liberation", in *The Hebrew Bible* (n. 101 above), 126-39.

struggle for the rights of women, the editorial board of a committee charged with the revision of the Bible produced "The Woman's Bible" in two volumes (New York 1885, 1898). This movement took on fresh life in the 1970's and has since undergone an enormous development in connection with the movement for the liberation of women, especially in North America. To be precise, several forms of feminist biblical hermeneutics have to be distinguished, for the approaches taken are very diverse. All unite around a common theme, woman, and a common goal: the liberation of women and the acquisition on their part of rights equal to those enjoyed by men.

We can here mention three principal forms of feminist biblical hermeneutics: the radical form, the neo-orthodox form and the critical form.

The *radical* form denies all authority to the Bible, maintaining that it has been produced by men simply with a view to confirming man's age-old domination of woman (androcentrism).

The *neo-orthodox* form accepts the Bible as prophetic and as potentially of service, at least to the extent that it takes sides on behalf of the

---

*Woman's Bible*[128]. In the 1960s and 1970s it developed new emphases, as the liberation of women began anew in North America. The Commission distinguishes three forms of this approach: (a) a radical form, which denies all authority to the Bible, because it was composed by men and seeks to dominate women[129]; (b) a neo-orthodox form, which accepts the Bible as prophetic and recognizes that it at time sides with the oppressed (women); in effect, this form results in a "canon within the canon"; and (c) a critical form, which uses a subtle methodology that seeks to rediscover the equal status and role of women among the disciples of Jesus and the first

---

[128] See E. C. Stanton, *The Woman's Bible* (2 vols.; New York: European Publ. Co, 1885, 1898; repr., 2 vols. in one; New York: Arno, 1972). This Bible was produced by twenty women suffragists under Elizabeth Cady Stanton. The women's movement can actually be traced back earlier in that century, to Sarah Grimké, who in 1837 complained about biblical interpretation as a means of keeping women in subjection. See S. M. Grimké, *Letters on the Equality of the Sexes and the Condition of Woman: Addressed to Mary S. Parker, President of the Boston Female Anti-Slavery Society* (Boston: Isaac Knapp, 1838; repr. New York: Source Book Press, 1970) 17-18, 91-97, 116-19.

[129] See M. Daly, *The Church and the Second Sex* (New York/Evanston, IL: Harper & Row, 1968) 32- 42, 138-49; and even more radically in *Beyond God the Father: Toward a Philosophy of Women's Liberation* (Boston, MA: Beacon, 1973) 13-22, 98-131; *Gyn/Ecology: The Metaethics of Radical Feminism* (Boston: Beacon, 1978); *Pure Lust: Elemental Feminist Philosophy* (Boston: Beacon, 1984).

oppressed and thus also of women; this orientation is adopted as a "canon within the canon", so as to highlight whatever in the Bible favors the liberation of women and the acquisition of their rights.

The *critical* form, employing a subtle methodology, seeks to rediscover the status and role of women disciples within the life of Jesus and in the Pauline churches. At this period, it maintains, a certain equality prevailed. But this equality has for the most part been concealed in the writings of the New Testament, something which came to be more and more the case as a tendency towards patriarchy and androcentrism became increasingly dominant.

Feminist hermeneutic has not developed a new methodology. It employs the current methods of exegesis, especially the historical-critical method. But it does add two criteria of investigation.

The first is the feminist criterion, borrowed from the women's liberation movement, in line with the more general direction of liberation theology. This criterion involves a hermeneutic of suspicion: since history was normally written by the victors, establishing the full truth requires that one does not simply trust texts as they stand but look for signs which may reveal something quite different.

---

Christians, a status that has been obscured by New Testament writings dominated by patriarchalism and androcentrism[130].

The feminist approach does not have a methodology of its own, but

---

[130] See A. Yarbro Collins (ed.), *Feminist Perspectives on Biblical Scholarship* (Biblical Scholarship in North America 10; Chico, CA: Scholars, 1985); D. L. Carmody, *Biblical Woman: Contemporary Reflections on Scriptural Texts* (New York: Crossroad, 1988); C. E. Cypser, *Taking off the Patriarchal Glasses* (New York: Vantage, 1987); P. Demers, *Women as Interpreters of the Bible* (New York/Mahwah, NJ: Paulist, 1992); J. C. Exum, *Fragmented Women: Feminist (Sub)versions of Biblical Narratives* (Valley Forge, PA: Trinity Press International, 1993); R. Haughton, *The Re-creation of Eve* (Springfield, IL: Tempelgate, 1985); A. L. Laffey, *An Introduction to the Old Testament: A Feminist Perspective* (Philadelphia, PA: Fortress, 1988); V. R. Mollenkott, *The Divine Feminine: The Biblical Imagery of God as Female* (New York: Crossroad, 1983); M. V. Rienstra, *Swallow's Nest: A Feminine Reading of the Psalms* (Grand Rapids, MI: Eerdmans, 1992); L. M. Russell (ed.), *Feminist Interpretation of the Bible* (Philadelphia, PA: Westminster, 1985); E. Schüssler Fiorenza, *Bread Not Stone: The Challenge of Feminist Biblical Interpretation* (Boston, MA: Beacon, 1984); *But She Said: Feminist Practices of Biblical Interpretation* (Boston, MA: Beacon, 1992); "Toward a Feminist Biblical Hermeneutics: Biblical Interpretation and Liberation Theology", *The Challenge of Liberation Theology: A First World Response* (ed. B. Mahan and L. D. Richesin; Maryknoll, NY: Orbis, 1981) 91-112; "Feminist Hermeneutics", *ABD* 2. 783-91; P. Trible, *God and the Rhetoric of Sexuality* (Overtures to Biblical Theology; Philadelphia, PA: Fortress, 1978; London: SCM, 1992); *Texts of Terror: Literary-Feminist Readings of Biblical Narratives* (Philadelphia, PA: Fortress, 1984; London: SCM, 1992).

The second criterion is sociological; it is based on the study of societies in the biblical times, their social stratification and the position they accorded to women.

With respect to the New Testament documents, the goal of study, in a word, is not the idea of woman as expressed in the New Testament but the historical reconstruction of two different situations of woman in the first century: that which was the norm in Jewish and Greco-Roman society and that which represented the innovation that took shape in the public life of Jesus and in the Pauline churches, where the disciples of Jesus formed "a community of equals". *Gal* 3:28 is a text often cited in defense of this view. The aim is to rediscover for today the forgotten history of the role of women in the earliest stages of the Church.

Feminist exegesis has brought many benefits. Women have played a more active part in exegetical research. They have succeeded, often better than men, in detecting the presence, the significance and the role of women in the Bible, in Christian origins and in the Church. The world-view of today, because of its greater attention to the dignity of women and to their role in society and in the Church, ensures that new questions are put to the biblical text, which in turn occasions new discoveries. Feminine sensitivity helps to unmask and correct certain commonly accepted interpretations which were tendentious and sought to justify the male domination of women.

---

uses the historical-critical method, to which it adds two criteria: (a) a criterion borrowed from the women's liberation movement, a hermeneutic of suspicion: Since history has normally been written by victors, one cannot trust texts as they stand; one has to read them for the signs that reveal something different. In this case, the story of early Christianity has been written (consciously or unconsciously) in the New Testament by male clerical victors, and its text has to be read for clues free of such bias. (b) The second criterion is sociological: the study of societies in biblical times reveals their social stratification and the place accorded to women. When applied to the New Testament, this approach seeks to uncover the normal situation of women in first-century Jewish and Greco-Roman society as well as the innovation that was introduced during the public ministry of Jesus and in Pauline churches where Christian disciples formed a community of equals, to which Gal 3:28 is said to bear witness[131]. Thus is recov-

---

[131] It is debatable whether Gal 3:28 can be understood in the *political* sense in which it is often quoted, because Paul there affirms an ethnic, social, and sexual equality of Christians (who are "in Christ Jesus"). For his thinking about political status, see Rom 13:1,3bc,6.

With regard to the Old Testament, several studies have striven to come to a better understanding of the image of God. The God of the Bible is not a projection of a patriarchal mentality. He is Father, but also the God of tenderness and maternal love.

Feminist exegesis, to the extent that it proceeds from a preconceived judgment, runs the risk of interpreting the biblical texts in a tendentious and thus debatable manner. To establish its positions, it must often, for want of something beer, have recourse to arguments *ex silentio*. As is well known, this type of argument is generally viewed with much reserve: it can never suffice to establish a conclusion on a solid basis. On the other

---

ered the forgotten role of women in the earliest stages of the Church.

Many benefits have come from this approach to the Bible. Today, there are many female interpreters of the Bible, and they have brought to light the proper significance and role of women in the Bible and in the early Church. They have made all interpreters and readers sensitive to the way in which the Bible had often been translated in the past and to the way in which it has often been tendentiously interpreted to justify the male domination of women. Feminist interpretations of biblical images of the Deity, especially in the Old Testament, have corrected a male-oriented picture of God. He may be Father, but is also the God of tenderness and maternal love.

The Commission, however, notes some of the problems that this approach to the Bible can cause[132]. Four are mentioned: (a) To the extent that it stems from a preconceived judgment, it runs the risk of interpreting the Bible tendentiously and in a debatable way. (b) It often has to interpret texts *ex silentio*, using the hermeneutic of suspicion. That mode of argumentation, however, can never be sufficient for a sound conclusion. (c) The feminist reconstruction of early Christianity, employing such a hermeneutic and based on fleeting hints in the text, remains questionable[133]. It is not really the fruit of "exegesis" and cannot be a

---

[132] See further P. J. Milne, "Feminist Interpretations of the Bible: Then and Now", *BRev* 8/5 (1992) 38-43, 52-55; M. Hayter, *The New Eve in Christ: The Use and Abuse of the Bible in the Debate about Women in the Church* (Grand Rapids, MI: Eerdmans, 1987).

[133] Some would adduce as an example E. Schüssler Fiorenza, *In Memory of Her: A Feminist Theological Reconstruction of Christian Origins* (New York: Crossroad, 1983). According to her, early Christian history in the New Testament was written as male clerical history. Cf. M. R. D'Angelo, "A Feminist Reading of Scripture", *The Ecumenist* 23 (1985) 86-89; R. M. Grant, "The Reconstruction of Christian Origins", *JR* 65 (1985) 83-88; G. Segalla, "L'Ermeneutica biblica feminista di E. Schüssler Fiorenza", *SPatav* 37 (1990) 147-61.

hand, the attempt made, on the basis of fleeting indications in the texts, to reconstitute an historical situation which these same texts are considered to have been designed to hide — this does not correspond at all to the work of exegesis properly so called. It entails rejecting the content of the inspired texts in preference for a hypothetical construction, quite different in nature.

Feminist exegesis often raises questions of power within the Church, questions which, as is obvious, are matters of discussion and even of confrontation. In this area, feminist exegesis can be useful to the Church only to the degree that it does not fall into the very traps it denounces and that it does not lose sight of the evangelical teaching concerning power as service, a teaching addressed by Jesus to all disciples, men and women[2].

## F. **Fundamentalist Interpretation**

Fundamentalist interpretation starts from the principle that the Bible, being the Word of God, inspired and free from error, should be read and

---

[2] Out of 19 votes cast, the text of this last paragraph received 11 in favor, 4 against and there were 4 abstentions. Those who voted against it asked that the result of the vote be published along with the text. The Commission consented to this.

---

substitute for the story told in the inspired text of the New Testament itself; it is and will always remain a hypothetical construct, excogitated in the twentieth century, which can never be taken as a norm of Christian faith and praxis. (d) This approach to the Bible often stems from a political agenda of women in the Church. It can be "useful to the Church only to the degree that it does not fall into the very traps it denounces and that it does not lose sight of the evangelical teaching concerning power as service, a teaching addressed by Jesus to all disciples, men and women"[134].

## F. **Fundamentalist Reading of the Bible**

The English translation of this section of the Commission's document bears the title "Fundamentalist Interpretation", whereas the original

---

[134] Not all members of the Commission agreed with the formulation of the last paragraph. A footnote in the document records the vote on it. Those who disagreed with its formulation thought that it was touching on a sensitive issue in the Church today and that it was inappropriate for those in power (the entirely male, clerical members of the Commission) to issue an admonition on humility to others (women exegetes) who do not currently

interpreted literally in all its details. But by "literal interpretation" it understands a naively literalist interpretation, one, that is to say, which excludes every effort at understanding the Bible that takes account of its historical origins and development. It is opposed, therefore, to the use of the historical-critical method, as indeed to the use of any other scientific method for the interpretation of Scripture.

The fundamentalist interpretation had its origin at the time of the Reformation, arising out of a concern for fidelity to the literal meaning of

---

French text has "Lecture fondamentaliste". The difference is important, because there was a discussion during the drafting of this part of the document whether "Fundamentalism" should be put on the same level as the other Methods and Approaches that had been discussed earlier. It was decided to speak rather about the "fundamentalist reading" of the Bible; hence the correct French title.

The fundamentalist reading of the Bible is a literalist understanding of the biblical text, which takes the final form of it as the verbatim expression of the Word of God and regards it as clear, plain, and unambiguous. It normally refuses to use the historical-critical method or any other would-be scientific method of interpretation and takes little account of the Bible's historical origins, the development of its text, or its diverse literary forms.

This way of reading the Bible stems ultimately from an emphasis on the literal sense of Scripture at the time of the Reformation, in reaction to the allegorical interpretation of the late Middle Ages. In the period after the Enlightenment, however, it emerged formally among Protestants as a bulwark against liberal nineteenth-century exegesis. The name "Fundamentalism" is derived from a document issued by the Niagara Bible Congress held at Niagara, NY in 1895[135]. In it conservative Protestants, reacting against Darwinism, scientific advances in biology and geology, and nineteenth-century liberal interpretation of the Bible, formulated a five-point statement on doctrines to be held, which later came to be called "Five Points of Fundamentalism". The five points were the verbal inerrancy of Scripture, divinity of Christ, virgin birth, substitutionary

---

enjoy similar status in the Church. The text seemed to them to be talking down to women from a male point of view.

[135] See L. W. Munhall, "The Niagara Bible Conference", *Moody Bible Institute Bulletin* 22 (1921-22) 1104-5.

Scripture. After the century of the Enlightenment, it emerged in Protestantism as a bulwark against liberal exegesis. The actual term "fundamentalist" is connected directly with the American Biblical Congress held at Niagara, New York, in 1895. At this meeting, conservative Protestant exegetes defined "five points of fundamentalism": the verbal inerrancy of Scripture, the divinity of Christ, his virginal birth, the doctrine of

---

atonement, and the bodily resurrection and second coming of Christ[136]. To insure these points, one insisted on "what the Bible says" in a literally factual sense. ("Islamic Fundamentalism", a phenomenon very much in the news today, is unrelated, save for its borrowing of the name from biblical fundamentalism).

This fundamentalist reading of the Bible is rightly oriented in its insistence on the inspiration of the Bible, the inerrancy of the Word of God, and other biblical truths in the "Five Points". But its way of presenting these truths is rooted in an ideology that is not biblical, despite the claims of its proponents. For it demands an unyielding adherence to rigid doctrinal attitudes and an unquestioning, uncritical reading of the Bible as the sole source of teaching about Christian life and salvation[137].

---

[136] See further F. A. Schaeffer, *The God Who Is There: Speaking Historic Christianity into the Twentieth Century* (Downers Grove, IL: Inter-Varsity, 1968); *No Final Conflict: The Bible Without Error in All That It Affirms* (Baton Rouge, LA: Louisiana State University, 1976).

[137] See further S. G. Cole, *The History of Fundamentalism* (New York: R. R. Smith, 1931; repr., Westport, CT: Greenwood, 1971); N. F. Furniss, *The Fundamentalist Controversy, 1918-1931* (New Haven, CT: Yale University; 1954; repr., Hamden, CT: Archon Books, 1963); E. R. Sandeen, *The Roots of Fundamentalism: British and American Millenarianism 1800-1930* (Chicago, IL: Chicago University, 1970); J. I. Packer, *"Fundamentalism" and the Word of God: Some Evangelical Principles* (Grand Rapids, MI: Eerdmans, 1958); E. H. Alan, *The Presbyterian Conflict* (New York: Garland, 1940; repr., 1988); K. C. Boone, *The Bible Tells Them So: The Discourse of Protestant Fundamentalism* (Albany, NY: State University of New York, 1989; London: SCM, 1990); D. R. McLachlan, *Reclaiming Authentic Fundamentalism* (Independence, MO: American Association of Christian Schools, 1993); J. I. Packer, *"Fundamentalism" and the Word of God: Some Evangelical Principles* (Grand Rapids, MI: Eerdmans, 1976); B. Silverstein, *Fundamentalism: A Monographic Bibliography* (Washington, DC: Information Access Group, 1989); *Evangelicalism and Fundamentalism: A Bibliography Selected from the ATLA Religion Database* (Chicago, IL: American Theological Library Association, 1982); B. Secondin, "Die unumstössliche Wahrheit: Herausforderungen und Gefahren des Fundamentalismus", *IKZ "Communio"* 20 (1991) 134-47; cf. *TD* 40 (1993) 3-7; F. Galindo, "Fundamentalismus — Die Alternative zur lückenhaften Evangelisierung Lateinamerikas?" *Ordensnachrichten* 30/5 (1991) 50-60; cf. *TD* 40 (1993) 9-14.

vicarious expiation and the bodily resurrection at the time of the second coming of Christ. As the fundamentalist way of reading the Bible spread to other parts of the world, it gave rise to other ways of interpretation, equally "literalist", in Europe, Asia, Africa and South America. As the 20th century comes to an end, this kind of interpretation is winning more and more adherents, in religious groups and sects, as also among Catholics.

Fundamentalism is right to insist on the divine inspiration of the Bible, the inerrancy of the Word of God and other biblical truths included in its five fundamental points. But its way of presenting these truths is rooted in an ideology which is not biblical, whatever the proponents of this approach might say. For it demands an unshakeable adherence to rigid doctrinal points of view and imposes, as the only source of teaching for Christian life and salvation, a reading of the Bible which rejects all questioning and any kind of critical research.

The basic problem with fundamentalist interpretation of this kind is that, refusing to take into account the historical character of biblical revelation, it makes itself incapable of accepting the full truth of the Incarnation itself. As regards relationships with God, fundamentalism seeks to escape any closeness of the divine and the human. It refuses to admit that the inspired Word of God has been expressed in human language and that this Word has been expressed, under divine inspiration, by human authors possessed of limited capacities and resources. For this reason, it tends to treat the biblical text as if it had been dictated word for word by the Spirit. It fails to recognize that the Word of God has been formulated in language and expression conditioned by various periods. It pays no attention to the literary forms and to the human ways of thinking to be found in the biblical texts, many of which are the result of a process extending over long

---

Its appeal is to "common sense", because God's book can have no mistakes in it, hence no historical mistakes. It intolerantly exerts an influence on people that is almost that of an extremist "cult" or "sect".

In failing to take into account the historical character of biblical revelation, the fundamentalist reading cannot admit that God's Word has been expressed, under inspiration, in the language of human authors who may have had either extraordinary or limited capabilities and who wrote in diverse literary forms. Consequently, it tends to treat the biblical text as if it had been dictated word for word by the Spirit and the human author as a mere scribe who has recorded the divine message. Moreover, it places undue emphasis on the inerrancy of details, especially those supposedly

periods of time and bearing the mark of very diverse historical situations.

Fundamentalism also places undue stress upon the inerrancy of certain details in the biblical texts, especially in what concerns historical events or supposedly scientific truth. It often historicizes material which from the start never claimed to be historical. It considers historical everything that is reported or recounted with verbs in the past tense, failing to take the necessary account of the possibility of symbolic or figurative meaning.

Fundamentalism often shows a tendency to ignore or to deny the problems presented by the biblical text in its original Hebrew, Aramaic or

---

concerning historical events or scientific matters[138]. It ignores the problems presented by the original Hebrew, Aramaic, or Greek texts, and it is often tied to one fixed translation or edition of the Bible[139]. In the inter-

---

[138] The so-called Monkey Trial of 1925 in Dayton, TN is a good example of the disaster that the fundamentalist reading of the Bible can cause. The State Legislature of Tennessee had passed a law forbidding the teaching of evolution, and it was signed by the governor on 13 March 1925. It stated that it was unlawful for any teacher to teach a theory that "denies the story of the divine creation of man as taught in the Bible and... that man has descended from a lower order of animals". John T. Scopes, a biology teacher in Rhea High School of Dayton, TN, had been teaching evolution and was indicted by the public prosecutor. The famous lawyer, William Jennings Bryan, came to assist the prosecutor. The defense was headed by another famous criminal lawyer, Clarence S. Darrow. The trial lasted eleven days and reached a climax, when Darrow summoned Bryan himself to the stand and subjected him to a grueling cross-examination on his fundamentalist beliefs, which became a shouting-match and in which Bryan was forced to contradict himself on the literalist understanding of the early chapters of Genesis. The experience hastened the death of Bryan, who died five days after the trial's end and the conviction of Scopes. See L. H. Allen (ed.), *Bryan and Darrow at Dayton* (New York: Russell & Russell, 1925; repr. 1967) 133ff. W. B. Gatewood, Jr. (ed.), *Controversy in the Twenties: Fundamentalism, Modernism, and Evolution* (Nashville, TN: Vanderbilt University, 1969) 331-67 ("Modernists and Fundamentalists at Armageddon: The Scopes Case"). Cf. L. W. Levine, *Defender of the Faith, William Jennings Bryan: The Last Decade 1915-1925* (New York: Oxford University, 1965); R. Ginger, *Six Days or Forever? Tennessee v. John Thomas Scopes* (Boston, MA: Beacon, 1958; repr., New York: Oxford University, 1974); T. McGowen, *The Great Monkey Trial: Science versus Fundamentalism in America* (New York: Franklin Watts, 1990); C. Darrow, *The Story of My Life* (New York: Scribner's Sons, 1932) 244-78.

[139] See K. C. Boone, *The Bible Tells Them So* (n. 137 above), 32, 40. Cf. J. A. Price, *The King James Only Controversy in American Fundamentalism since 1950* (Chattanooga, TN: Dissertation, Temple Baptist Theological Seminary, 1990). In the United States much of the fundamentalist reading of the Bible has been linked to the *Scofield Reference Bible* (New York: Oxford University, 1909; 2d ed., 1945). C. I. Scofield was a fundamentalist of the dispensationalist sort; he annotated the *King James Version* of the Bible and thus made the *KJV* the only English Bible to use.

Greek form. It is often narrowly bound to one fixed translation, whether old or present-day. By the same token, it fails to take account of the "re-readings" (*relectures*) of certain texts which are found within the Bible itself.

In what concerns the Gospels, fundamentalism does not take into account the development of the gospel tradition, but naively confuses the final stage of this tradition (what the evangelists have written) with the initial (the words and deeds of the historical Jesus). At the same time fundamentalism neglects an important fact: the way in which the first Christian communities themselves understood the impact produced by Jesus of Nazareth and his message. But it is precisely there that we find a witness to the apostolic origin of the Christian faith and its direct expression. Fundamentalism thus misrepresents the call voiced by the gospel itself.

Fundamentalism likewise tends to adopt very narrow points of view. It accepts the literal reality of an ancient, out-of-date cosmology, simply because it is found expressed in the Bible; this blocks any dialogue with a

---

pretation of the Gospels, it equates the final stage of the gospel tradition (what the evangelists wrote down, ca. A.D. 65-95) with the first stage of it (what Jesus of Nazareth did and said, ca. A.D. 1-33)[140]. Consequently, it ignores the way the first Christian communities understood the impact produced by Jesus and his message[141]. As a result, this literalist reading of the Bible has little to do with the genuine literal sense of Scripture (to be discussed below).

Joined to this literalist reading of the Bible is the principle *Scriptura sola*, "Scripture alone", and so the fundamentalist position tends to discount the genuine Tradition that has grown out of the Bible under the guidance of the Holy Spirit within the Christian faith-community. As a result, fundamentalists can be anti-Church, distrusting even the ancient creeds and early conciliar decisions.

In speaking of this fundamentalist reading of the Bible and its consequences, the Commission does not mince words. It regards it as "dange-

---

[140] See p. 22 above.

[141] Cf. J. Barr, *Fundamentalism* (London: SCM, 1977; Philadelphia, PA: Westminster, 1978); *Escaping from Fundamentalism* (London: SCM, 1984); *Beyond Fundamentalism* (Philadelphia, PA: Westminster, 1984); J. S. Spong, *Rescuing the Bible from Fundamentalism: A Bishop Rethinks the Meaning of Scripture* (San Francisco, CA: HarperSan Francisco, 1991); D. G. Stevick, *Beyond Fundamentalism* (Richmond, VA: John Knox, 1964); L. W.

broader way of seeing the relationship between culture and faith. Its relying upon a non-critical reading of certain texts of the Bible serves to reinforce political ideas and social attitudes that are marked by prejudices — racism, for example — quite contrary to the Christian gospel.

Finally, in its attachment to the principle "Scripture alone", fundamentalism separates the interpretation of the Bible from the Tradition, which, guided by the Spirit, has authentically developed in union with Scripture in the heart of the community of faith. It fails to realize that the New Testament took form within the Christian Church, and that it is the Holy Scripture of this Church, the existence of which preceded the composition of the texts. Because of this, fundamentalism is often anti-

---

rous", despite the attraction that it may have for people who would look to the Bible for ready answers to problems in human life here on earth. It speaks of the "intellectual suicide" often associated with it, because it is, in effect, an invitation not to think, not to query the text of the Bible, and thus fosters a false certitude. The aftermath of being taken in by this mode of reading the Bible, which has occurred time and again, is that many such persons inevitably grow up intellectually and realize that one cannot read the Bible that way and, as a result, have simply thrown over all faith commitments[142].

Unfortunately, Catholics in recent times have been developing their own form of fundamentalist reading of the Bible[143]. This is, on the one

---

Countryman, *Biblical Authority or Biblical Tyranny: Scripture and the Christian Pilgrimage* (Valley Forge, Pa: Trinity Press International; Cambridge, MA: Cowley Publications, 1994); R. Bergeron, *Les fondamentalistes et la Bible: Quand la lettre se fait prison* (Montreal: Fides, 1887); H. M. Teeple, *The Historical Approach to the Bible* (Truth in Religion 2; Evanston, IL: Religion and Ethics Institute, 1982).

[142] See J. L. Lane, *The Influence of Higher Education on Fundamentalist Religious Beliefs of College Students* (Tallahassee, FL: Thesis, Florida State University, 1965); J. S. Brent, *The Experience of Leaving Protestant Fundamentalism: An Existential-Phenomenological Analysis* (Columbus, OH: Thesis, Ohio State University, 1990).

[143] See M. Paple, *Catholics and Fundamentalists: What's the Difference?* (Milwaukee, WI: Hi-Time, 1991); P. M. Arnold, "The Reemergence of Fundamentalism in the Catholic Church", *The Fundamentalist Phenomenon: A View from Within, A Response from Without* (ed. N. J. Cohen: Grand Rapids, MI: Eerdmans, 1990) 172-91; J. A. Coleman, "Who Are the Catholic 'Fundamentalists'?" *Commonweal* 116 (1989) 42-47.

Cf. K. Keating, *Catholicism and Fundamentalism: The Attack on "Romanism" by "Bible Christians"* (San Francisco, CA: Ignatius, 1989); P. Stenhouse, *Catholic Answers to Bible Christians: A Light on Biblical Fundamentalism* (Kensington, N.S.W.: Chevalier, 1988); S. B. Marrow, *The Words of Jesus in Our Gospels: A Catholic Response to Fundamentalism* (New York/Ramsey, NJ: Paulist, 1979).

Church; it considers of little importance the creeds, the doctrines and liturgical practices which have become part of Church tradition, as well as the teaching function of the Church itself. It presents itself as a form of private interpretation which does not acknowledge that the Church is founded on the Bible and draws its life and inspiration from Scripture.

The fundamentalist approach is dangerous, for it is attractive to people who look to the Bible for ready answers to the problems of life. It can deceive these people, offering them interpretations that are pious but illusory, instead of telling them that the Bible does not necessarily contain an immediate answer to each and every problem. Without saying as much in so many words, fundamentalism actually invites people to a kind of intellectual suicide. It injects into life a false certitude, for it unwittingly confuses the divine substance of the biblical message with what are in fact its human limitations.

---

hand, a return to a pre-critical way of reading the Bible, which was part of the post-Tridentine Catholic and Counter-Reformation (i.e. anti-Protestant) heritage. On the other, it has resulted from the present-day confusion that reigns in the Catholic interpretation of the Bible, of which the Commission speaks in its Introduction. Like others, Catholics are in this regard victims of fadism and are affected by currents of the contemporary search for a guarantee against life's problems. So they too are turning to the Bible for quick answers and running the same risks.

## II. HERMENEUTICAL QUESTIONS

### A. Philosophical Hermeneutics

In its recent course exegesis has been challenged to some rethinking in the light of contemporary philosophical hermeneutics, which has stressed the involvement of the knowing subject in human understanding, especially as regards historical knowledge. Hermeneutical reflection took new life with the publication of the works of Friedrich Schleiermacher, Wilhelm Dilthey and, above all, Martin Heidegger. In the footsteps of these philosophers, but also to some extent moving away from them, various authors have more deeply developed contemporary hermeneutical theory and its applications to Scripture. Among them we will mention especially Rudolf Bultmann, Hans Georg Gadamer and Paul Ricœur. It is not possible to give a complete summary of their thought here. It will be

---

## II. HERMENEUTICAL QUESTIONS

The foregoing survey of methods of interpretating the Bible, of different approaches to it, and of the fundamentalist reading of it leads naturally to a further question about the philosophical underpinnings of any interpretation of the Bible. What is one up to, when one tries to interpret the Bible? In an attempt to answer such a question, the Commission next considers such topics as (A) philosophical hermeneutics and its modern perspectives and usefulness for exegesis; (B) the meaning of inspired Scripture and its literal, spiritual, and fuller senses.

### A. Philosophical Hermeneutics

As logic is to thinking and grammar is to speaking, so hermeneutics is to exegesis. It is a manner of second reflection on what one is about when one interprets a text. "Hermeneutics" is derived from Greek *hermēneia*, "interpretation", and seeks to set forth the laws of interpreting, as logic

enough to indicate certain central ideas of their philosophies which have had their impact on the interpretation of biblical texts[3].

---

[3] The hermeneutic of the Word developed by Gerhard Ebeling and Ernst Fuchs adopts a different approach and proceeds from another field of thought. It involves more a theological rather than a philosophical hermeneutic. Ebeling agrees however with such authors as Bultmann and Ricœur in affirming that the World of God finds its true meaning only in the encounter with those to whom it is addressed.

---

formulates those of thinking and grammar those of speaking or writing[144]. "Hermeneutics" is an English way of expressing what is called in German *Hermeneutik*; hence the use of it as a singular noun. As applied to Scripture, it denotes the theory of interpretation of the biblical text, the theory of rules that govern the exegesis of the Bible.

"Hermeneutics", in general, refers to the modern mode of philosophical reflection on interpretation that stems from the writings of the German theologian, Friedrich Daniel Ernst Schleiermacher (1768-1834)[145], the German philosopher of culture and history, Wilhelm Dilthey (1833-1911)[146], and the German existentialist philosopher, Martin Heidegger (1889-1976)[147]. More recent developments in hermeneutics, especially

---

[144] This is the meaning of *hermēneia* in the strict sense. However, the Greek word was at times used also in the sense of "translation", and even of "explanation, commentary".

[145] See F. D. E. Schleiermacher, *Hermeneutik* (ed. H. Kimmerle; Heidelberg: Winter, 1959); in English, *Hermeneutics: The Handwritten Manuscripts* (AARTTS 1; tr. J. Duke and J. Forstman; Missoula, MT: Scholars, 1977); R. O. Palmer, *Hermeneutics: Interpretation Theory in Schleiermacher, Dilthey, Heidegger, and Gadamer* (Evanston, IL: Northwestern University, 1969); K. Mueller-Vollmer (ed.), *The Hermeneutics Reader: Texts of the German Tradition from the Enlightenment to the Present* (New York: Continuum, 1985).

Cf. D. S. Ferguson, *Biblical Hermeneutics: An Introduction* (Atlanta, GA: John Knox, 1986); D. K. McKim (ed.), *A Guide to Contemporary Hermeneutics: Major Trends in Biblical Interpretation* (Grand Rapids, MI: Eerdmans, 1986); R. W. Funk, *Language, Hermeneutic, and Word of God* (New York: Harper & Row, 1966); R. Marlé, *Introduction to Hermeneutics* (New York: Herder and Herder, 1967); B. C. Lategan, "Hermeneutics", *ABD* 3. 149-54; R. E. Brown and S. M. Schneiders, "Hermeneutics", *NJBC* art. 71 (pp. 1146-65).

[146] See W. Dilthey, *Gesammelte Schriften* (14 vols.; ed. B. Groethuysen; Stuttgart: Teubner; Göttingen: Vandenhoeck & Ruprecht, 1959-68), esp. 7. 205-20. Cf. H. A. Hodges, *Wilhelm Dilthey: An Introduction* (New York: H. Fertig, 1944; repr. 1989); *The Philosophy of Wilhelm Dilthey* (London: Routledge & Kegan Paul, 1952); I. N. Bulhof, *Wilhelm Dilthey: A Hermeneutic Approach to the Study of History and Culture* (The Hague/Boston, MA: Nijhoff Publishers, 1980).

[147] See M. Heidegger, *Sein und Zeit* (Tübingen: Neomarius Verlag, 1927); in English, *Being and Time* (London: SCM; New York: Harper & Bros., 1962). Cf. H. M. Sass, *Heidegger-Bibliographie* (Meisenheim am Glan: A. Hain, 1968).

## 1. *Modern Perspectives*

Conscious of the cultural distance between the world of the first century and that of the twentieth, *Bultmann* was particularly anxious to make the reality of which the Bible treats speak to his contemporaries. He insisted upon the "pre-understanding" necessary for all understanding and elaborated the theory of the existential interpretation of the New Testament writings. Relying upon the thinking of Heidegger, Bultmann insisted that it is not possible to have an exegesis of a biblical text without presuppositions which guide comprehension. "Pre-understanding" (*"Vorverständnis"*) is founded upon the life-relationship (*"Lebensverhältnis"*) of the interpreter to the reality of which the text speaks. To avoid subjectivism, however, one must allow preunderstanding to be deepened and enriched — even to be modified and corrected — by the reality of the text.

---

in the application of such reflection to biblical interpretation, are found in the writings of the German New Testament exegete, Rudolf Bultmann (1884-1976)[148], the German philosopher, Hans Georg Gadamer (1900--)[149], and the French philosopher, Paul Ricœur (1913--)[150].

## 1. *Modern Perspectives*

To each of the last three scholars the Commission now devotes some attention. Of the three, the most important is the first. Bultmann was himself an exegete, who wrestled with the text and sought to interpret it in commentaries, whereas the other two, Gadamer and Ricœur, are philosophers, not known for biblical commentaries. Hence their writings are always to be read with requisite discernment.

In addition to his contribution to the form-critical study of the Gospels, Bultmann developed a hermeneutics, especially in his book,

---

[148] See n. 151 below. Cf. J. Macquarrie, *An Existentialist Theology: A Comparison of Heidegger and Bultmann* (London: SCM, 1955).

[149] See H. G. Gadamer, *Wahrheit und Methode: Grundzüge einer philosophischen Hermeneutik* (Tübingen: Mohr [Siebeck], 1960; 2d ed., 1965). Cf. his *Kleine Schriften* (2 vols.; Tübingen: Mohr [Siebeck], 1967); *Philosophical Hermeneutics* (Berkeley, CA: University of California, 1976).

[150] See P. Ricœur, *Le conflit des interprétations: Essais d'herméneutique* (Paris: Editions du Seuil, 19690; in English, *The Conflict of Interpretations: Essays in Hermeneutics* (ed. D. Ihde; Evanston, IL: Northwestern University, 1974). Cf. *Essays on Biblical Interpretation* (ed. L. S. Mudge; Philadelphia, PA: Fortress, 1980).

Bultmann asked what might be the most appropriate frame of thought for defining the sort of questions that would render the texts of Scripture understandable to people of today. He claimed to have found the answer in the existential analysis of Heidegger, maintaining that Heideggerian existential principles have a universal application and offer structures and concepts most appropriate for the understanding of human existence as revealed in the New Testament message.

*Gadamer* likewise stresses the historical distance between the text and its interpreter. He takes up and develops the theory of the hermeneutical circle. Anticipations and preconceptions affecting our understanding stem from the tradition which carries us. This tradition consists in a mass of historical and cultural data which constitute our life context and our horizon of understanding. The interpreter is obliged to enter into dia-

---

*Jesus*[151], in which he depicted Jesus as summoning human beings to an *Entscheidung*, "decision", challenging them to respond to his radical preaching, because in him God was presenting salvation in a final, decisive way[152]. Bultmann's approach to the Gospels was developed out of a *Vorverständnis*, "pre-understanding", which has already been described (p. 46 above). For him this meant a demythologizing reading of the Gospels (à la D. F. Strauss), a Lutheran *sola fides* doctrine, a New Testament theology that begins only with the primitive kerygma[153], and a

---

[151] See n. 69 above. Also *Glauben und Verstehen* (4 vols.; Tübingen: Mohr [Siebeck], 1933-65); part of vol. 1 appeared in English as *Faith and Understanding* (ed. R. W. Funk; New York: Harper & Row, 1969); part of vol. 2 as *Essays, Philosophical and Theological* (London: SCM, 1955); *Existence and Faith: Shorter Writings of Rudolf Bultmann* (ed. S. M. Ogden; New York: Meridian Books, 1960).

Cf. K. Barth, *Rudolf Bultmann: Ein Versuch ihn zu verstehen* (Zurich: Evangelischer V., 1952); C. W. Kegley, *The Theology of Rudolf Bultmann* (New York: Harper & Row, 1966); R. Marlé, *Bultmann et l'interprétation du Nouveau Testament* (Théologie 33; Paris: Aubier, 1956; 2d ed., 1966); A. Malet, *Mythos et logos: La pensée de Rudolf Bultmann* (Geneva: Labor et Fides, 1962); in English, *The Thought of Rudolf Bultmann* (Shannon: Irish University; Garden City, NY: Doubleday, 1969); W. Schmithals, *Die Theologie Rudolf Bultmanns* (2d ed.; Tübingen: Mohr [Siebeck], 1967); in English, *An Introduction to the Theology of Rudolf Bultmann* (Minneapolis, MN: Augsburg, 1968); L. Malevez, *The Christian Message and Myth: The Theology of Rudolf Bultmann* (London: SCM, 1958); G. Miegge, *L'Evangile et le mythe dans la pensée de Rudolf Bultmann* (Bibliothèque théologique; Neuchâtel: Delachaux et Niestlé, 1958); J. Macquarrie, *The Scope of Demythologizing: Bultmann and His Critics* (London: SCM, 1960).

[152] See also his *Theology of the New Testament* (n. 69 above) 1. 9.

[153] Ibid., 1. 3.

logue with the reality at stake in the text. Understanding is reached in the fusion of the differing horizons of text and reader (*"Horizontverschmelzung"*). This is possible only to the extent that there is a "belonging" (*"Zugehörigkeit"*), that is, a fundamental affinity, between the interpreter and his or her object. Hermeneutics is a dialectical process: the understanding of a text always entails an enhanced understanding of oneself.

With regard to the hermeneutical thought of *Ricœur*, the principal thing to note is the highlighting of the function of distantiation. This is the necessary prelude to any correct appropriation of a text. A first distancing occurs between the text and its author, for, once produced, the text takes on a certain autonomy in relation to its author; it begins its own career of meaning. Another distancing exists between the text and its successive readers; these have to respect the world of the text in its otherness. Thus the methods of literary and historical analysis are necessary for interpretation. Yet the meaning of a text can be fully grasped only as it is actualized in the lives of readers who appropriate it. Beginning with their situation, they are summoned to uncover new meanings, along the fundamental line of meaning indicated by the text. Biblical knowledge should not stop short at language; it must seek to arrive at the reality of which the language speaks. The religious language of the Bible is a symbolic language which "gives rise to thought" (*"donne à penser"*), a language the full richness of which one never ceases to discover, a language which points to a transcendent reality and which, at the same time, awakens human beings to the deepest dimensions of personal existence.

---

form of existentialist philosophy borrowed from the younger Heidegger. This enabled Bultmann to concentrate on Stage III of the gospel tradition and to sever from it all interest in Stage I (what the Jesus of history did and said). To such an approach Bultmann added his demythologization of the Gospels. Thus he was able to present the New Testament message as a meaningful challenge to modern, twentieth-century readers which would enable them to come to a decision about God's demand, a decision by which they would affirm their authentic existence. So Bultmann thought he had bridged "the cultural distance between the world of the first century and that of the twentieth". He thus clothed the New Testament message in a Heideggerian existentialist philosophy and a radical demythologization of the text in an effort to bring the meaning of the New Testament to people of the twentieth century.

Both Gadamer and Ricœur likewise address themselves to the problem of the distance between the historical text of the Bible and the mo-

## 2. Usefulness for Exegesis

What is to be said about these contemporary theories of the interpretation of texts? The Bible is the Word of God for all succeeding ages. Hence the absolute necessity of a hermeneutical theory which allows for the incorporation of the methods of literary and historical criticism within a broader model of interpretation. It is a question of overcoming the distance between the time of the authors and first addressees of the biblical texts and our own contemporary age, and of doing so in a way that permits a correct actualization of the scriptural message so that the Christian life of faith may find nourishment. All exegesis of texts is thus summoned to make itself fully complete through a "hermeneutics" understood in this modern sense.

The Bible itself and the history of its interpretation point to the need for a hermeneutics — for an interpretation, that is, that proceeds from and addresses our world today. The whole complex of the Old and New Testament writings show themselves to be the product of a long process where founding events constantly find reinterpretation through connection with the life of communities of faith. In Church tradition, the Fathers, as first interpreters of Scripture, considered that their exegesis of texts was complete only when it had found a meaning relevant to the situation of Christians in their own day. Exegesis is truly faithful to proper intention of biblical texts when it goes not only to the heart of their formulation to find the reality of faith there expressed but also seeks to link this reality to the experience of faith in our present world.

Contemporary hermeneutics is a healthy reaction to historical positiv-

---

dern reader, or what Bultmann called "a circle", the "hermeneutical circle", which in the work of Gadamer and Ricœur becomes rather a spiral, a circle that moves on different levels.

## 2. Usefulness for Exegesis

The Commission recognizes the need of a contemporary hermeneutical theory for the interpretation of the Bible, because it is the Word of God for all ages, and not just for the people for whom the message was immediately and directly formulated. In other words, historical and literary criticism of the Bible have to be subsumed under a broader theory of interpretation, which facilitates the passage of its message from the human author to his first addressees and then to people of every age and genera-

ism and to the temptation to apply to the study of the Bible the purely objective criteria used in the natural sciences. On the one hand, all events reported in the Bible are interpreted events. On the other, all exegesis of the accounts of these events necessarily involves the exegete's own subjectivity. Access to a proper understanding of biblical texts is only granted to the person who has an affinity with what the text is saying on the basis of life experience. The question which faces every exegete is this: which hermeneutical theory best enables a proper grasp of the profound reality of which Scripture speaks and its meaningful expression for people today?

We must frankly accept that certain hermeneutical theories are inadequate for interpreting Scripture. For example, Bultmann's existentialist interpretation tends to enclose the Christian message within the constraints of a particular philosophy. Moreover, by virtue of the presuppositions insisted upon in this hermeneutic, the religious message of the Bible is for the most part emptied of its objective reality (by means of an excessive "demythologization") and tends to be reduced to an anthropological message only. Philosophy becomes the norm of interpretation, rather than

---

tion. The Commission thus speaks of "a correct actualization of the scriptural message" in which modern Christian faith can find its proprer nourishment, a notion to which it will return later in the document.

The Church Fathers, the first interpreters of the Christian Bible, used a similar hermeneutics to bring its message to the people of their day. Hence the exegesis of biblical texts is rightly oriented "when it goes not only to the heart of their formulation to find the reality of faith there expressed but also seeks to link this reality to the experience of faith in our present world". There is, moreover, a necessary relationship between the "interpreted events" in the biblical story and the subjective understanding of the interpreter that is brought to the task. The latter can only be an "affinity with what the text is saying on the basis of life experience", which is nothing less than the empathy of Christian faith, as one reads the biblical text today.

Consequently, the Commission finds the existentialist and demythologizing philosophical hermeneutics of Bultmann to be inadequate, because his interpretation has, in effect, reduced the New Testament to an anthropological message, to a mere teaching about humanity[154].

---

[154] See further N. A. Dahl, "Rudolf Bultmann's Theology of the New Testament", *The Crucified Messiah and Other Essays* (Minneapolis, MN: Augsburg, 1974) 90-128, esp. 113-15.

an instrument of understanding the central object of all interpretation: the person of Jesus Christ and the saving events accomplished in human history. An authentic interpretation of Scripture, then, involves in the first place a welcoming of the meaning that is given in the events and, in a supreme way, in the person of Jesus Christ.

This meaning is expressed in the text. To avoid, then, purely subjective readings, an interpretation valid for contemporary times will be founded on the study of the text and such an interpretation will constantly submit its presuppositions to verification by the text.

Biblical hermeneutics, for all that it is a part of the general hermeneutics applying to every literary and historical text, constitutes at the same time a unique instance of general hermeneutics. Its specific characteristics stem from its object. The events of salvation and their accomplishment in the person of Jesus Christ give meaning to all human history. New interpretations in the course of time can only be the unveiling or unfolding of this wealth of meaning. Reason alone cannot fully comprehend the account of these events given in the Bible. Particular presuppositions, such as the faith lived in ecclesial community and the light of the Spirit, control its interpretation. As the reader matures in the life of the Spirit, so there grows also his or her capacity to understand the realities of which the Bible speaks.

---

In contrast, "an authentic interpretation of Scripture" for Christians is one that welcomes the meaning given to salvific events, especially in the person of Jesus of Nazareth. That, in effect, means an interpretation born of Christian faith, but based on the message expressed in the text of the New Testament and guided by the light of the Spirit in a community of faith. This is what it means to read the Bible as the Word of God, as the Word of God speaking to me[155].

Although biblical hermeneutics is part of the general hermeneutics that governs the interpretation of any literary or historical text, it has a specific orientation of its own, because it deals with the unique events of salvation accomplished in Jesus Christ, who gives meaning to all human history. Those events so oriented are not comprehended by reason alone, but are seen by the eyes of faith. That specific orientation can never be neglected.

---

[155] See G. Martin, *Reading Scripture as the Word of God: Practical Approaches and Attitudes* (2d ed.; Ann Arbor, MI: Servant Books, 1982); R. M. Brown, *The Bible Speaks to You* (Philadelphia, PA: Westminster, 1955).

## B. The Meaning of Inspired Scripture

The contribution made by modern philosophical hermeneutics and the recent development of literary theory allows biblical exegesis to deepen its understanding of the task before it, the complexity of which has become ever more evident. Ancient exegesis, which obviously could not take into account modern scientific requirements, attributed to every text of Scripture several levels of meaning. The most prevalent distinction was that between the literal sense and the spiritual sense. Medieval exegesis distinguished within the spiritual sense three different aspects, each relating, respectively, to the truth revealed, to the way of life commended and to the final goal to be achieved. From this came the famous couplet of Augustine of Denmark (13th century):

> *"Littera gesta docet, quid credas allegoria,*
> *moralis quid agas, quid speres anagogia".*

In reaction to this multiplicity of senses, historical-critical exegesis adopted, more or less overtly, the thesis of the one single meaning: a text cannot have at the same time more than one meaning. All the effort of historical-critical exegesis goes into defining "the" precise sense of this or that biblical text seen within the circumstances in which it was produced.

---

## B. The Meaning of Inspired Scripture

Having discussed modern modes of interpreting the Bible, the hermeneutical presuppositions of such interpretation, and the need of a proper contemporary hermeneutics, the Commission turns to some implications of that hermeneutical reflection. In particular, to the question whether the written Word of God can have more than one meaning.

This question is raised because in the history of the interpretation of the Bible, more than one meaning was often given to it. Indeed, for long periods of Church history multiple senses of Scripture dominated the understanding of the Bible, and several levels of meaning were attributed to its texts. Consequently, that raises the modern question about the viability of multiple senses of Scripture today, especially in view of the way the historical-critical method has developed and is presently practised within the Church. Can one admit allegorical interpretations of the written Word of God today? Or can passages of the Bible today take on a meaning different from that which they had when first composed?

The Commission begins by recalling the distinction between the lite-

But this thesis has now run aground on the conclusions of theories of language and of philosophical hermeneutics, both of which affirm that written texts are open to a plurality of meaning.

---

ral and the spiritual sense of Scripture. Because "spiritual sense" can be understood in various ways, it is important to understand the way in which the Commission at first uses it. That refers to the medieval distinction, which spoke of four senses of Scripture, three of them being aspects or subdivisions of the "spiritual sense"[156]. The four senses came to be summed up in the late thirteenth-century distich,

> Littera gesta docet, quid credas allegoria,
> moralis quid agas, quid speres anagogia[157],
> The literal teaches facts; the allegorical, what you are to believe;
> the moral, what you are to do, the anagogical, what you are to hope for[158].

According to this way of interpreting Scripture, every verse could have four senses: the literal, the allegorical, the moral, and the anagogical (or eschatological). This way of understanding Scripture grew out of an earlier tripartite sense (historia, moralis, allegoria) and from what Origen had called the "spiritual" or "mystical" sense of Scripture[159]. The allegorical sense is actually found as early as in the Ep. Barnabas 9.7, where such an interpretation is given to the number 318, the number of the men circumcised by Abraham, understood as referring to the cross of Jesus Christ.

There were, however, always people in the Christian Church who reacted against such allegorizing or spiritualizing of Scripture, e.g. the Antiochene School in the fourth century, Nicholas of Lyra in the late Middle Ages, the Reformers Luther and Calvin, and those today who use

---

[156] See H. de Lubac, Exégèse médiévale: Les quatre sens de l'Ecriture (2 double vols.; Théologie 41, 41, 42, 59; Paris: Aubier, 1959, 1959, 1961, 1964); "Sens spirituel", RSR 36 (1949) 542-76. Cf. F. Ohly, Vom geistigen Sinn des Wortes im Mittelalter (Darmstadt: Wissenschaftliche Buchgesellschaft, 1966).

[157] It is usually attributed to Augustine of Dacia, O.P., who was of Scandinavian origin (Denmark) and died in 1282. In 1260 he published a compendium of theology entitled Rotulus Pugillaris. See A. Walz, "Augustini de Dacia O.P. 'Rotulus Pugillaris'", Angelicum 6 (1929) 253-78, 548-74. Cf. A. Vaccari, "Auctor versuum de quattuor Scripturae sensibus", VDom 9 (1929) 212-14.

[158] As it is quoted in Nicholas of Lyra, Postilla in Gal. 4.3, the last clause reads rather quo tendas anagogia, "the anagogical, whither you are headed", which does not alter the sense.

[159] See Peri Archōn 5.3.5; GCS 22. 331; SC 268. 362. Cf. H. de Lubac, Exégèse médiévale (n. 156 above), 1/1. 198-207.

The problem is not simple, and it arises in different ways in regard to different types of texts: historical accounts, parables, oracular pronouncements, laws, proverbs, prayers, hymns, etc. Nevertheless, while keeping in mind that considerable diversity of opinion also prevails, some general principles can be stated.

## 1. *The Literal Sense*

It is not only legitimate, it is also absolutely necessary to seek to define the precise meaning of texts as produced by their authors — what is called the "literal" meaning. St. Thomas Aquinas had already affirmed the fundamental importance of this sense (*S. Th.* I, q. 1, a. 10, ad 1).

The literal sense is not to be confused with the "literalist" sense to which fundamentalists are attached. It is not sufficient to translate a text word for word in order to obtain its literal sense. One must understand the

---

a properly-oriented form of the historical-critical method[160]. That is why the Commission admits that "all the effort of historical-critical exegesis" has been to define "'the' precise sense of this or that biblical text seen within the circumstances in which it was produced", in other words the "literal" sense.

And yet, modern theories of language and philosophical hermeneutics have shown that at times one has to reckon with "a plurality of meaning" in a written text, even if to admit that creates a "problem", depending on the variety of biblical texts (historical, legal, proverbial, etc.) and the diversity of opinion prevailing in hermeneutical theories. For this reason the Commission devotes space to an explanation of the literal, spiritual, and fuller senses of Scripture.

## 1. *The Literal Sense*

One has to recognize the need to determine "the precise meaning of texts as produced by their authors", what Thomas Aquinas called the "li-

---

[160] Even Thomas Aquinas, who used the four senses of Scripture, wrote to this effect: "All the senses are based on one, namely the literal, from which alone an argument can be drawn, and not from those which are said by way of allegory... Yet nothing is lost to sacred Scripture because of this, because nothing necessary for faith is contained in the spiritual sense, which Scripture does not clearly pass on elsewhere by the literal sense" (*S.T.* I, q. 1, a. 10 ad 1). Cf. *Quaestiones Quodlibetales* VII, q. 16, a. 14-16.

text according to the literary conventions of the time. When a text is metaphorical, its literal sense is not that which flows immediately from a word to word translation (e.g., "Let your loins be girt": *Luke* 12:35), but that which corresponds to the metaphorical use of these terms ("Be ready for action"). When it is a question of a story, the literal sense does not necessarily imply belief that the facts recounted actually took place, for a story need not belong to the genre of history but be instead a work of imaginative fiction.

The literal sense of Scripture is that which has been expressed directly by the inspired human authors. Since it is the fruit of inspiration, this sense is also intended by God, as principal author. One arrives at this sense by means of a careful analysis of the text, within its literary and historical context. The principal task of exegesis is to carry out this analy-

---

teral sense", and what Pius XII labelled in the same way[161]. The Commission now defines it as "that which has been expressed directly by the inspired human author". It is the sense ascertained by a careful analysis of the text, within its literary and historical context, according to its ancient literary genre and according to the literary convention of its time of composition. In the case of the Gospels it would mean the sense of the evangelists, and not necessarily the sense of the words as used by Jesus of Nazareth a generation earlier. Moreover, that sense could differ depending on the way it is used by different evangelists.

This may seem at first sight to be as comprehensive as what Pius XII meant when he stated that the foremost endeavor of the Catholic exegete was to "define clearly that sense of the biblical words which is called literal... so that the mind of the author may be made abundantly clear" (§23). More recent hermeneutical studies, however, have made it clear that the authorial intention of a text is not always so apparent[162]. Hence the Commission does not state that the literal sense is that which has been *intended* by the inspired human author; it is rather that which has been *expressed* by him. Some of his intention may be gauged by what he has expressed, but that scarcely leads to a full manifestation of his intention, especially when

---

[161] See preceding note and also the quotation of *Divino afflante Spiritu* on p. 43. Although at times in the past the literal sense was distinguished from the metaphorical sense, it is normally understood today to include that sense (e.g. "Behold, the Lamb of God", John 1:36).

[162] To say this, however, does not mean that one accepts uncritically the modern literary theory about "authorial intention" as a fallacy. Cf. E. D. Hirsch, *Validity in Interpretation* (New Haven, CT: Yale University, 1967).

sis, making use of all the resources of literary and historical research, with a view to defining the literal sense of the biblical texts with the greatest possible accuracy (cf. *Divino Afflante Spiritu: EB*, 550). To this end, the study of ancient literary genres is particularly necessary (*ibid.*, 560).

Does a text have only one literal sense? In general, yes; but there is no question here of a hard and fast rule, and this for two reasons. First, a

---

one is dealing with such ancient texts as those in the Old and New Testament, written in languages of long ago[163].

The "literal" sense, however, is not to be confused with a "literalist" reading of a biblical text in any fundamentalistic way. For the literal sense has to include metaphorical, figurative or symbolic, even fictive and imaginative modes of expression common to all human language. Due regard must be had, then, for the literary form that the human author has used. Again, not everything narrated in the past tense is necessarily to be taken as expressive of historic reality. For example, "The veil of the Temple was torn in two, from top to bottom" (Mark 15:38) may well have more of a symbolic meaning than a historical affirmation. The truth of a statement is always gauged by the literary form employed[164].

It is important to realize that at times the literal sense of Scripture is quite obvious and that no sophistication is required in the reader to comprehend it. Paul says, "We write to you nothing but what you can read and understand" (2 Cor 1:13). This would be true, for instance, of many of the psalms and proverbs in the Old Testament, as well as many of its straightforward historical narratives; the same could be said of simple narratives about the life and ministry of Jesus in the Gospels or uncomplicated accounts in the Acts of the Apostles. But the literal sense is not always so easily comprehended, especially when the biblical text in its ancient original language is not clear or has used complicated words and phrases or when it demands a knowledge of the time, culture, and mode of expression related to the context in which it was composed. In this case no little sophistication is needed to comprehend the literal sense, and this is the reason for the work of the professional interpreter or exegete.

---

[163] The Commission also recognizes that what has been expressed by the human author is what is intended by God, the principal author. In saying that, the Commission is merely reaffirming the normal Catholic understanding of biblical inspiration. This will have ramifications in the discussion of the *sensus plenior* below.

[164] As A. Bea once put it, "Sua cuique generi litterario est veritas" (Every literary genre has its own truth); see *De Scripturae Sacrae inspiratione quaestiones historicae et dogmaticae* (2d ed.; Rome: Biblical Institute, 1935) §90.

human author can intend to refer at one and the same time to more than one level of reality. This is in fact normally the case with regard to poetry. Biblical inspiration does not reject this capacity of human psychology and language; the Fourth Gospel offers numerous examples of it. Secondly, even when a human utterance appears to have only one meaning, divine inspiration can guide the expression in such way as to create more than one meaning. This is the case with the saying of Caiaphas in *John* 11:50: at one and the same time it expresses both an immoral political ploy and a divine revelation. The two aspects belong, both of them, to the literal sense, for they are both made clear by the context. Although this example may be extreme, it remains significant, providing a warning against adopting too narrow a conception of the inspired text's literal sense.

One should be especially attentive to the *dynamic aspect* of many texts. The meaning of the royal psalms, for example, should not be limited strictly to the historical circumstances of their production. In speaking of the king, the psalmist evokes at one and the same time both the institution as it actually was and an idealized vision of kingship as God intended it to be; in this way the text carries the reader beyond the institution of kingship in its actual historical manifestation. Historical-critical exegesis has

---

Does a biblical text have only one literal sense? The Commission finds that, in general, this is so, while recognizing that a human author can speak or write on more than one level of reality, as in poetry, or as often in the Johannine Gospel[165]. At times, one has to reckon with a "plurality of meaning", but that does not mean that one can find a plurality everywhere in the Bible. To admit that would open the gates to a multitude of subjective meanings. Moreover, divine inspiration can add a meaning, as in the prediction of Caiaphas in John 11:50, which simultaneously expresses "an immoral political ploy and a divine revelation". Even though the Commission notes the significance of this rare example as a warning not to give too narrow a meaning to an inspired text's literal sense, it is the evangelist himself who in this instance (vv. 51-52) calls the reader's attention to the double meaning of v. 50, the unconscious prediction of the high priest.

Moreover, biblical texts have at times a *dynamic aspect*, which carries a meaning transcending their precise historical circumstances, which can

---

[165] E.g. the meaning of *anōthen* in John 3:3,4,7; of "living water" in 4:10-14; of "going up" in 7:8. Cf. R. E. Brown, *The Gospel according to John* (AB 29, 29A; Garden City, NY: Doubleday, 1966, 1970) 1. cxxxv.

too often tended to limit the meaning of texts by tying in too rigidly to precise historical circumstances. It should seek rather to determine the direction of thought expressed by the text; this direction, far from working towards a limitation of meaning, will on the contrary dispose the exegete to perceive extensions of it that are more or less foreseeable in advance.

One branch of modern hermeneutics has stressed that human speech gains an altogether fresh status when put in writing. A written text has the capacity to be placed in new circumstances, which will illuminate it in different ways, adding new meanings to the original sense. This capacity of written texts is especially operative in the case of the biblical writings, recognized as the Word of God. Indeed, what encouraged the believing community to preserve these texts was the conviction that they would continue to be bearers of light and life for generations of believers to come. The literal sense is, from the start, open to further developments, which are produced through the "re-reading" ("*relectures*") of texts in new contexts.

---

be open to "extensions" not immediately foreseeable. This can be found especially in royal psalms. In such cases the historical-critical method has to remain open to the direction of such an aspect of biblical texts. However, the Commission has significantly not used of the royal psalms the term "messianic", undoubtedly realizing the tendency all too prevalent today to read a (Christian) connotation into poetic creations that did not stem from such contexts in pre-Christian Judaism. When a royal psalm (e.g. Psalm 2) is used of Jesus, the (Christian) Messiah, in the New Testament (e.g. in Acts 13:33), then the psalm itself takes on a messianic connotation. But that does not mean that the messianic meaning was already denoted by the psalm in its pre-Christian Old Testament context. The interpreter of such an Old Testament psalm may have to realize, however, that its dynamic aspect may point to such a foreseeable understanding.

More important, however, is the recognition of the process of "re-reading" found in Scripture itself. Called in French *relecture*, it is found especially in written texts, when words, phrases, or themes are used in new circumstances that add new meanings to the original sense. Thus the literal sense of the written text would have to be regarded as open to such further meaning, and it has been preserved in the believing community precisely because of this. For instance, motifs from the Exodus are taken up in Deutero-Isaiah to give consolation to the people of Israel returning from Babylonian Captivity (e.g. the motifs of Exod 15:1-18 so used in Isa 42:10-13; or those of Exodus 14–15 so used in Isa 43:16-17; 41:17-20); or

It does not follow from this that we can attribute to a biblical text whatever meaning we like, interpreting it in a wholly subjective way. On the contrary, one must reject as unauthentic every interpretation alien to the meaning expressed by the human authors in their written text. To admit the possibility of such alien meanings would be equivalent to cutting off the biblical message from its root, which is the Word of God in its historical communication; it would also mean opening the door to interpretation of a wildly subjective nature.

## 2. The Spiritual Sense

There are reasons, however, for not taking "alien" in so strict a sense as to exclude all possibility of higher fulfilment. The paschal event, the

---

when motifs from the plagues of Egypt and deliverance from Egypt are taken up in Wisdom 11–19[166]. This process is particularly important at times in the use of Old Testament motifs in the New Testament and plays a major role in the canonical interpretation of Scripture[167].

Having admitted these various ways in which the literal sense of Scripture may at times have to be understood and broadened, the Commission finally cautions that none of these broadening aspects can be invoked to "attribute to a biblical text whatever meaning we like, interpreting it in a wholly subjective way". For these would be "alien meanings", alien to the biblical message and not rooted in its historical communication.

## 2. The Spiritual Sense

Along with the literal sense of Scripture, there has also been in the Catholic tradition of interpreting the Bible a "spiritual sense". The trouble

---

[166] An analogous re-reading of Scripture can be found in the way the Jewish authors of the Qumran community composed their sectarian commentaries (pěšārîm) on prophetic writings or the psalms. See M. P. Horgan, *Pesharim: Qumran Interpretations of Biblical Books* (CBQMS 8; Washington, DC: Catholic Biblical Association, 1979). Cf. M. Fishbane, *Biblical Interpretation in Ancient Israel* (Oxford: Clarendon, 1985); and *It Is Written: Scripture Citing Scripture: Essays in Honour of Barnabas Lindars, SSF* (ed. D. A. Carson and H. G. M. Williamson; Cambridge, UK: Cambridge University, 1988).

[167] To admit this, however, does not mean that the re-reading of Old Testament passages in the New Testament was all of one sort, because sometimes it was typological, sometimes allegorical, sometimes using the *sensus plenior*, and often christological.

death and resurrection of Jesus, has established a radically new historical context, which sheds fresh light upon the ancient texts and causes them to undergo a change in meaning. In particular, certain texts which in ancient

with that term is that it is a weasel word, and it is not always used with a univocal meaning. Hence one has to distinguish current uses of the term.

First, it has been used at times loosely to designate what is more properly called an "accommodated sense" of Scripture, which is really an alien meaning imposed on a biblical text[168]. Such a "spiritual" sense will, however, always remain alien because of its subjective nature; it cannot be accorded any legitimacy in the interpretive endeavor[169]. The Commission significantly says nothing about the accommodated sense or the possibility of its being a "spiritual" sense, as it cautions against subjective interpretations stemming from imaginative speculation.

Second, as the Commission uses the term, it is the traditional meaning of "spiritual sense", which was made popular by Origen, if it did not originate with him[170]. It denotes the meaning given to Old Testament texts by the paschal mystery, the death and resurrection of Jesus, i.e. "the

---

[168] It has been applied to the accommodated sense given by Pope John Paul II to Col 3:3, which speaks of a Christian's share in the risen life of Christ as a "life hidden with Christ in God", when he applied it to Mary living with Jesus during his Hidden Life: "During the years of Jesus" hidden life in the house at Nazareth, Mary's life, too, is 'hid with Christ in God' (cf. Col. 3:3) through faith" (*Redemptoris Mater* §17; *AAS* 79 [1987] 380; *Origins* 16 [1986-87] 752; *The Pope Speaks* 32 [1987] 169).

[169] "No place is found in *sacra doctrina* for what has been called the "accommodated" sense, or the meaning given by artifice to a biblical text not warranted by its context in Scripture or in Tradition but adjusted to an adventitious situation. Though perhaps fruitful for private meditation or for a sermon on a special occasion it forms no part of the Church's public teaching" ("The Senses of Scripture", in *St Thomas Aquinas: Summa Theologica 1. 1a 1* [Blackfriars Edition, ed. T. Gilby; London: Eyre & Spottiswoode; New York: McGraw-Hill, 1964] 141). The accommodated sense is, in reality, eisegesis, the opposite of exegesis, for it reads into the biblical text a more-than-literal sense, quite alien to it, as it makes the Bible responsible for pious thoughts and fancies extraneous to it. Yet it has been characteristic of much patristic and liturgical usage.

[170] See Origen, *Peri Archōn* 4.3.5; GCS 22. 331; SC 268. 362. There Origen says that all Scripture has a spiritual (*pneumatikon*) sense, but not all of it has a bodily (*sōmatikon*) sense. On Origen's exegesis, see J. Quasten, *Patrology* (Westminster, MD; Utrecht/Antwerp: Spectrum) 2 (1953) 48; J. Daniélou, *Origen* (New York: Sheed and Ward, 1955); P. Nautin, *Origène: Sa vie et son oeuvre* (Paris: Beauchesne, 1977); H. de Lubac, *Histoire et Esprit: L'Intelligence de l'Ecriture d'après Origène* (Paris: Aubier, 1950); R. Gögler, *Zur Theologie des biblischen Wortes bei Origenes* (Düsseldorf: Patmos, 1963); H. Crouzel, *Origène* (Paris: Lethielleux; Namur: Culture et verité, 1985).

times had to be thought of as hyperbole (e.g., the oracle where God, speaking of a son of David, promised to establish his throne "forever": *2 Sam* 7:12-13; *1 Chr* 17:11-14), these texts must now be taken literally, because "Christ, having been raised from the dead, dies no more" (*Rom*

---

meaning expressed by the biblical texts when read, under the influence of the Holy Spirit, in the context of the paschal mystery of Christ and of the new life which flows from it". In other words, this traditional "spiritual sense" of Scripture is the christological sense of Old Testament texts[171]. This is the sense, too, in which Pius XII used the term in *Divino afflante Spiritu* §26, which he admits can be a genuine meaning of the Christian Scriptures (§27). In this sense the New Testament often recognizes the fulfillment of the Scriptures, i.e. of the Old Testament[172].

A good example is given of such a spiritual sense: God's promise to establish the dynastic throne "forever" for a son of David (2 Sam 7:12-13; 1 Chr 17:12). The divine promise might there have seemed to be a hyperbole, but it already possessed a dynamic aspect. Its spiritual sense is found in Christ's everlasting rule: "Christ, raised from the dead, dies no more" (Rom 6:9); though "son of David according to the flesh" (Rom 1:3), he rules "forever", but not on the earthly throne of David.

The Commission, however, recognizes that such ancient christological exegesis strained at times to find a spiritual sense even in the minutest details of the biblical text, using either rabbinic techniques or Hellenistic allegory. But it warns that, despite the pastoral concern that may govern such an effort, that kind of allegorical interpretation cannot be used today[173].

---

[171] See A. T. Hanson, *Jesus Christ in the Old Testament* (London: SPCK, 1965); R. H. Judd, *Jesus Christ in the Old Testament* (Oregon, IL: National Bible Institution, 1928).

[172] Recall the formula quotations of the Matthean Gospel, introduced by, "Thus were fulfilled the words of the prophet, saying..." or "In order that the words of the prophet... might be fulfilled" (Matt 1:22; 2:5, 15, 17, 23, etc.). These fulfillment formulas are developed from such Old Testament passages as 1 Kgs 2:27 or 2 Chr 36:21, but they are strikingly absent from any Qumran texts, where one might have expected them to show up. Cf. J. A. Fitzmyer, "The Use of Explicit Old Testament Quotations in Qumran Literature and in the New Testament", *ESBNT*, 3-58, esp. 13-14.

[173] Reference is made to *Divino afflante Spiritu* §27, where Pius XII cautioned Catholic exegetes and preachers to refrain scrupulously from proposing as the genuine meaning of Scripture alien figurative senses, adding that such a use of Scripture "is, as it were, extrinsic to it and accidental, and... especially in these days, it is not free from danger" (*EB* §553; *RSS* §553).

6:9). Exegetes who have a narrow, "historicist" idea about the literal sense will judge that here is an example of an interpretation alien to the original. Those who are open to the dynamic aspect of a text will recognize here a profound element of continuity as well as a move to a different level: Christ rules forever, but not on the earthly throne of David (cf. also *Ps* 2:7-8; 110:1-4).

In such cases one speaks of "the spiritual sense". As a general rule, we can define the spiritual sense, as understood by Christian faith, as the meaning expressed by the biblical texts when read, under the influence of the Holy Spirit, in the context of the paschal mystery of Christ and of the new life which flows from it. This context truly exists. In it the New Testament recognizes the fulfilment of the Scriptures. It is therefore quite acceptable to re-read the Scriptures in the light of this new context, which is that of life in the Spirit.

The above definition allows us to draw some useful conclusions of a more precise nature concerning the relationship between the spiritual and literal senses:

Contrary to a current view, there is not necessarily a distinction between the two senses. When a biblical text relates directly to the paschal mystery of Christ or to the new life which results from it, its literal sense is already a spiritual sense. Such is regularly the case in the New Testament.

---

Third, the literal sense of Scripture can also be its "spiritual" sense, because the literal sense is the meaning intended by God and the inspired human author to feed the religious lives of God's people. Thus the literal sense of the New Testament, which is directly related to "the paschal mystery of Christ or to the new life which results from it", is already its spiritual sense.

In a similar way, the Commission admits that there are already many texts in the Old Testament, the literal meaning of which is a "spiritual sense", because Christian faith recognizes in them "an anticipatory relationship to the new life brought by Christ". Because of that relationship one can understand the continuity and the "fulfillment" of Scripture, and its transition to a higher level, especially in the New Testament. One wonders, however, how this anticipatory relationship really differs from the traditional meaning of "spiritual sense" mentioned above (in sense 2), because it is, in effect, a relationship to the paschal mystery. In this regard, the Commission's text is not wholly clear.

Fourth, there is a spiritual sense that the Commission has not fully considered. If, as it recognizes, there is a distinction between the spiritual

It follows that it is most often in dealing with the Old Testament that Christian exegesis speaks of the spiritual sense. But already in the Old Testament, there are many instances where texts have a religious or spiritual sense as their literal sense. Christian faith recognizes in such cases an anticipatory relationship to the new life brought by Christ.

While there is a distinction between the two senses, the spiritual sense can never be stripped of its connection with the literal sense. The latter remains the indispensable foundation. Otherwise, one could not speak of the "fulfilment" of Scripture. Indeed, in order that there be fulfilment, a relationship of continuity and of conformity is essential. But it is also necessary that there be transition to a higher level of a reality.

The spiritual sense is not to be confused with subjective interpretations stemming from the imagination or intellectual speculation. The spiritual sense results from setting the text in relation to real facts which are not foreign to it: the paschal event, in all its inexhaustible richness, which constitutes the summit of the divine intervention in the history of Israel, to the benefit of all mankind.

Spiritual interpretation, whether in community or in private, will discover the authentic spiritual sense only to the extent that it is kept within these perspectives. One then holds together three levels of reality: the

---

sense (as defined in the second and third meanings above) and the literal sense, which remains "the indispensable foundation" of the other senses, there arises a further question: Does not the literal sense of the Old Testament, apart from its relation to the paschal mystery or any anticipatory relationship, bear a spiritual meaning in itself? For the literal sense of the Old Testament was also "intended and ordained by God" (*Divino afflante Spiritu* §27). The Hebrew Scriptures were meant to feed the spiritual lives of God's people long before the Christ-event, just as the literal sense of the New Testament is intended to feed the lives of Christians of all generations and is for them a spiritual sense. So there must be a way in which the literal sense of the Old Testament has to be understood as its spiritual sense. Joining this to what has been said above about the New Testament, one can see that the literal sense of all Scripture is, indeed, a genuine spiritual sense. This would mean too that even Christians can find food for their spiritual lives in the literal sense of Old Testament texts. Moses and the prophets of old, who addressed their message to Israel, still address it to Christians of today. The christological sense of the Old Testament would, then, really be an added spiritual sense.

biblical text, the paschal mystery and the present circumstances of life in the Spirit.

Persuaded that the mystery of Christ offers the key to interpretation of all Scripture, ancient exegesis labored to find a spiritual sense in the minutest details of the biblical text — for example, in every prescription of the ritual law — making use of rabbinic methods or inspired by Hellenistic allegorical exegesis. Whatever its pastoral usefulness might have been in the past, modern exegesis cannot ascribe true interpretative value to this kind of procedure (cf. *Divino Afflante Spiritu: EB*, 553).

One of the possible aspects of the spiritual sense is the typological. This is usually said to belong not to Scripture itself but to the realities expressed by Scripture: Adam as the figure of Christ (cf. *Rom* 5:14), the flood as the figure of baptism (*1 Pet* 3:20-21), etc. Actually, the connection involved in typology is ordinarily based on the way in which Scripture describes the ancient reality (cf. the voice of Abel: *Gen* 4:10; *Heb* 11:4; 12:24) and not simply on the reality itself. Consequently, in such a case one can speak of a meaning that is truly scriptural.

---

If there is any validity to the foregoing distinctions, it would mean that just as there were three medieval ways of understanding the "spiritual sense" of Scripture, so too there are three modern ways of doing so, even if they do not coincide.

Finally, the Commission distinguishes the "spiritual sense" of Scripture from its "typical sense" or its typology. This sense is predicated not of the words of Scripture, but of the things or realities (persons, places, events) as described in Scripture, when they are seen as foreshadowing future "things" in God's work of salvation. Hence it is not the meaning of biblical words or phrases, but of things as described in the Bible: e.g. Jonah in the belly of the fish (Jonah 2:1) is understood as a "type" (*typos*) of the buried Christ (Matt 12:40), who is the corresponding "antitype"; or the bronze serpent on the pole (Num 21:9), as the type of the lifted up Son of Man (John 3:14); or Adam, as the type of Christ (Rom 5:14); or the flood, as the type of baptism (1 Pet 3:20-21)[174].

---

[174] See further J. Daniélou, "Qu'est-ce que la typologie?" *L'Ancien Testament et les chrétiens* (ed. P. Auvray et al.; Paris: Editions du Cerf, 1951) 199-205; G. W. H. Lampe and K. J. Woollcombe, *Essays on Typology* (SBT 22; Naperville, IL: Allenson, 1957). Cf. L. Goppelt, *Typos: The Typological Interpretation of the Old Testament in the New* (Grand Rapids, MI: Eerdmans, 1982).

### 3. *The Fuller Sense*

The term "fuller sense" (*sensus plenior*), which is relatively recent, has given rise to discussion. The fuller sense is defined as a deeper meaning of the text, intended by God but not clearly expressed by the human author. Its existence in the biblical text comes to be known when one studies the text in the light of other biblical texts which utilize it or in its relationship with the internal development of revelation.

It is then a question either of the meaning that a subsequent biblical author attributes to an earlier biblical text, taking it up in a context which confers upon it a new literal sense, or else it is a question of the meaning that an authentic doctrinal tradition or a conciliar definition gives to a biblical text. For example, the context of *Matt* 1:23 gives a fuller sense to the prophecy of *Isa* 7:14 in regard to the *almah* who will conceive, by using the translation of the Septuagint (*parthenos*): "The *virgin* will conceive". The Patristic and conciliar teaching about the Trinity expresses the fuller sense of the teaching of the New Testament regarding God the Father, the Son and the Holy Spirit. The definition of original sin by the Council of

---

### 3. *The Fuller Sense*

The theory of *sensus plenior*, "the fuller sense" of Scripture is of relatively recent vintage, and because it was given serious consideration only in the early part of this century, it does not have the venerable status of the literal or the spiritual senses[175]. The Commission defines *sensus plenior* as the "deeper meaning of the text, intended by God but not clearly expressed by the human author". Here the Commission is building on the Catholic understanding of biblical inspiration, which distinguishes between God as the primary author of Scripture and the inspired human writer as the secondary author. With such a distinction one can see how God could have moved a human writer to formulate something, the *sensus plenior* of which would only become apparent in the light of subsequent reference to or use of such a formulation, and of which the original human

---

[175] The term was first coined by A. Fernández in 1925. See further R. E. Brown, *The Sensus Plenior of Sacred Scripture* (Baltimore, MD: St. Mary's University, 1955); "The Sensus Plenior in the Last Ten Years", *CBQ* 15 (1963) 262-85; "The Problems of the 'Sensus Plenior'", *ETL* 43 (1967) 460-69; "Hermeneutics", *NJBC* art. 71, §49-51. Cf. J. Coppens, *Le problème du sens plénier des Saintes Ecritures* (Louvain: Publications Universitaires de Louvain, 1958).

Trent provided the fuller sense of Paul's teaching in *Rom* 5:12-21 about the consequences of the sin of Adam for humanity. But when this kind of control — by an explicit biblical text or by an authentic doctrinal tradition — is lacking, recourse to a claimed fuller sense could lead to subjective interpretation deprived of validity.

In a word, one might think of the "fuller sense" as another way of indicating the spiritual sense of a biblical text in the case where the spiritual sense is distinct from the literal sense. It has its foundation in the fact that the Holy Spirit, principal author of the Bible, can guide human authors in the choice of expressions in such a way that the latter will express a truth the fullest depths of which the authors themselves do not perceive. This deeper truth will be more fully revealed in the course of time — on the one hand, through further divine interventions which clarify the meaning of texts and, on the other, through the insertion of texts into the canon of Scripture. In these ways there is created a new context, which brings out fresh possibilities of meaning that had lain hidden in the original context.

---

author would have had no inkling. In admitting this sense of Scripture, the Commission formulates its own all-important proviso: the *sensus plenior* is not a meaning that anyone can assign to a passage of Scripture, but is that which becomes apparent only when a text is understood in light of other biblical texts that subsequently use it or when it is comprehended in "its relationship with the internal development of revelation". The last clause refers to the way a biblical text has been taken up into a genuine doctrinal Tradition, which has developed in Church teaching (e.g. in a patristic teaching or a conciliar definition). As an example of the former, the subsequent biblical usage, the Commission cites the meaning given to *'almāh*, "young girl" (Isa 7:14), as it is interpreted as *parthenos*, "virgin", in the Septuagint and in Matt 1:23. Because of that later use, "virgin" becomes the *sensus plenior* of Isa 7:14. As examples of the latter, the use in Tradition, it cites the patristic explanation of the Trinity (three persons in one God) as the *sensus plenior* of the New Testament teaching about the Father, Son, and Holy Spirit, and the Tridentine definition of Original Sin as the *sensus plenior* of Rom 5:12-21[176]. In effect, the *sensus plenior* is only a modern way of expressing a certain kind of "spiritual sense" (in its traditional meaning, #2 above) in given instances.

---

[176] See *Decretum de peccato originali* (17 June 1546); DS §1510-16, esp. 1512.

## III. CHARACTERISTICS OF CATHOLIC INTERPRETATION

Catholic exegesis does not claim any particular scientific method as its own. It recognizes that one of the aspects of biblical texts is that they are the work of human authors, who employed both their own capacities for expression and the means which their age and social context put at their disposal. Consequently, Catholic exegesis freely makes use of the scientific methods and approaches which allow a better grasp of the meaning of texts in their linguistic, literary, socio-cultural, religious and historical contexts, while explaining them as well through studying their sources and attending to the personality of each author (cf. *Divino Afflante Spiritu: EB*, 557). Catholic exegesis actively contributes to the development of new methods and to the progress of research.

What characterizes Catholic exegesis is that it deliberately places itself within the living tradition of the Church, whose first concern is fidelity to the revelation attested by the Bible. Modern hermeneutics has made clear, as we have noted, the impossibility of interpreting a text without starting from a "pre-understanding" of one type or another. Catholic exegetes approach the biblical text with a pre-understanding which holds closely together modern scientific culture and the religious tradition emanating from Israel and from the early Christian community. Their inter-

---

## III. CHARACTERISTICS OF CATHOLIC INTERPRETATION

In their use of the historical-critical method of interpretation and of other scientific methods or approaches, Catholic interpreters of the Bible today do not differ from their Jewish or Protestant peers. This was not always so, because prior to the encyclical of Pius XII Catholic interpreters were still interpreting the Bible as did their forebears since the days of the Counter-Reformation (with a method that was akin to a fundamentalist reading of the Bible). Moreover, they were deterred from using modern interpretive methods because of the Church's general reaction to nineteenth-century rationalism and the Modernist crisis in the early decades of

pretation stands thereby in continuity with a dynamic pattern of interpretation that is found within the Bible itself and continues in the life of
the Church. This dynamic pattern corresponds to the requirement that
there be a lived affinity between the interpreter and the object, an affinity
which constitutes, in fact, one of the conditions that makes the entire exegetical enterprise possible.

All pre-understanding, however, brings dangers with it. As regards
Catholic exegesis, the risk is that of attributing to biblical texts a meaning
which they do not contain but which is the product of a later development
within the tradition. The exegete must beware of such a danger.

## A. **Interpretation in the Biblical Tradition**

The texts of the Bible are the expression of religious traditions which
existed before them. The mode of their connection with these traditions is

---

the twentieth century[177]. That, of course, changed with the encyclical of
Pius XII in 1943.

Catholic interpretation of the Bible, however, "deliberately places
itself within the living tradition of the Church, whose first concern is
fidelity to the revelation attested by the Bible" (p. 132). For this reason,
the *Vorverständnis* or presupposition that Catholic exegetes bring to their
interpretation is a faith-commitment that holds closely together current
exegetical techniques, modern scientific culture, and the religious tradition emanating from Israel and the early Christian community. This
implies a continuity with the dynamic pattern of interpretation that is
found within the Bible itself and that persists in the life of the Church, but
that also demands caution, lest one attribute to the Bible what is only a
product of a later development.

## A. **Interpretation in the Biblical Tradition**

Since that presupposition uses as its starting point the dynamic
pattern of interpretation found in the Bible itself, the Commission tries to

---

[177] One need only read the encyclical of Pope Benedict XV, *Spiritus Paraclitus* (*EB*
§440-95; *RSS* §440-95), to become aware of the restricted nature of Catholic biblical interpretation in the 1920s. For a picture of the dismal situation in the United States, see G. P.
Fogarty, *American Catholic Biblical Scholarship: A History from the Early Republic to Vatican II* (San Francisco, CA: Harper & Row, 1989) 171-98 ("Anti-Modernism in the United
States: 1910-1940").

different in each case, with the creativity of the authors shown in various degrees. In the course of time, multiple traditions have flowed together little by little to form one great common tradition. The Bible is a privileged expression of this process: it has itself contributed to the process and continues to have controlling influence upon it.

The subject, "Interpretation in the Biblical Tradition", can be approached in very many ways. The expression can be taken to include the manner in which the Bible interprets fundamental human experiences or the particular events of the history of Israel, or again the manner in which the biblical texts make use of their sources, written or oral, some of which may well come from other religions or cultures — through a process of reinterpretation. But our subject is the interpretation of the Bible; we do not want to treat here these very broad questions but simply to make some observations about the interpretation of biblical texts that occurs within the Bible itself.

## 1. *Re-readings* (Relectures)

One thing that gives the Bible an inner unity, unique of its kind, is the fact that later biblical writings often depend upon earlier ones. These more recent writings that allude to older ones create "re-readings" (*relectures*), which develop new aspects of meaning, sometimes quite different from the original sense. A text may also make explicit reference to older passages, whether it is to deepen their meaning or to make known their fulfilment.

---

describe that pattern. The Bible grew out of preexistent religious traditions, oral and written, and it bears witness to them and to the complex formulations resulting from them. This has especially been brought to light by modern source criticism, which has been able to distinguish the diversity of such traditions. Yet the Bible constitutes a privileged expression of the process of conflated and interpreted traditions. Still more important, however, is the process of interpretation of biblical texts that appears within the Bible.

## 1. *Re-readings* (Relectures)

The inner unity of the Bible stems in part from the dependence of more recent biblical writings on older ones. They thus create *relectures*, which bring new meanings or nuances, sometimes different from the

Thus it is that the inheritance of the land, promised by God to Abraham for his offspring (*Gen* 15:7, 18), becomes entrance into the sanctuary of God (*Exod* 15:17), a participation in God's "rest" (*Ps* 132:7-8) reserved for those who truly have faith (*Ps* 95:8-11; *Heb* 3:7–4:11) and, finally, entrance into the heavenly sanctuary (*Heb* 6:12, 18-20), "the eternal inheritance" (*Heb* 9:15).

The prophecy of Nathan, which promised David a "house", that is a dynastic succession, "secure forever" (*2 Sam* 7:12-16), is recalled in a number of re-phrasings (*2 Sam* 23:5; *1 Kings* 2:4; 3:6; *1 Chr* 17:11-14), arising especially out of times of distress (*Ps* 89:20-38), not without significant changes; it is continued by other prophecies (*Ps* 2:7-8; 110:1, 4; *Amos* 9:11; *Isa* 7:13-14; *Jer* 23:5-6; etc.), some of which announce the return of the kingdom of David itself (*Hos* 3:5; *Jer* 30:9; *Ezek* 34:24; 37:24-25; cf. *Mark* 11:10). The promised kingdom becomes universal (*Ps* 2:8; *Dan* 2:35, 44; 7:14; cf. *Matt* 28:18). It brings to fullness the vocation of human beings (*Gen* 1:28; *Ps* 8:6-9; *Wis* 9:2-3; 10:2).

The prophecy of Jeremiah concerning the 70 years of chastisement incurred by Jerusalem and Judah (*Jer* 25:11-12; 29:10) is recalled in *2 Chr* 25:20-23, which affirms that this punishment has actually occurred. Nonetheless, much later, the author of Daniel returns to reflect upon it once more, convinced that this word of God still conceals a hidden meaning that could throw light upon the situation of his own day (*Dan* 9:24-27).

The basic affirmation of the retributive justice of God, rewarding the good and punishing the evil (*Ps* 1:1-6; 112:1-10; *Lev* 26:3-33; etc.), flies in the face of much immediate experience, which often fails to bear it out. In the face of this, Scripture allows strong voices of protestation and argument to be heard (*Ps* 44; *Job* 10:1-7; 13:3-28; 23–24), as little by little it plumbs more profoundly the full depths of the mystery (*Ps* 37; *Job* 38–42; *Isa* 53; *Wis* 3–5).

---

original sense. Four examples of such re-readings are cited: (1) how the inheritance of the land promised to Abraham (Gen 15:7, 18) develops within the Old and the New Testament; (2) how the oracle of Nathan (2 Sam 7:12-16) about the guaranteed Davidic succession is gradually continued in prophecies about kingship in a universal sense; (3) how Jeremiah's prophecy of 70 years of chastisement of Jerusalem (Jer 25:11-12; 29:10) is recalled in 2 Chr 25:20-23 and becomes a motivation even in the days of Daniel (Dan 9:2, 24-27); and (4) how the mystery of God's retributive justice (Ps 1:1-6; 112:1-10), rewarding good and punishing evil, is gradually unfolded.

*2. Relationships between the Old Testament and the New*

Intertextual relationships become extremely dense in the writings of the New Testament, thoroughly imbued as it is with the Old Testament through both multiple allusion and explicit citation. The authors of the New Testament accorded to the Old Testament the value of divine revelation. They proclaimed that this revelation found its fulfillment in the life, in the teaching and above all in the death and resurrection of Jesus, source of pardon and of everlasting life. "Christ died for our sins *according to the Scriptures* and was buried; he was raised on the third day *according to the Scriptures* and appeared..." (*1 Cor* 15:3-5): such is the center and core of the apostolic preaching (*1 Cor* 15:11).

As always, the relationship between Scripture and the events which bring it to fulfilment is not one of simple material correspondence. On the contrary, there is mutual illumination and a progress that is dialectic: what becomes clear is that Scripture reveals the meaning of events and that events reveal the meaning of Scriptures, that is, they require that certain aspects of the received interpretation be set aside and a new interpretation adopted.

Right from the start of his public ministry, Jesus adopted a personal and original stance different from the accepted interpretation of his age, that "of the scribes and Pharisees" (*Matt* 5:20). There is ample evidence of this: the antitheses of his Sermon on the Mount (*Matt* 5:21-48); his

---

*2. Relationships between the Old Testament and the New*

That interpretation within the biblical tradition takes on a special form when the New Testament not only explicitly quotes the Old Testament, but becomes a tissue of allusions to it[178]. This intertexuality reveals how New Testament writers recognized in the Old Testament its value as a source of divine revelation, a revelation whose fulfillment was the Christ-event. The fragment of the primitive apostolic proclamation preserved in 1 Cor 15:3-5 shows how even the death and resurrection of Jesus Christ were understood "according to the Scriptures". For the New Testament often records events which are understood as fulfilling the Old

---

[178] Though there is not one explicit quotation from the Old Testament in the Book of Revelation, its Greek text is a *cento* of allusions to Old Testament passages. See A. Vanhoye, "L'Utilisation du livre d'Ezéchiel dans l'Apocalypse", *Bib* 43 (1962) 436-76.

sovereign freedom with respect to Sabbath observance (*Mark* 2:27-28 and parallels); his way of relativizing the precepts of ritual purity (*Mark* 7:1-23 and parallels); on the other hand, the radicality of his demand in other areas (*Matt* 10:2-12 and parallels; 10:17-27 and parallels) and, above all, his attitude of welcome to "the tax-collectors and sinners" (*Mark* 2:15-17 and parallels). All this was in no sense the result of a personal whim to challenge the established order. On the contrary, it represented a most profound fidelity to the will of God expressed in Scripture (cf. *Matt* 5:17; 9:13; *Mark* 7:8-13 and parallels; 10:5-9 and parallels).

Jesus' death and resurrection pushed to the very limit the interpretative development he had begun, provoking on certain points a complete break with the past, alongside unforeseen new openings. The death of the Messiah, "king of the Jews" (*Mark* 15:26 and parallels), prompted a transformation of the purely earthly interpretation of the royal psalms and messianic prophecies. The resurrection and heavenly glorification of Jesus as Son of God lent these texts a fullness of meaning previously unimaginable. The result was that some expressions which had seemed to be hyperbole had now to be taken literally. They came to be seen as divine preparations to express the glory of Christ Jesus, for Jesus is truly "Lord" (*Ps* 110:1), in the fullest sense of the word (*Acts* 2:36; *Phil* 2:10-11; *Heb* 1:10-12); he is Son of God (*Ps* 2:7; *Mark* 14:62; *Rom* 1:3-4), God with God (*Ps* 45:7; *Heb* 1:8; *John* 1:1; 20:28); "his reign will have no end" (*Luke* 1:32-33; cf. *1 Chr* 17:11-14; *Ps* 45:7; *Heb* 1:8) and he is at the same time "priest forever" (*Ps* 110:4; *Heb* 5:6-10; 7:23-24).

It is in the light of the events of Easter that the authors of the New

---

Testament in a mutual, dialectic process: "Scripture reveals the meaning of events and... events reveal the meaning of Scripture, that is, they require that certain aspects of the received interpretation be set aside and a new interpretation adopted". The Commission illustrates this by citing examples of how Jesus' interpretive preaching as preserved in various Gospels altered an understanding of the Scriptures of old (e.g. in the antitheses of Matt 5:21-48). Jesus' death and resurrection further provoked an interpretation of the Hebrew Scriptures, when royal psalms were transformed into messianic prophecies, thus lending to such Old Testament texts a meaning previously unimaginable. Thus "lord" in Ps 110:1 was given a new meaning in Acts 2:36; and in Phil 2:10-11 it became the title par excellence for the risen Christ; "my son" in Ps 2:7 acquired a new nuance in Rom 1:3-4 (becoming Son of God with power); "O God" in Ps 45:7 became a title by which Jesus is addressed in Heb 1:8; and "priest

Testament read anew the scriptures of the Old. The Holy Spirit, sent by the glorified Christ (cf. *John* 15:26; 16:7), led them to discover the spiritual sense. While this meant that they came to stress more than ever the prophetic value of the Old Testament, it also had the effect of relativizing very considerably its value as a system of salvation. This second point of view, which already appears in the Gospels (cf. *Matt* 11:11-13 and parallels; 12:41-42 and parallels; *John* 4:12-14; 5:37; 6:32), emerges strongly in certain Pauline letters as well as in the Letter to the Hebrews. Paul and the author of the Letter to the Hebrews show that the Torah itself, insofar as it is revelation, announces its own proper end as a legal system (cf. *Gal* 2:15–5:1; *Rom* 3:20-21; 6:14; *Heb* 7:11-19; 10:8-9). It follows that the pagans who adhere to faith in Christ need not be obliged to observe all the precepts of biblical law, from now on reduced in its entirety simply to the status of a legal code of a particular people. But in the Old Testament as the Word of God they have to find the spiritual sustenance that will assist them to discover the full dimensions of the paschal mystery which now governs their lives (cf. *Luke* 24:25-27, 44-45; *Rom* 1:1-2).

All this serves to show that within the one Christian Bible, the relationships that exist between the New and the Old Testament are quite

---

forever" in Ps 110:4 took on a new meaning when applied to Christ in Heb 5:6-10; 7:23-24. This reading of the Hebrew Scriptures anew is attributed to the work of the Holy Spirit among early Christians, which led them to discover this "spiritual sense" or christological sense of the Scriptures of old.

More importantly, however, the christological reading of the Old Testament has "had the effect of relativizing very considerably its value as a system of salvation". In this connection, the Commission refers to utterances of Jesus preserved in Matt 11:11-13 (and parallels); 12:41-42 (and parallels); John 4:12-14; 5:37; 6:32; to statements of Paul in Gal 2:15-5:1; Rom 3:20-21; 6:14; and to passages in Heb 7:11-19; 10:8-9 to emphasize that a new form of salvation has now come from God to human beings through Jesus Christ. Accordingly, the Commission distinguishes between the Old Testament as a "legal code" destined for the Jewish people and "the Word of God" with sustenance for the spiritual lives of all, Gentiles and Jews, who will find in it "the full dimension of the paschal mystery", which may now govern their lives as followers of Jesus Christ, as Luke 24:25-27, 44-45 and Rom 1:1-2 suggest. Hence for Christians, there is a sense in which some aspects of the Old Testament, legal or dietary, cease to be normative, whereas there is also a sense in which the Old Testament

complex. When it is a question of the use of particular texts, the authors of the New Testament naturally have recourse to the ideas and procedures for interpretation current in their time. To require them to conform to modern scientific methods would be anachronistic. Rather, it is for the exegete to acquire a knowledge of ancient techniques of exegesis, so as to be able to interpret correctly the way in which a scriptural author has used them. On the other hand, it remains true that the exegete need not put absolute value in something which simply reflects limited human understanding.

Finally, it is worth adding that within the New Testament, as already within the Old, one can see the juxtaposing of different perspectives that sit sometimes in tension with one another: for example, regarding the status of Jesus (*John* 8:29; 16:32 and *Mark* 15:34) or the value of the Mosaic Law (*Matt* 5:17-19 and *Rom* 6:14) or the necessity of works for justification (*James* 2:24 and *Rom* 3:28; *Eph* 2:8-9). One of the characteristics of the Bible is precisely the absence of a sense of systematization and the presence, on the contrary, of things held in dynamic tension. The Bible is a repository of many ways of interpreting the same events and reflecting upon the same problems. In itself it urges us to avoid excessive simplification and narrowness of spirit.

---

continues to bring God's salvific Word to Christians as it did to the Jewish people of old[179].

As a result, the relations between the Old and the New Testament within the Christian Bible are complex. Moreover, when New Testament writers interpreted the Old Testament, they did so not according to modern standards of exegesis or interpretation, but according to the interpretive ideas and procedures current in their own day[180]. Furthermore, dynamic tensions are detected within the Bible between different ways of speaking about the same event or person, because of the diverse origin of the viewpoints expressed. These have to be reckoned with[181].

---

[179] See p. 74 above. Cf. A. Vanhoye, "Salut universel par le Christ et validité de l'Ancienne Alliance", *NTR* 116 (1994) 815-35.

[180] See J. A. Fitzmyer, "The Use of Explicit Old Testament Quotations" (n. 172 above), 3-58.

[181] The Commission cites as examples the way different evangelists express Jesus' relation to the Father (John 8:29, "He who sent me is with me; he has not left me alone"; but Mark 15:34, "My God, my God, why have you forsaken me"); or the way different New Testament writers speak of the law of Moses (Matt 5:17-19, "not an iota or a dot will pass from the law"; but Paul in Rom 6:14 writes, "You are not under law but under grace"); or the different way deeds are related to justification in Jas 2:24 and Rom 3:28.

### 3. *Some Conclusions*

From what has just been said, one can conclude that the Bible contains numerous indications and suggestions relating to the art of interpretation. In fact, from its very inception the Bible has been itself a work of interpretation. Its texts were recognized by the communities of the Former Covenant and by those of the apostolic age as the genuine expression of the common faith. It is in accordance with the interpretative work of these communities and together with it that the texts were accepted as Sacred Scripture (thus, e.g., the Song of Songs was recognized as Sacred Scripture when applied to the relation between God and Israel). In the course of the Bible's formation, the writings of which it consists were in many cases reworked and reinterpreted, so as to make them respond to new situations, previously unknown.

The way in which Sacred Scripture reveals its own interpretation of texts suggests the following observations:

Sacred Scripture has come into existence on the basis of a consensus in the believing communities recognizing in the texts the expressions of revealed faith. This means that, for the living faith of the ecclesial communities, the interpretation of Scripture should itself be a source of consensus on essential matters.

Granted that the expression of faith, such as it is found in the Sacred Scripture acknowledged by all, has had to renew itself continually in order to meet new situations — which explains the "re-readings" of many of the biblical texts — the interpretation of the Bible should likewise involve an aspect of creativity; it ought also to confront new questions, so as to respond to them out of the Bible.

Granted that tensions can exist in the relationship between various texts of Sacred Scripture, interpretation must necessarily show a certain pluralism. No single interpretation can exhaust the meaning of the whole, which is a symphony of many voices. Thus the interpretation of one particular text has to avoid seeking to dominate at the expense of others.

Sacred Scripture is in dialogue with communities of believers: it has come from their traditions of faith. Its texts have been developed in rela-

---

### 3. *Some Conclusions*

The conclusions that the Commission draws from the preceding considerations are rather clear and call for little comment. The Bible not only

tion to these traditions and have contributed, reciprocally, to the development of the traditions. It follows that interpretation of Scripture takes place in the heart of the Church: in its plurality and its unity, and within its tradition of faith.

Faith traditions formed the living context for the literary activity of the authors of Sacred Scripture. Their insertion into this context also involved a sharing in both the liturgical and external life of the communities, in their intellectual world, in their culture and in the ups and downs of their shared history. In like manner, the interpretation of Sacred Scripture requires full participation on the part of exegetes in the life and faith of the believing community of their own time.

Dialogue with Scripture in its entirety, which means dialogue with the understanding of the faith prevailing in earlier times, must be matched by a dialogue with the generation of today. Such dialogue will mean establishing a relationship of continuity. It will also involve acknowledging differences. Hence the interpretation of Scripture involves a work of sifting and setting aside; it stands in continuity with earlier exegetical traditions, many elements of which it preserves and makes its own; but in other matters it will go its own way, seeking to make further progress.

---

contains indications and suggestions about the art of its interpretation, but is itself "a work of interpretation". For it came into existence because a consensus in faith-communities, among Jews and then early Christians, recognized their texts as expressions of their common faith. The interpretation of texts by such communities brought it about that they were accepted. Hence Scripture should itself be a source of consensus on essential matters. Moreover, because the expression of faith found in Scripture has had to renew itself to meet new situations (hence the *relectures*), the interpretation of Scripture has to have a measure of creativity as it confronts new questions and responds to them out of the Bible. Furthermore, since tensions exist at times between different parts of Scripture, its interpretation has to be pluralistic, because Scripture is a symphony of many voices, which resists a procrustean interpretation. Scripture must also be understood as in dialogue with such faith-communities, and it is rightly interpreted only in the heart of them, together with their faith-traditions. But in all these respects the interpretation of it calls for interpreters who share the life and faith of the believing communities of their own time.

## B. Interpretation in the Tradition of the Church

The Church, as the People of God, is aware that it is helped by the Holy Spirit in its understanding and interpretation of Scripture. The first disciples of Jesus knew that they did not have the capacity right away to understand the full reality of what they had received in all its aspects. As they persevered in their life as a community, they experienced an ever-deepening and progressive clarification of the revelation they had received. They recognized in this the influence and the action of "the Spirit of truth", which Christ had promised them, to guide them to the fullness of the truth (*John* 16:12-13). Likewise the Church today journeys onward, sustained by the promise of Christ: "The Paraclete, the Holy Spirit, which the Father will send in my name, will teach you all things and will make you recall all that I have said to you" (*John* 14:26).

---

## B. Interpretation in the Tradition of the Church

The Church, as the new people of God, is aided by the Spirit in its interpretation of Scripture. This is evident from the start, because the New Testament itself records how it took time for Jesus' disciples to come to a proper understanding of what Jesus had said: "When he was raised from the dead, his disciples remembered that he had said this, and they came to believe the Scripture and the word Jesus had spoken" (John 2:22). Later on John's Gospel explains this fuller understanding as a guidance of the Holy Spirit: "The Paraclete, the holy Spirit that the Father will send in my name, will teach you all things and remind you of all that I have told you" (John 14:26); "The Spirit of Truth will guide you to all truth; he will not speak on his own, but will say to you what he has heard" (John 16:13). Thus the Johannine Jesus assured the community of his followers about the Spirit-guided assistance it would always have in the understanding of the Word of God. This includes, of course, the interpretation of Scripture and of the Tradition that has grown out of it. A further explanation of this understanding of divine revelation can be found in *Dei Verbum* §8.

## 1. *Formation of the Canon*

Guided by the Holy Spirit and in the light of the living Tradition which it has received, the Church has discerned the writings which should be regarded as Sacred Scripture in the sense that, "having been written under the inspiration of the Holy Spirit, they have God for author and have been handed on as such to the Church" (*Dei Verbum*, 11) and contain "that truth which God wanted put into the Sacred Writings for the sake of our salvation" (*ibid.*).

The discernment of a "canon" of Sacred Scripture was the result of a long process. The communities of the Old Covenant (ranging from particular groups, such as those connected with prophetic circles or the priesthood, to the people as a whole) recognized in a certain number of texts the Word of God capable of arousing their faith and providing guidance for daily life; they received these texts as a patrimony to be preserved and handed on. In this way these texts ceased to be merely the expression of a particular author's inspiration; they became the common property of the whole people of God. The New Testament attests its own reverence for these sacred texts, received as a precious heritage passed on by the Jewish people. It regards these texts as "Sacred Scripture" (*Rom* 1:2), "inspired" by the Spirit of God (2 *Tim* 3:16; cf. *2 Pet* 1:20-21), which "can never be annulled" (*John* 10:35).

To these texts, which form "the Old Testament" (cf. *2 Cor* 3:14), the Church has closely associated other writings: first, those in which it recog-

---

## 1. *Formation of the Canon*

Under the guidance of that Spirit, the Church came to recognize the collection of its normative writings as a canon. That recognition meant that such books were "written under the inspiration of the Holy Spirit..., [and] have God as their author and have been handed on as such to the Church"; they teach, moreover, "that truth which God wanted put into the Sacred Writings for the sake of our salvation"[182]. That recognition of

---

[182] *Dei Verbum* §11 (*The Documents of Vatican II*, 118-19). The first quotation defines the sense of the Bible's inspiration, and the second the sense of its inerrancy. Cf. J. Ratzinger et al., "Dogmatic Constitution on Divine Revelation", *Commentary on the Documents of Vatican II* (ed. H. Vorgrimler; 5 vols.; New York: Herder and Herder, 1967-69) 3 (1968) 155-272, esp. 228-37.

nized the authentic witness, coming from the apostles (cf. *Luke* 1:2; *1 John* 1:1-3) and guaranteed by the Holy Spirit (cf. *1 Pet* 1:12), concerning "all that Jesus began to do and teach" (*Acts* 1:1) and, secondly, the instructions given by the apostles themselves and other disciples for the building up of the community of believers. This double series of writings subsequently came to be known as "the New Testament".

Many factors played a part in this process: the conviction that Jesus — and the apostles along with him — had recognized the Old Testament as inspired Scripture and that the paschal mystery is its true fulfilment; the conviction that the writings of the New Testament were a genuine reflection of the apostolic preaching (which does not imply that they were all composed by the apostles themselves); the recognition of their conformity with the rule of faith and of their use in the Christian liturgy; finally, the experience of their affinity with the ecclesial life of the communities and of their potential for sustaining this life.

In discerning the canon of Scripture, the Church was also discerning and defining her own identity. Henceforth Scripture was to function as a mirror in which the Church could continually rediscover her identity and assess, century after century, the way in which she constantly responds to the gospel and equips herself to be an apt vehicle of its transmission (cf. *Dei Verbum*, 7). This confers on the canonical writings a salvific and

---

the canon, however, was the result of a long, drawn-out process in which Jewish communities of the First Covenant gradually appropriated texts as the normative Word of God so that they became in time the common property of the people of God, challenging their fidelity and guiding their religious lives. In turn, Christians, as the new people of God, appropriated these writings and thereby acknowledged the precious heritage passed on to them by the Jewish people. To these they added other writings of their own, Gospels and apostolic instructions, which came to be known as the New Testament, in contrast to the inherited Old Testament[183]. Part of the Christian appropriation was based on the way Jesus (and his apostles) had used the Old Testament; part of it too was regulated by the way the New Testament writings were gradually being recognized as a genuine reflection of apostolic preaching and as compositions consonant with the *regula fidei* then in vogue and with the community's life and liturgy. As a result, the Christian Bible began to function as a mirror in which the Chris-

---

[183] See J. A. Sanders, "Canon", *ABD* 1. 837-52; B. M. Metzger, *The Canon of the New Testament: Its Origin, Development, and Significance* (Oxford: Clarendon, 1987).

theological value completely different from that attaching to other ancient texts. The latter may throw much light on the origins of the faith. But they can never substitute for the authority of the writings held to be canonical and thus fundamental for the understanding of the Christian faith.

## 2. *Patristic Exegesis*

From earliest times it has been understood that the same Holy Spirit, who moved the authors of the New Testament to put in writing the message of salvation (*Dei Verbum*, 7; 18), likewise provided the Church with continual assistance for the interpretation of its inspired writings (cf. Ire-

---

tian Church could discover its identity and assess its continuous response to the gospel century after century. In this way, the canon continues to be a unique criterion, exercising a unique salvific role and possessing a unique theological value and heritage.

## 2. *Patristic Exegesis*

The interpretation of the Bible in the Church began with what is called today patristic exegesis. The work of the Fathers of the Church in the early centuries of its existence not only helped fashion the Christian canon, which is still in use, but their interpretation of the Bible greatly aided in shaping the Tradition that has grown out of the Bible and that accompanies it[184]. For that Tradition together with the Bible forms the norm of Christian faith for all subsequent centuries[185]. Patristic exegesis

---

[184] The Commission does not specify who are meant by "the Fathers of the Church". The earliest list of them is found in the sixth-century *Decretum Gelasianum de recipiendis et non recipiendis libris* (cited in part in DS §353). From this document one has derived the four qualifications regarded as necessary to call an early writer a "Father": orthodoxy of doctrine, holiness of life, ecclesiastical approval, and antiquity. See further J. Quasten, *Patrology* (n. 170 above), 1. 9-12. Other ancient writers were called *ecclesiae scriptores* or *scriptores ecclesiastici*, a term derived from Jerome, *De viris illust.*, prologue. Among these would be writers like Tertullian, Origen, and Rufinus. Cf. B. Altaner and A. Stuiber, *Patrologie: Leben, Schriften und Lehre der Kirchenväter* (8th ed.; Freiburg im B.: Herder, 1978) 1-6.

[185] Not, however, in the same sense. For Scripture acts as the *norma normans non normata*, "the norm that norms but is not normed", whereas Tradition is the *norma normata*, "the norm that is normed (by Scripture)". See further K. Rahner, "Scripture and Theology", *Theological Investigations* 6 (Baltimore, MD: Helicon, 1969) 89-97, esp. 93; also "Bible. B. Theology", *Sacramentum mundi* (6 vols.; New York: Herder and Herder, 1968-70) 1. 171-78, esp. 176-77.

naeus, *Adv. Haer.*, 3.24.1; cf. 3.1.1; 4.33.8; Origen, *De Princ.*, 2.7.2; Tertullian, *De Praescr.*, 22).

The Fathers of the Church, who had a particular role in the process of the formation of the canon, likewise have a foundational role in relation to the living tradition which unceasingly accompanies and guides the Church's reading and interpretation of Scripture (cf. *Providentissimus*: *EB*, 110-111; *Divino afflante Spiritu*, 28-30: *EB*, 554; *Dei Verbum*, 23; PBC, *Instruction concerning the Historical Truth of the Gospels*, 1). Within the broader current of the great Tradition, the particular contribution of

---

cannot be simply identified with that Tradition, but it drew out "from the totality of Scripture the basic orientations which shaped the doctrinal tradition of the Church" and "provided a rich theological teaching for the instruction and spiritual sustenance of the faithful". Such interpretation is found in the Fathers' commentaries and apologetic writings, and above all in homilies delivered in the course of liturgical celebrations or catechetical instructions, in which both the Christian community and individuals would use the Bible for study, prayer, and worship.

Three main characteristics are found in the patristic interpretation of the written Word of God. First, the Bible is for the Fathers *God's book*, the single work of a single author. Though they on occasion spoke of the active involvement of human authors and of the diversity of their inspired compositions, they were little interested in the way God's revelation historically developed or in the way it was gradually formulated on occasions of different date. Second, many Fathers understood the *Logos*, the Word of God (as presented in the prologue of the Johannine Gospel), to be the author of the Old Testament. This enabled them to give a christological interpretation to all of Scripture. Third, apart from the Antiochene School, which espoused a more literal interpretation[186], many Fathers interpreted Scripture freely and arbitrarily, taking phrases or sentences out of their contexts to emphasize some revealed truth that they found ex-

---

[186] This school was founded by Lucian of Antioch (d. A.D. 312), who was famous for his Greek translation of the Old Testament; see Eusebius, *HE* 9.6.3. Its philosophy was Aristotelian, and it sought to interpret Scripture more according to the sense expressed by the inspired author. This school opposed the allegorical interpretation of Scripture and its search for figures of Christ and hidden meanings in the Old Testament, which was espoused by Origen and the School of Alexandria. Other exponents of the Antiochene literal interpretation were Marcellus of Ancyra (d. ca. 374), Diodore of Tarsus (d. ca. 390), John Chrysostom (347-407), Theodore of Mopsuestia (350-428), Theodoret of Cyrrhus (393-466), and Nestorius (d. ca. 451). The Antiochene school never achieved the prominence or influence of the Alexandrian school.

patristic exegesis consists in this: to have drawn out from the totality of Scripture the basic orientations which shaped the doctrinal tradition of the Church, and to have provided a rich theological teaching for the instruction and spiritual sustenance of the faithful.

The Fathers of the Church placed a high value upon the reading of Scripture and its interpretation. This can be seen, first of all, in works directly linked to the understanding of Scripture, such as homilies and commentaries. But it is also evident in works of controversy and theology, where appeal is made to Scripture in support of the main argument.

For the Fathers the chief occasion for reading the Bible is in church, in the course of the liturgy. This is why the interpretations they provide are always of a theological and pastoral nature, touching upon relationship with God, so as to be helpful both for the community and the individual believer.

The Fathers look upon the Bible above all as the Book of God, the single work of a single author. This does not mean, however, that they

---

pressed in it[187]. Characteristic of this patristic approach was the traditional "spiritual sense", i.e. a christological understanding of the Old Testament.

In other words, the Fathers felt at liberty to indulge in what is called today "eisegesis", the opposite of exegesis; they read meanings about revealed truth *into* passages. This they did in controversy with Jewish interpreters and with Christian theological opponents. The Commission, however, bends over backward to give a benign interpretation of this patristic method of interpretation, which is, it admits, "a virtually inextricable" mixture of typology and allegory. This allegorical interpretation is seen to result from a pastoral concern to regard nothing in the biblical text as out of date or devoid of meaning. For God was thought to be constantly addressing a message through it that was pertinent to the Christians of their day. The Fathers were convinced that everything had been written "for our instruction" (alluding to 1 Cor 10:11), even if the words bore little relation to the topic under discussion.

---

[187] This was chiefly true of the School of Alexandria, dominated by Origen. Its philosophy was Platonic or Neo-Platonic, which resulted in a "spiritual" or "mystical" interpretation of Scripture, especially of the Old Testament. The chief exponents of this mode of interpretation, often called "allegorical", were, in addition to Origen, Clement of Alexandria (150-250), Dionysius the Great (d. 264), Athanasius (296-373), Didymus the Blind (313-398), Gregory of Nyssa (330-395), Basil (330-379), Cyril of Alexandria (d. 444), and Gregory the Great (540-604).

reduce the human authors to nothing more than passive instruments; they are quite capable, also, of according to a particular book its own specific purpose. But their type of approach pays scant attention to the historical development of revelation. Many Fathers of the Church present the *Logos*, the Word of God, as author of the Old Testament and in this way insist that all Scripture has a christological meaning.

Setting aside certain exegetes of the School of Antioch (Theodore of Mopsuestia, in particular), the Fathers felt themselves at liberty to take a sentence out of its context in order to bring out some revealed truth which they found expressed within it. In apologetic directed against Jewish positions or in theological dispute with other theologians, they did not hesitate to rely on this kind of interpretation.

Their chief concern being to live from the Bible in communion with their brothers and sisters, the Fathers were usually content to use the text of the Bible current in their own context. What led Origen to take a systematic interest in the Hebrew Bible was a concern to conduct arguments with Jews from texts which the latter found acceptable. Thus, in his praise for the *hebraica veritas*, St. Jerome appears, in this respect, a somewhat untypical figure.

As a way of eliminating the scandal which particular passages of the Bible might provide for certain Christians, not to mention pagan adversar-

---

For all his allegorical or spiritual interpretation, Origen was really the early Church scholar who fostered the textual criticism of the Old Testament, even though the motivation for his work was apologetic[188], and some of his interpretations did bring out the literal sense. What Origen thus began led to Jerome's respect for the *hebraica veritas*, by which he meant the normative meaning of the Hebrew text of the Old Testament over against that of the Latin translation current in his day, the *Vetus Itala*. Jerome's great contribution was the fresh translation of that Hebrew text into Latin, which became in time the famous Latin Vulgate[189].

The Commission, however, has finally to admit that "convinced that they are dealing with the book of God and therefore with something of inexhaustible meaning, the Fathers hold that any particular passage is open to any particular interpretation on an allegorical basis. But they also

---

[188] See p. 27 above for his work on the *Hexapla*.
[189] See further J. Griboment, "The Translations: Jerome and Rufinus", *Patrology* (ed. A. di Bernardino; Westminster, MD: Christian Classics, Inc., 1986) 195-254, esp. 224-27.

ies of Christianity, the Fathers had recourse fairly frequently to the allegorical method. But they rarely abandoned the literalness and historicity of texts. The Fathers' recourse to allegory transcends for the most part a simple adaptation to the allegorical method in use among pagan authors.

Recourse to allegory stems also from the conviction that the Bible, as God's book, was given by God to his people, the Church. In principle, there is nothing in it which is to be set aside as out of date or completely lacking meaning. God is constantly speaking to his Christian people a message that is ever relevant for their time. In their explanations of the Bible, the Fathers mix and weave together typological and allegorical interpretations in a virtually inextricable way. But they do so always for a pastoral and pedagogical purpose, convinced that everything that has been written, has been written for our instruction (cf. *1 Cor* 10:11).

Convinced that they are dealing with the book of God and therefore with something of inexhaustible meaning, the Fathers hold that any particular passage is open to any particular interpretation on an allegorical

---

consider that others are free to offer something else, provided only that what is offered respects the analogy of faith". That, of course, is a sweeping admission scarcely saved by what is stated in the final sentence. For one has to ask how "any particular interpretation on an allegorical basis" differs from what the Commission labelled earlier "purely subjective readings" (cf. p. 116 above).

It is not surprising, then, that the Commission frankly admits the risk that this sort of allegorical interpretation runs: it is "something of an embarrassment to people today". In other words, we find it difficult to understand how that could ever have passed for a legitimate mode of interpreting Scripture[190]. In this context we must add: *Admirandum, sed non imitandum*, "It is to be admired, but not imitated".

And yet, in the history of the Church, in periods of less sophistication, the Fathers' mode of interpreting Scripture sought "to read the Bible theologically, within the heart of a living Tradition, with an authentic Christian spirit". In other words, what the Fathers thus strove to

---

[190] For an assessment of patristic exegesis, see Y. M.-J. Congar, *La tradition et les traditions: Essai théologique* (Paris: Librairie Arthème Fayard, 1963) 154-57. Cf. F. Sadowski, *The Church Fathers on the Bible: Selected Readings* (New York: Alba House, 1987); M. Simonetti, *Profilo storico dell'esegesi patristico* (Rome: Istituto Patristico Augustinianum, 1981); *Biblical Interpretation in the Early Church: An Historical Introduction to Patristic Exegesis* (Edinburgh: Clark, 1994); J. W. Trigg, *Biblical Interpretation* (Message of the Fathers of the Church 9; Wilmington, DE: Glazier, 1988).

basis. But they also consider that others are free to offer something else, provided only that what is offered respects the analogy of faith.

The allegorical interpretation of Scripture so characteristic of patristic exegesis runs the risk of being something of an embarassment to people today. But the experience of the Church expressed in this exegesis makes a contribution that is always useful (cf. *Divino Afflante Spiritu*, 31-32; *Dei Verbum*, 23). The Fathers of the Church teach to read the Bible theologically, within the heart of a living Tradition, with an authentic Christian spirit.

### 3. *The Roles of Various Members of the Church in Interpretation*

The Scriptures, as given to the Church, are the communal treasure of the entire body of believers: "Sacred Tradition and Sacred Scripture form one sacred deposit of the Word of God, entrusted to the Church. Holding fast to this deposit, the entire holy people, united with its pastors, remains steadfastly faithful to the teaching of the apostles..." (*Dei Verbum*, 10; cf. also 21). It is true that the familiarity with the text of Scripture has been more notable among the faithful at some periods of the Church's history than in others. But Scripture has been at the forefront of all the important

---

accomplish by their allegorical interpretation is still a legitimate goal of all biblical interpretation. If the sophisticated historical-critical method of interpretation is "indispensable" and actually required today, it still has to be practised with the same goal and motivation as characterized the patristic method just described[191].

### 3. *The Roles of Various Members of the Church in Interpretation*

The Bible has been given to the Church as a whole, to "the entire body of believers". After citing various conciliar and biblical statements to

---

[191] What is surprisingly missing in the Commission's discussion of patristic exegesis is a reference to the interpretation of the Bible according to "the unanimous consent of the Fathers". That norm for Catholic interpretation surfaced in the Tridentine *Decretum de vulgata editione Bibliorum et de modo interpretandi s. Scripturam* of 8 April 1546 (DS §1507) and in the *Professio fidei Tridentina* (DS §1863) and was repeated in Vatican Council I, *Constitutio dogmatica "Dei Filius" de fide catholica* of 24 April 1870 (DS §3007). That way of referring to patristic interpretation as normative was corrected by Pius XII in 1943, when he wrote, "There are but few texts whose sense has been defined by the authority of the Church; nor are those more numerous about which the teaching of the Holy Fathers is unanimous" (*Divino afflante Spiritu* §47; DS §3831; *EB* §565; *RSS* §565).

moments of renewal in the life of the Church, from the monastic movement of the early centuries to the recent era of the Second Vatican
Council.

This same Council teaches that all the baptised, when they bring their
faith in Christ to the celebration of the Eucharist, recognize the presence
of Christ also in his word, "for it is he himself who speaks when the holy
Scriptures are read in the Church" (*Sacrosanctum Concilium*, 7). To this
hearing of the word, they bring that "sense of the faith" (*sensus fidei*)
which characterizes the entire People (of God). (...) For by this sense of
faith aroused and sustained by the Spirit of truth, the People of God,
guided by the sacred Magisterium which it faithfully follows, accepts not a
human word but the very Word of God (cf. *1 Thess* 2:13). It holds fast
unerringly to the faith once delivered to the saints (cf. *Jude* 3), it pene-
trates it more deeply with accurate insight and applies it more thoroughly
to Christian life" (*Lumen Gentium*, 12).

Thus all the members of the Church have a role in the interpretation
of Scripture. In the exercise of their pastoral ministry, *bishops*, as successors of the apostles, are the first witnesses and guarantors of the living
tradition within which Scripture is interpreted in every age. "Enlightened
by the Spirit of truth, they have the task of guarding faithfully the Word of
God, of explaining it and through their preaching making it more widely
known" (*Dei Verbum*, 9; cf. *Lumen Gentium*, 25). As co-workers with the
bishops, *priests* have as their primary duty the proclamation of the Word
(*Presbyterorum Ordinis*, 4). They are gifted with a particular charism for
the interpretation of Scripture, when, transmitting not their own ideas,
but the Word of God, they apply the eternal truth of the Gospel to the
concrete circumstances of daily life (*ibid.*). It belongs to *priests* and to
*deacons*, especially when they administer the sacraments, to make clear
the unity constituted by Word and Sacrament in the ministry of the
Church.

As those who preside at the eucharistic community and as educators
in the faith, the ministers of the Word have as their principal task, not
simply to impart instruction, but also to assist the faithful to understand
and discern what the Word of God is saying to them in their hearts when

---

support this idea, the Commission discusses the way bishops, priests and
deacons, ministers of the Word, and even individual Christians contribute
to the common interpretation of the Bible in the Church.

Bishops, as successors of the Apostles, are the first witnesses and
guarantors of the living tradition within which Scripture is interpreted.

they hear and reflect upon the Scriptures. Thus the *local church* as a whole, on the pattern of Israel, the People of God (*Exod* 19:5-6), becomes a community which knows that it is addressed by God (cf. *John* 6:45), a community that listens eagerly to the Word with faith, love and docility (*Deut* 6:4-6). Granted that they remain ever united in faith and love with the wider body of the Church, such truly-listening communities become in their own context vigorous sources of evangelisation and of dialogue, as well as agents for social change (*Evangelii nuntiandi*, 57-58; CDF, *Instruction concerning Christian Freedom and Liberation*, 69-70).

The Spirit is, assuredly, also given to *individual Christians*, so that their hearts can "burn within them" (*Luke* 24:32), as they pray and prayerfully study the Scripture within the context of their own personal lives. This is why the Second Vatican Council insisted that access to Scripture be facilitated in every possible way (*Dei Verbum*, 22; 25). This kind of reading, it should be noted, is never completely private, for the believer always reads and interprets Scripture within the faith of the Church and then brings back to the community the fruit of that reading, for the enrichment of the common faith.

The entire biblical tradition and, in a particular way, the teaching of Jesus in the Gospels indicates as privileged hearers of the Word of God those whom the world considers *people of lowly status*. Jesus acknowleged that things hidden from the wise and learned have been revealed to the simple (*Matt* 11:25; *Luke* 10:21) and that the Kingdom of God belongs to those who make themselves like little children (*Mark* 10:14 and parallels).

Likewise, Jesus proclaimed: "Blessed are you poor, because the

---

They must guard the Word of God faithfully, explain it, and through their preaching make it more widely known. Priests have as their primary duty the proclamation of the Word, and when they and deacons administer the sacraments, they must make clear the unity of Word and Sacrament in the ministry of the Church[192]. Ministers of the Word must assist the faithful to

---

[192] Noteworthy here is the primacy given to "the proclamation of the Word". From the rest of the paragraph, which mentions the administration of the Sacraments, one gathers that the Commission gives priority to the priest's obligation to proclaim the Word and preach it. In this connection, one might recall words of the apostle Paul himself in 1 Cor 1:14-17, who proclaimed that "Christ did not send me to baptize, but to preach the gospel". The Commission also speaks of priests being gifted with a particular charism for the interpretation of Scripture. This, of course, may be true, but the actual quality of preaching is not thereby guaranteed. See P. Hebbelthwaite, "New Scripture Document 'Thinking in Centuries'", *National Catholic Reporter* 30/21 (25 March 1994) 13-14, esp. 14.

Kingdom of God is yours" (*Luke* 6:20; cf. *Matt* 5:3). One of the signs of the messianic era is the proclamation of the Good News to the poor (*Luke* 4:18; 7:22; *Matt* 11:5; cf. CDF, *Instruction concerning Christian Freedom and Liberation*, 47-48). Those who, in their powerlessness and lack of human resources, find themselves forced to put their trust in God alone and in his justice have a capacity for hearing and interpreting the Word of God which should be taken into account by the whole Church; it demands a response on the social level as well.

Recognizing the diversity of gifts and functions which the Spirit places at the service of the community, especially the gift of teaching (*1 Cor* 12:28-30; *Rom* 12:6-7; *Eph* 4:11-16), the Church expresses its esteem for those who display a particular ability to contribute to the building up of the Body of Christ through their expertise in interpreting Scripture (*Divino Afflante Spiritu*, 46-48: *EB*, 564-565; *Dei Verbum*, 23; PBC, *Instruction concerning the Historical Truth of the Gospels*, Introd.). Although their labors did not always receive in the past the encouragement that is given them today, *exegetes* who offer their learning as a service to the Church find that they are part of a rich tradition which stretches from the first centuries, with Origen and Jerome, up to more recent times, with Père Lagrange and others, and continues right up to our time. In particular, the discovery of the literal sense of Scripture, upon which there is now so much insistence, requires the combined efforts of those who have expertise in the fields of ancient languages, of history and culture, of textual criticism and the analysis of literary forms, and who know how to make good use of the methods of scientific criticism. Beyond this attention to the text in its original historical context, the Church depends on exegetes, animated by the same Spirit as inspired Scripture, to ensure that "there be as great a number of servants of the Word of God as possible capable of effectively providing the people of God with the nourishment of the Scriptures" (*Divino Afflante Spiritu*, 24; 53-55; *EB*, 551, 567; *Dei Verbum*, 23; Paul VI, *Sedula Cura* [1971]). A particular cause for satisfaction in our times is the growing number of *women exegetes*; they frequently contribute new and penetrating insights to the interpretation of Scripture and rediscover features which had been forgotten.

If, as noted above, the Scriptures belong to the entire Church and are part of "the heritage of the faith", which all, pastors and faithful, "pre-

---

understand what the Word of God is saying to them in their hearts when they listen to and meditate on Scripture. Individual Christians, to whom the Spirit is also given, are guided by it in their prayer, reading, and study of the Scriptures. The Commission wisely adds that this kind of individual

serve, profess and put into practice in a communal effort", it nevertheless remains true that "responsibility for authentically interpreting the Word of God, as transmitted by Scripture and Tradition, has been entrusted solely to the living Magisterium of the Church, which exercises its authority in the name of Jesus Christ" (*Dei Verbum*, 10). Thus, in the last resort it is the Magisterium which has the responsibility of guaranteeing the authenticity of interpretation and, should the occasion arise, of pointing out instances where any particular interpretation is incompatible with the au-

---

reading of the Bible is never completely private, because the believer reads and interprets Scripture within the faith-community of the Church and brings to that community the fruit of such reading and prayer. As examples of individual Christians who turn to the Bible the Commission singles out people of lowly status and the poor, who have a capacity to hear the Word, which needs to be heard. It also singles out in a special way exegetes, making special mention of women exegetes. These are individuals who have put their knowledge, learning, and skills in the interpretation of Scripture to the service of the Church. Such were persons like Origen and Jerome in the patristic period, and like Marie-Joseph Lagrange, O.P. in modern times[193].

Recognizing the Scriptures as part of the heritage of faith in the Church and following the lead of the Second Vatican Council, the Commission acknowledges that the responsiblity for interpreting Scripture authentically lies with the Church's living teaching office or *magisterium*[194]. For this very purpose it consults exegetes, theologians,

---

[193] He founded the famous Ecole Biblique in Jerusalem in 1890 and was in reality the one who, despite much opposition and persecution from contemporary Integrists in the Catholic Church, showed how the historical-critical method could be used in biblical interpretation without any detriment to Christian and Catholic faith. See his *La méthode historique surtout à propos de l'Ancien Testament* (Paris: Lecoffre, 1903; édition augmentée, 1904); in English, *Historical Criticism and the Old Testament* (London: Catholic Truth Society, 1905). This book was attacked by A.-J. Delattre, *Autour de la Question Biblique: Une nouvelle école d'exégèse et les autorités qu'elle invoque* (Liége: Dessain, [1904]). To this attack Lagrange replied in *Eclaircissement sur le Méthode Historique: A propos d'un livre du R. P. Delattre, S.J.* (Paris: Victor Lecoffre, 1905). To which Delattre replied in *Le Criterium à l'usage de la nouvelle exégèse biblique* (Liége: Dessain, [1907]).

See M.-J. Lagrange, *L'Ecriture en église: Choix de portraits et d'exégèse spirituelle (1890-1937)* (Lectio divina 142; ed. M. Gilbert; Paris: Cerf, 1990); *Exégète à Jérusalem: Nouveaux Mélanges d'histoire religieuse (1890-1939)* (Cahiers de la RB 29; ed. M. Gilbert; Paris: Gabalda, 1991). Cf. L.-H. Vincent, "Le Père Lagrange", *RB* 47 (1938) 321-54; F.-M. Braun, *The Work of Père Lagrange* (Milwaukee, WI: Bruce, 1963).

[194] See *Dei Verbum* §10.

thentic Gospel. It discharges this function within the *koinonia* of the Body, expressing officially the faith of the Church, as a service to the Church; to this end it consults theologians, exegetes and other experts, whose legitimate liberty it recognizes and with whom it remains united by reciprocal relationship in the common goal of "preserving the people of God in the truth which sets them free" (CDF, *Instruction concerning the Ecclesial Vocation of the Theologian*, 21).

## C. The Task of the Exegete

The task of Catholic exegetes embraces many aspects. It is an ecclesial task, for it consists in the study and explanation of Holy Scripture in a way that makes all its riches available to pastors and the faithful. But it is at the same time a work of scholarship, which places the Catholic exegete in contact with non-Catholic colleagues and with many areas of scholarly research. Moreover, this task includes at the same time both research and teaching. And each of these normally leads to publication.

### 1. *Principal Guidelines*

In devoting themselves to their task, Catholic exegetes have to pay due account to the *historical character* of biblical revelation. For the two

---

and other experts, whose liberty it respects and whose work contributes to the common goal of preserving the people of God in the biblical truth.

## C. The Task of the Exegete

In recent decades the Church has often issued instructions for professional interpreters of the Bible[195], and the Commission adds its own comments about their task, which is at once ecclesial and scholarly, and devoted to research and teaching.

### 1. *Principal Guidelines*

Four points are singled out: (I) Exegetes have to respect the *historical character* of biblical revelation, because the two Testaments bear the

---

[195] See *Providentissimus Deus* §II D 4 (*EB* §128-32; *RSS* 128-32); *Divino afflante spiritu* §23-48 (*EB* §550-65; *RSS* §550-65); Biblical Commission, *Instruction on the Historical Truth of the Gospels*, §IV-XII (see n. 12 above).

Testaments express in human words bearing the stamp of their time the historical revelation communicated by God in various ways, concerning himself and his plan of salvation. Consequently, exegetes have to make use of the historical-critical method. They cannot, however, accord to it a sole validity. All methods pertaining to the interpretation of texts are entitled to make their contribution to the exegesis of the Bible.

In their work of interpretation, Catholic exegetes must never forget that what they are interpreting is the *Word of God*. Their common task is not finished when they have simply determined sources, defined forms or explained literary procedures. They arrive at the true goal of their work only when they have explained the meaning of the biblical text as God's word for today. To this end, they must take into consideration the various hermeneutical perspectives which help towards grasping the contemporary meaning of the biblical message and which make it responsive to the needs of those who read Scripture today.

Exegetes should also explain the christological, canonical and ecclesial meanings of the biblical texts.

The *christological* significance of biblical texts is not always evident; it must be made clear whenever possible. Although Christ established the New Covenant in his blood, the books of the First Covenant have not lost their value. Assumed into the proclamation of the Gospel, they acquire and display their full meaning in the "mystery of Christ" (*Eph* 3:4); they shed light upon multiple aspects of this mystery, while in turn being illuminated by it themselves. These writings, in fact, served to prepare the people of God for his coming (cf. *Dei Verbum*, 14-16).

Although each book of the Bible was written with its own particular end in view and has its own specific meaning, it takes on a deeper meaning when it becomes part of the *canon* as a whole. The exegetical task includes therefore bringing out the truth of Augustine's dictum:

> "*Novum Testamentum in Vetere latet,*
> *et in Novo Vetus patet*"
> ["The New Testament lies hidden in the Old,
> and the Old becomes clear in the New"]
> (cf. *Quaest. in Hept.*, 2, 73: *CSEL* 28, III, 3, p. 141).

Exegetes have also to explain the relationship that exists between the Bible and the *Church*. The Bible came into existence within believing

---

stamp of the varied times of God's revelation of himself and his plan of salvation, and hence they must use all available means of interpretation.

communities. In it the faith of Israel found expression, later that of the early Christian communities. United to the living Tradition which preceded it, which accompanies it and is nourished by it (cf. *Dei Verbum*, 21), the Bible is the privileged means which God uses yet again in our own day to shape the building up and the growth of the Church as the People of God. This ecclesial dimension necessarily involves an openness to ecumenism.

Moreover, since the Bible tells of God's offer of salvation to all people, the exegetical task necessarily includes a universal dimension. This means taking account of other religions and of the hopes and fears of the world of today.

## 2. *Research*

The exegetical task is far too large to be successfully pursued by individual scholars working alone. It calls for a division of labor, especially in *research*, which demands specialists in different fields. Interdisciplinary

---

(2) Exegetes are to remember that they are interpreting the *Word of God* and arrive at their goal only when they have explained the meaning of the biblical text as God's word for today, making use of proper hermeneutical principles. (3) Exegetes are to make clear the *christological* meaning of biblical texts, whenever possible. Though Old Testament writings have not lost their value, they acquire a special meaning from their being taken up into the proclamation of the gospel and related to the "mystery of Christ", and hence their canonical relationship is important. (4) Exegetes have to explain the relation of the Bible to the *Church*. For the Bible came into being within believing communities: the Old Testament as the record of Israel's faith, and the New as the record of that of early Christian communities. "United to the living Tradition which preceded it, which accompanies it and is nourished by it..., the Bible is the privileged means which God uses yet again in our day to shape the building up and the growth of the Church as the People of God". This ecclesial aspect has ramifications for relations with other Christians and other religions.

## 2. *Research*

The vast task of exegesis requires individuals who specialize in some of its aspects, and the research of specialists becomes necessary for the

collaboration will help overcome any limitations that specialisation may tend to produce.

It is very important for the good of the entire Church, as well as for its influence in the modern world, that a sufficient number of well-prepared persons be committed to research in the various fields of exegetical study. In their concern for the more immediate needs of the ministry, bishops and religious superiors are often tempted not to take sufficiently seriously the responsibility incumbent upon them to make provision for this fundamental need. But a lack in this area exposes the Church to serious harm, for pastors and the faithful then run the risk of being at the mercy of an exegetical scholarship which is alien to the Church and lacks relationship to the life of faith. In stating that "the *study* of Sacred Scripture" should be "as it were the soul of Theology" (*Dei Verbum*, 24), the Second Vatican Council has indicated the crucial importance of exegetical research. By the same token, the Council has also implicitly reminded Catholic exegetes that their research has an essential relationship to theology, their awareness of which must also be evident.

### 3. *Teaching*

The declaration of the Council made equally clear the fundamental role which belongs to the *teaching* of exegesis in the Faculties of Theology,

---

good of the entire Church. The Commission calls this to the attention of bishops and religious superiors, who have to provide for this fundamental need. For the study of Sacred Scripture has to be, as it were, the soul of Theology[196].

### 3. *Teaching*

Along with research the exegete's task is one of teaching, especially in faculties of theology, seminaries, and houses of study of religious orders

---

[196] The Commission thus echoes Vatican Council II (*Dei Verbum* §24) and Pope Leo XIII (*Providentissimus Deus*, *ASS* 26 [1893-94] 283; *EB* §411). The idea of Scripture as the soul of Theology is, in fact, much older than Leo XIII. It has been traced to the seventeenth century, to the Thirteenth General Congregation of the Society of Jesus held in Rome in 1687, where it is found in Decree 15. See M. Gilbert, "Cinquant'anni di magistero romano", *Chiesa e Sacra Scrittura* (n. 4 above), 17; cf. J. M. Lera, "'Sacrae paginae studium sit veluti anima Sacrae Theologiae' (Notas sobre el origen y procedencia de este frase)", *Palabra y vida: Homenaje a J. Alonso Díaz* (ed. A. Vargas-Machuca and G. Ruiz; Madrid: UPCM, 1984) 409-22.

the Seminaries and the Religious Houses of Studies. It is obvious that the level of these studies will not be the same in all cases. It is desirable that the teaching of exegesis be carried out by both men and women. More technical in university faculties, this teaching will have a more directly pastoral orientation in seminaries. But it can never be without an intellectual dimension that is truly serious. To proceed otherwise would be to show disrespect towards the Word of God.

Professors of exegesis should communicate to their students a profound appreciation of Sacred Scripture, showing how it deserves the kind of attentive and objective study which will allow a better appreciation of its literary, historical, social and theological value. They cannot rest content simply with the conveying of a series of facts to be passively absorbed but should give a genuine introduction to exegetical method, explaining the principal steps, so that students will be in a position to exercise their own personal judgment. Given the limited time at a teacher's disposal, it is appropriate to make use of two alternative modes of teaching: on the one hand, a synthetic exposition to introduce the student to the study of whole books of the Bible, omitting no important area of the Old or New Testament; on the other hand, in-depth analyses of certain, well-chosen texts, which will provide at the same time an introduction to the practice of exegesis. In either case, care must be taken to avoid a one-sided approach that would restrict itself, on the one hand, to a spiritual commentary empty of historical-critical grounding or, on the other, to a historical-critical commentary lacking doctrinal or spiritual content (cf. *Divino Afflante Spiritu*: *EB*, 551-552; PBC, *De Sacra Scriptura recte docenda*: *EB*, 598). Teaching should at one and the same time show forth the historical roots of the biblical writings, the way in which they constitute the personal word of the heavenly Father addressing his children with love (cf. *Dei Verbum*, 21) and their indispensable role in the pastoral ministry (cf. *2 Tim* 3, 16).

---

or congregations. As teachers, exegetes are to instill the techniques of exegesis, a profound appreciation of Scripture itself, and an introduction to all the books of the Bible.

## 4. *Publications*

As the fruit of research and a complement to teaching, publications play a highly important role in the advancement and spread of exegetical work. Beyond printed texts, publication today embraces other more powerful and more rapid means of communication (radio, television, other electronic media); it is very advantageous to know how to make use of these things.

For those engaged in research, publication at a high academic level is the principal means of dialogue, discussion and cooperation. Through it, Catholic exegesis can interact with other centers of exegetical research as well as with the scholarly world in general.

There is another form of publication, more short-term in nature, which renders a very great service by its ability to adapt itself to a variety of readers, from the well-educated to children of catechism age, reaching biblical groups, apostolic movements and religious congregations. Exegetes who have a gift for popularization provide an extremely useful and fruitful work, one that is indispensable if the fruit of exegetical studies is to be dispersed as widely as need demands. In this area, the need to make the biblical message something real for today is ever more obvious. This requires that exegetes take into consideration the reasonable demands of educated and cultured persons of our time, clearly distinguishing for their benefit what in the Bible is to be regarded as secondary detail conditioned by a particular age, what must be interpreted as the language of myth and what is to be regarded as the true historical and inspired meaning. The biblical writings were not composed in modern language or in the style of the 20th century. The forms of expression and literary genres employed in the Hebrew, Aramaic or Greek text must be made meaningful to men and women of today, who otherwise would be tempted to lose all interest in the Bible or else to interpret it in a simplistic way that is literalist or simply fanciful.

In all this variety of tasks, the Catholic exegete has no other purpose than the service of the Word of God. The aim of the exegete is not to

---

## 4. *Publications*

The fruit of research and teaching should also be publication, at all levels and in all manners. Here a call is made for popularization, an adaptation of the biblical message to the cultural and educational level of people today. The Commission recommends that such popularization must concern itself with what might be secondary or time-conditioned in the

substitute for the biblical texts the results of his or her work, whether that involve the reconstruction of ancient sources used by the inspired authors or up-to-date presentation of the latest conclusions of exegetical science. On the contrary, the aim of the exegete is to shed more and more light on the biblical texts themselves, helping them to be better appreciated for what they are in themselves and understood with ever more historical accuracy and spiritual depth.

## D. Relationships with Other Theological Disciplines

Being itself a theological discipline, *"fides quaerens intellectum"*, exegesis has close and complex relationships with other fields of theological learning. On the one hand, systematic theology has an influence upon the presuppositions with which exegetes approach biblical texts. On the other hand, exegesis provides the other theological disciplines with data fundamental for their operation. There is, accordingly, a relationship of dialogue between exegesis and the other branches of theology, granted always a mutual respect for that which is specific to each.

### 1. *Theology and Presuppositions regarding Biblical Texts*

Exegetes necessarily bring certain presuppositions (Fr. *précompréhension*) to biblical writings. In the case of the Catholic exegete, it is a

---

Bible or what might be couched in "the language of myth" and distinguish such affirmations from its "true historical and inspired meaning". In all of this, however, exegetes who engage in such popularization have to guard against a reading of the Bible in a simplistic, literalist, or fanciful way.

In this variety of tasks, exegetes have only one purpose, the service of the Word of God and shedding of light on the meaning of the biblical text.

## D. Relationships with Other Theological Disciplines

Because exegesis is a theological discipline, it is related to dogmatic and moral theology, even though each of these disciplines has its own methodology and autonomous status.

### 1. *Theology and Presuppositions regarding Biblical Texts*

The presuppositions with which the Catholic exegete approaches the biblical text have been developed over the centuries by theological reflec-

question of presuppositions based on the certainties of faith: the Bible is a text inspired by God, entrusted to the Church for the nurturing of faith and guidance of the Christian life. These certainties of faith do not come to an exegete in an unrefined, raw state, but only as developed in the ecclesial community through the process of theological reflection. The reflection undertaken by systematic theologians upon the inspiration of Scripture and the function it serves in the life of the Church provides in this way direction for exegetical research.

But correspondingly, the work of exegetes on the inspired texts provides them with an experience which systematic theologians should take into account as they seek to explain more clearly the theology of scriptural inspiration and the interpretation of the Bible within the Church. Exegesis creates, in particular, a more lively and precise awareness of the historical character of biblical inspiration. It shows that the process of inspiration is historical, not only because it took place over the course of the history of Israel and of the early Church, but also because it came about through the agency of human beings, all of them conditioned by their time and all, under the guidance of the Spirit, playing an active role in the life of the people of God.

Moreover, theology's affirmation of the strict relationship between inspired Scripture and Tradition has been both confirmed and made more precise through the advance of exegetical study, which has led exegetes to pay increasing attention to the influence upon texts of the life-setting ("*Sitz im Leben*") out of which they were formed.

---

tion. This relation of biblical interpretation to theology is, therefore, very important, because the presuppositions are theological. They concern the inspiration of the Bible, its consignment to the Church, and its goal of nurturing Christian faith and guiding Christian life. It is the bailiwick of systematic theology to work out and clarify these relationships. But because there is a danger that the systematic theologian may try to explain such relationships in a vacuum, the exegete has to bring to such reflection the concrete shape that the relationships take: a precise awareness of the historical character of biblical inspiration, which has involved human authors of varied times, places, and cultures, who were moved by the Spirit to play an active role in God's people; the relationship of Scripture to Tradition, which has been enhanced by new advances in exegetical study that have made possible the study of the vital contexts out of which biblical texts have taken shape and the bearing they have on the developing Tradition.

## 2. *Exegesis and Systematic Theology*

Without being the sole *locus theologicus*, Sacred Scripture provides the privileged foundation of theological studies. In order to interpret Scripture with scholarly accuracy and precision, theologians need the work of exegetes. From their side, exegetes must orientate their research in such fashion that "the study of Sacred Scripture" can be in reality "as it were the soul of Theology" (*Dei Verbum*, 24). To achieve this, they ought to pay particular attention to the religious content of the biblical writings.

Exegetes can help systematic theologians avoid two extremes: on the one hand, a dualism, which would completely separate a doctrinal truth from its linguistic expression, as though the latter were of no importance; on the other hand, a fundamentalism, which, confusing the human and the divine, would consider even the contingent features of human discourse to be revealed truth.

To avoid these two extremes, it is necessary to make distinctions without at the same time making separations — thus to accept a continuing tension. The Word of God finds expression in the work of human authors. The thought and the words belong at one and the same time both to God and to human beings, in such a way that the whole Bible comes at once from God and from the inspired human author. This does not mean,

---

## 2. *Exegesis and Systematic Theology*

Because Scripture is the "soul of Sacred Theology" and provides the privileged foundation for all theological study, systematic theologians need the accurate and precise work of exegetes; and exegetes have to orient their work so that the study of Scripture really becomes the animating principle of theology. For this reason, exegetes have to pay particular attention to the religious content of all biblical writings.

Exegetes can help systematic theologians avoid two extremes: a dualism that would separate doctrinal truth from its linguistic or philological expression, and a fundamentalism that would confuse the human and the divine and consider contingent features of human discourse as revealed truth. For there is an ongoing tension between these two elements: the Word of God finds expression in the words of human authors, whereas the thoughts and the words belong at once to both God and human beings. Yet God has not thereby given an absolute value to the historical conditioning of the message. It is still open to interpretation and actualization so

however, that God has given the historical conditioning of the message a value which is absolute. It is open both to interpretation and to being brought up to date — which means being detached, to some extent, from its historical conditioning in the past and being transplanted into the historical conditioning of the present. The exegete performs the groundwork for this operation, which the systematic theologian continues by taking into account the other *loci theologici* which contribute to the development of dogma.

### 3. *Exegesis and Moral Theology*

Similar observations can be made regarding the relationship between exegesis and moral theology. The Bible closely links many instructions about proper conduct — commandments, prohibitions, legal prescriptions, prophetic exhortations and accusations, counsels of wisdom, and so forth — to the stories concerning the history of salvation. One of the tasks of exegesis consists in preparing the way for the work of moralists by assessing the significance of this wealth of material.

This task is not simple, for often the biblical texts are not concerned

---

that it can be transplanted to meet a present need or condition. Exegetes perform the groundwork for this operation, which systematic theologians must build on and continue by using other data (e.g. from Tradition, Church documents, or philosophy), which contribute to the development of the dogmatic Tradition.

### 3. *Exegesis and Moral Theology*

Similarly, exegetes can help moral theologians assess the significance of the many commandments, prohibitions, legal prescriptions, prophetic exhortations and admonitions, and sapiential counsels embedded in the stories that recount the history of salvation.

This assessment, however, is not simple, since the biblical texts do not distinguish universal moral principles from particular prescriptions (ritual purity or legal ordinances). Moreover, some writings of the Old Testament contain "imperfect and provisional" elements (*Dei Verbum* §15), which have to be evaluated in light of the progress of moral understanding and sensitivity that have developed over the years. And the data of the New Testament in the area of morality are at times paradoxical or even provocative, especially in the relation of the Mosaic law to Christian life.

to distinguish universal moral principles from particular prescriptions of ritual purity and legal ordinances. All is mixed together. On the other hand, the Bible reflects a considerable moral development, which finds its completion in the New Testament. It is not sufficient therefore that the Old Testament should indicate a certain moral position (e.g., the practice of slavery or of divorce, or that of extermination in the case of war) for this position to continue to have validity. One has to undertake a process of discernment. This will review the issue in the light of the progress in moral understanding and sensitivity that has occurred over the years. The writings of the Old Testament contain certain "imperfect and provisional" elements (*Dei Verbum*, 15), which the divine pedagogy could not eliminate right away. The New Testament itself is not easy to interpret in the area of morality, for it often makes use of imagery, frequently in a way that is paradoxical or even provocative; moreover, in the New Testament area the relationship between Christians and the Jewish Law is the subject of sharp controversy.

Moral theologians therefore have a right to put to exegetes many questions which will stimulate exegetical research. In many cases the response may be that no biblical text explicitly addresses the problem proposed. But even when such is the case, the witness of the Bible, taken within the framework of the forceful dynamic that governs it as a whole, will certainly indicate a fruitful direction to follow. On the most important points the moral principles of the Decalogue remain basic. The Old Testa-

---

Because of all this, moral theologians have a right to put to exegetes many questions that will stimulate further biblical study. Even when no direct answer is forthcoming from the Bible about some modern moral problems, it often supplies an outlook or a dynamic point of view that may indicate a direction to be followed, e.g. that human beings have been created "in the image of God" (Gen 1:27). As for the main points of morality, the Decalogue (Exod 20:1-17; Deut 5:6-21) remains basic, and such principles are further illumined by the New Testament teaching about God's love poured out through Jesus Christ and the holy Spirit[197].

---

[197] For the problem that biblical data sometimes create in the area of moral theology, see V. McNamara, *Faith and Ethics: Recent Roman Catholicism* (Dublin: Gill and Macmillan; Washington, DC: Georgetown University, 1985) 69-94. Cf. J. R. Donahue, "The Challenge of the Biblical Renewal to Moral Theology", *The Catholic Moral Tradition since Vatican II* (Washington, DC: Georgetown University, 1993) 59-80.

ment already contains the principles and the values which require conduct in full conformity with the dignity of the human person, created "in the image of God" (*Gen* 1:27). Through the revelation of God's love that comes in Christ, the New Testament sheds the fullest light upon these principles and values.

### 4. Differing Points of View and Necessary Interaction

In its 1988 document of the Interpretation of Theological Truths, the International Theological Commission recalled that a conflict has broken out in recent times between exegesis and dogmatic theology; it then notes the positive contribution modern exegesis has made to systematic theology (*The Interpretation of Theological Truths*, 1988, C.I, 2). To be more precise, it should be said that the conflict was provoked by liberal exegesis. There was no conflict in a generalised sense between Catholic exegesis and dogmatic theology but only some instances of strong tension. It remains true, however, that tension can degenerate into conflict when, from one side or the other, differing points of view, quite legitimate in themselves, become hardened to such an extent that they become in fact irreconcilable opposites.

The points of view of both disciplines are in fact different and rightly so. The primary task of the exegete is to determine as accurately as possible the meaning of biblical texts in their own proper context, that is, first of all, in their particular literary and historical context and then in the context of the wider canon of Scripture. In the course of carrying out this task, the exegete expounds the theological meaning of texts when such a meaning is present. This paves the way for a relationship of continuity between exegesis and further theological reflection. But the point of view is not the same, for the work of the exegete is fundamentally historical and descriptive and restricts itself to the interpretation of the Bible.

Theologians as such have a role that is more speculative and more systematic in nature. For this reason, they are really interested only in certain texts and aspects of the Bible and deal, besides, with much other

---

### 4. Differing Points of View and Necessary Interaction

The Biblical Commission comments on a statement made by the International Theological Commission in its 1988 document, *The Interpretation of Dogmas*, that conflict has broken out between exegesis and dogmatic theology, even though the latter acknowledges the positive contribu-

data which is not biblical — patristic writings, conciliar definitions, other documents of the magisterium, the liturgy — as well as systems of philosophy and the cultural, social and political situation of the contemporary world. Their task is not simply to interpret the Bible; their aim is to present an understanding of the Christian faith that bears the mark of a full reflection upon all its aspects and especially that of its crucial relationship to human existence.

Because of its speculative and systematic orientation, theology has often yielded to the temptation to consider the Bible as a store of *dicta*

---

tion that modern exegesis has made to systematic theology[198]. The Biblical Commission maintains, however, that that "conflict was provoked by liberal exegesis", which it does not otherwise explain[199], and that there have

---

[198] See Internationale Theologenkommission, "Die Interpretation der Dogmen", *IKZ* *"Communio"* 19 (1990) 246-66 (original German working-text), esp. 258-59 (C.I, 2); "On the Interpretation of Dogmas", *Origins* 20 (1990-91) 1-14, esp. 10; *ITQ* 56 (1990) 245-77, esp. 266-67; "L'Interpretazione dei dogmi", *CivCatt* 1990 (21 April 1990) 144-73, esp. 163-64; "De interpretatione dogmatum", *Gregorianum* 72 (1991) 5-37 (not well translated), esp. 25.

The text reads, "The conflict between exegesis and dogmatic theology is a modern phenomenon. In the wake of the Enlightenment, the tools of historical criticism were developed even with the intention of using them to achieve emancipation from ecclesiastical-dogmatic authority. This criticism became ever more comprehensive. Soon Scripture and dogma alone were no longer in conflict, but the very text of Scripture itself was subjected to further critical scrutiny to discover the 'dogmatic overcoatings' in Scripture itself. The development of historical criticism in sociopolitical and psychological criticism scrutinized the text for sociopolitical antagonisms or suppressed psychic data. Common to these different lines of criticism is the suspicion that the Church's dogma and even Scripture itself conceal a primitive reality, which can only be uncovered by means of critical inquiry.

"The positive side and results of Enlightenment criticism of tradition obviously should not be overlooked. The historical criticism of Scripture has been able to make it clear that Scripture itself is ecclesial; it has its roots in the *paradosis* of the early Church, and the fixing of its canonical limits was a process of decision in the Church. In that way exegesis was pointing the way back to dogma and tradition.

"Above all, historical criticism has never succeeded in showing that Jesus himself was absolutely 'undogmatic'. Even in historical criticism of the most rigorous sort, there remains a reasonably uncontestable historical core about the earthly Jesus. To this core belongs the claim expressed in the deeds and words of Jesus about his mission, his person, and his relation to God, his 'Abba'. That claim implies the later dogmatic development, which is already beginning in the New Testament and is the core of all dogmatic statements. For that very reason, the primitive form of Christian dogma is the confession central to the New Testament: Jesus the Christ is the Son of God (Matt 16:16)" [my translation of the original German].

[199] From the text of the Theological Commission's document quoted in the preceding note one gathers that the "liberal exegesis" was more at home outside the Catholic Church than in it.

*probantia* serving to confirm doctrinal theses. In recent times, theologians have become more keenly conscious of the importance of the literary and historical context for the correct interpretation of ancient texts and they are much more ready to work in collaboration with exegetes.

Inasmuch as it is the Word of God set in writing, the Bible has a richness of meaning that no one systematic theology can ever completely capture or confine. One of the principal functions of the Bible is to mount serious challenges to theological systems and to draw attention constantly to the existence of important aspects of divine revelation and human reality which have at times been forgotten or neglected in efforts at systematic

---

been only some instances of strong tension between Catholic exegesis and dogmatic theology[200]. But there is a danger that such tension could develop into opposition.

The tension rises from the different points of view of exegesis and systematic theology that have to be respected. The task of exegetes is to determine as accurately as possible the meaning of biblical texts in their proper literary and historical contexts, as well as in the context of the whole canon. This includes a determination of the theological meaning of texts, which would supply the groundwork for further (systematic) theological reflection. The exegetes' task, then, is fundamentally historical, literary, and descriptive, being restricted to the interpretation of the biblical text. But the task of systematic theologians is more speculative, and it may limit their interest to only some aspects of the biblical text, as they deal with other data, patristic, conciliar, liturgical, or ecclesiastical, or with philosophical and cultural concerns derived from the contemporary world. Their task is not simply to interpret the Bible, but to explain Christian faith as it bears on problems of modern human existence.

Yet this speculative and systematic orientation has often led theologians in the past to treat the Bible merely as a storehouse of proof-texts for their doctrinal theses, to pick and choose from it what they find useful to their purposes, and to disregard the basic thrust of biblical texts. More recently, however, theologians have become more conscious, in general, of the need to interpret ancient biblical texts "in the way it has to be done

---

[200] For example, J. Galot ascribes to Y. Congar the following statement: "Je respecte et j'interroge sans cesse la science des exégètes, mais je récuse leur magistère" (*Gregorianum* 70 [1989] 161). Cf. R. E. Brown, *Biblical Exegesis and Church Doctrine* (New York: Paulist, 1985); R. J. Neuhaus (ed.), *Biblical Interpretation in Crisis: The Ratzinger Conference on Bible and Church* (Grand Rapids, MI: Eerdmans, 1989).

reflection. The renewal that has taken place in exegetical methodology can make its own contribution to awareness in these areas.

In a corresponding way, exegesis should allow itself to be informed by theological research. This will prompt it to put important questions to texts and so discover their full meaning and richness. The critical study of the Bible cannot isolate itself from theological research, or from spiritual experience and the discernment of the Church. Exegesis produces its best results when it is carried out in the context of the living faith of the Christian community, which is directed toward the salvation of the entire world.

---

today and not in the way [one] used to do it in the good old days"[201]. As a result, there is much greater collaboration of theologians and exegetes, and so one wonders about the accusation of "conflict".

Yet, even so, the richness of the written Word of God can never be encapsulated in one system of theology. Hence the renewed exegetical methodology can challenge theological systems, while also contributing to new modes of theological reflection. By the same token, exegesis can be enhanced by proper systematic reflection on its relation to theology. For the critical study of the Bible cannot isolate itself from theological research or from the spiritual life and experience of the Church. In fact, it produces its best results in that mixed context.

---

[201] See K. Rahner, "Exegese und Dogmatik", *Stimmen der Zeit* 168 (1961) 241-62; repr. in *Schriften zur Theologie* (16 vols.; Einsiedeln: Benziger, 1954-84) 5 (1964) 82-111, esp. 93.

## IV. INTERPRETATION OF THE BIBLE IN THE LIFE OF THE CHURCH

Exegetes may have a distinctive role in the interpretation of the Bible but they do not exercise a monopoly. This activity within the Church has aspects which go beyond the academic analysis of texts. The Church, indeed, does not regard the Bible simply as a collection of historical documents dealing with its own origins; it receives the Bible as Word of God, addressed both to itself and to the entire world at the present time. This conviction, stemming from the faith, leads in turn to the work of actualizing and inculturating the Biblical message, as well as to various uses of the inspired text in liturgy, in "Lectio divina", in pastoral ministry and in the ecumenical movement.

### A. Actualization

Already within the Bible itself — as we noted in the previous chapter — one can point to instances of actualization: very early texts have been

---

## IV. INTERPRETATION OF THE BIBLE IN THE LIFE OF THE CHURCH

The interpretation of the Bible is not a monopolistic task of exegetes, because the Church has received the Bible as the Word of God addressed both to itself and to the world at large. Hence the Bible's role in the life of the Church involves actualization, inculturation, and use in liturgy, *lectio divina*, pastoral ministry, and ecumenism.

### A. Actualization

This term is derived from French *actualisation*, which means roughly "modernization". When the Commission was commenting on the forms of

re-read in the light of new circumstances and applied to the contemporary situation of the People of God. The same basic conviction necessarily stimulates believing communities of today to continue the process of actualization.

## 1. *Principles*

Actualization rests on the following basic principles:

Actualization is possible because the richness of meaning contained in the biblical text gives it a value for all time and all cultures (cf. *Isa* 40:8; 66:18-21; *Matt* 28:19-20). The biblical message can at the same time both relativize and enrich the value systems and norms of behavior of each generation.

Actualization is necessary because, although their message is of lasting value, the biblical texts have been composed with respect to circumstances of the past and in language conditioned by a variety of times and seasons. To reveal their significance for men and women of today, it is necessary to apply their message to contemporary circumstances and to express it in language adapted to the present time. This presupposes a hermeneutical endeavor, the aim of which is to go beyond the historical conditioning so as to determine the essential points of the message.

The work of actualization should always be conscious of the complex relationships that exist in the Christian Bible between the two Testaments, since the New Testament presents itself, at one and the same time, as both the fulfilment and the surpassing of the Old. Actualization takes place in line with the dynamic unity thus established.

---

*relecture* found in the Bible itself, it used this very term. It denotes a mode of applying biblical teaching to new, contemporary situations of the people of God; it is a way of applying sound hermeneutical theory.

## 1. *Principles*

Four principles of actualization are mentioned: (a) The wealth of meaning of the biblical text gives it a value for all times and cultures[202]. (b) Though the biblical text is of lasting value, it is often time-conditioned in

---

[202] This principle is based on the Bible itself: Isa 40:8, "Though grass withers and flowers wilt, the word of our God stands forever"; Isa 66:18, "I come to gather nations of every language"; Matt 28:19, "Make disciples of all nations".

It is the living tradition of the community of faith that stimulates the task of actualization. This community places itself in explicit continuity with the communities which gave rise to Scripture and which preserved and handed it on. In the process of actualization, tradition plays a double role: on the one hand, it provides protection against deviant interpretations; on the other hand, it ensures the transmission of the original dynamism.

Actualization, therefore, cannot mean manipulation of the text. It is not a matter of projecting novel opinions or ideologies upon the biblical writings, but of sincerely seeking to discover what the text has to say at the present time. The text of the Bible has authority over the Christian Church at all times, and, although centuries have passed since the time of its composition, the text retains its role of privileged guide not open to manipulation. The Magisterium of the Church "is not above the Word of God, but serves it, teaching only what has been handed on; by divine commission, with the help of the Holy Spirit, the Church listens to the text

---

its expression and needs hermeneutical analysis to determine its essential message, what it is saying to the present, actual situation. (c) Actualization has to respect the dynamic unity and complex relationship between the two Testaments of the Christian Bible, since the New Testament not only fulfills the Old, but often surpasses it. (d) The living tradition of the faith-community stimulates the actualization, protecting the Bible against deviant interpretations and ensuring the transmission of the Bible's original teaching and dynamism.

The danger in actualization is the manipulation of the sacred text, which might foist novel opinions upon it. Since the Bible has authority over the Christian Church at all times, it remains unmanipulable; the Christian community has to square itself with the written Word of God generation after generation, not the other way round. In this connection the Commission cites *Dei Verbum* §10, which admitted that not even the magisterium or teaching authority of the Church is in any way "above the Word of God[203]".

---

[203] The Council document uses "Word of God" in the broad sense of "revelation", which is not restricted to the written Word of God. But the phrase does not exclude the "written Word of God". Rather, it includes it, and that is what makes that statement in *Dei Verbum* §10 so important. The written Word of God cannot be manipulated even by the *magisterium*.

with love, watches over it in holiness and explains it faithfully" (*Dei Verbum*, 10).

## 2. *Methods*

Based on these principles, various methods of actualization are available.

Actualization, already practised within the Bible itself, was continued in the Jewish tradition through procedures found in the Targums and Midrashim: searching for parallel passages (*gezerah shawah*), modification in the reading of the text (*'al tiqrey*), appropriation of a second meaning (*tartey mishma'*), etc.

---

## 2. *Methods*

Four ways are singled out in which the actualization of the biblical text can be carried out: (a) By the use of Jewish exegetical techniques, such as *gĕzērāh šāwāh*, loosely defined as a search for parallel passages, *'al tiqrê*, a modification of the reading of the text, and *tartê mišma'*, a secondary meaning[204]. (b) By typology and allegory, such as were used by Fathers of the Church[205]. (c) By the interpretation of Scripture by Scripture, especially when Old Testament texts have been re-read in either the Old or the New Testament, or in light of the mystery of Christ and the Christian Church[206]. (d) By modern philosophical hermeneutics,

---

[204] *Gĕzērāh šāwāh* literally means "an equal decision", but in rabbinical hermeneutics it came to denote that one passage in the Torah could be used to interpret another, when they both have identical (and possibly unique) expressions or wording. *'Al tiqrê* means "Do not read (it thus, but rather...)". *Tartê mišma'* means "second hearing (of the text)", i.e. a second way of understanding it. See further H. L. Strack and G. Stemberger, *Introduction to the Talmud and Midrash* (Edinburgh: Clark, 1991). One must remember that these rabbinical hermeneutical rules date from a relatively late period. They are attested in writings that come from after A.D. 200, and it is a matter of debate how much older they may be. They could have already been part of the oral tradition of earlier rabbis, but no one can say for certain how much older they are.

[205] In recommending as a mode of actualization the patristic use of typology and allegory, the Commission does not intend to negate what it said earlier about the risk that the allegorical interpretation runs of being "an embarrassment to people today" (p. 150) and about it as a mode that cannot be used today (p. 126). In this regard, one should recall what Pius XII had to say about "figurative senses" (other than the literal sense or the spiritual [i.e. christological] sense of the Old Testament); see n. 173 (p. 126) above.

[206] The Commission cites as an example the manna mentioned in Exod 16:14-15, called in 16:4 "bread from heaven", which becomes in Wis 16:20 "food of angels" and "bread from heaven" (cf. Ps 78:24) and in John 6:41, 58 "the bread that came down from heaven", which is understood of the Eucharist.

In their turn, the Fathers of the Church made use of typology and allegory in order to actualize the biblical text in a manner appropriate to the situation of Christians of their time.

Modern attempts at actualization should keep in mind both changes in ways of thinking and the progress made in interpretative method.

Actualization presupposes a correct exegesis of the text, part of which is the determining of its *literal sense*. Persons engaged in the work of actualization who do not themselves have training in exegetical procedures should have recourse to good introductions to Scripture; this will ensure that their interpretation proceeds in the right direction.

The most sure and promising method for arriving at a successful actualization, is the interpretation of Scripture by Scripture, especially in the case of the texts of the Old Testament which have been re-read in the Old Testament itself (e.g., the manna of *Exodus* 16 in *Wis* 16:20-29) and/ or in the New Testament (*John* 6). The actualization of a biblical text in Christian life will proceed correctly only in relation to the mystery of Christ and of the Church. It would be inappropriate, for example, to propose to Christians as models of a struggle for liberation, episodes drawn solely from the Old Testament (*Exodus, 1–2 Maccabees*).

Based upon various forms of the philosophy of hermeneutics, the task of interpretation involves, accordingly, three steps: 1. to hear the Word from within one's own concrete situation; 2. to identify the aspects of the present situation highlighted or put in question by the biblical text; 3. to draw from the fullness of meaning contained in the biblical text those elements capable of advancing the present situation in a way that is productive and consonant with the saving will of God in Christ.

By virtue of actualization, the Bible can shed light upon many current issues: for example, the question of various forms of ministry, the sense of the Church as communion, the preferential option for the poor, liberation

---

as one listens to the Word from within one's own concrete situation, identifies aspects of it that are illumined or questioned by the biblical text, and draws upon the fullness of the text that might affect the situation in a way consonant with God's salvific will. When actualization is properly carried out, it can shed light on many issues in the life of the Church today: on ministry, the Church as communion, preferential option for the poor, the situation of women, human rights, protection of human life, preservation of nature, and world peace.

Yet, even in this section on methods of actualization, even before it comes to a discussion of its limits, the Commission expresses caution

theology, the situation of women. Actualization can also attend to values of which the modern world is more and more conscious, such as the rights of the human person, the protection of human life, the preservation of nature, the longing for world peace.

## 3. *Limits*

So as to remain in agreement with the saving truth expressed in the Bible, the process of actualization should keep within certain limits and be careful not to take wrong directions.

While every reading of the Bible is necessarily selective, care should be taken to avoid *tendentious interpretations*, that is, readings which, instead of being docile to the text, make use of it only for their own narrow purpose (as is the case in the actualization practised by certain sects, for example, Jehovah's Witnesses).

Actualization loses all validity, if it is grounded in *theoretical principles* which are at variance with the fundamental orientations of the Biblical text, as, for example, a rationalism which is opposed to faith or an atheistic materialism.

Clearly to be rejected also is every attempt at actualization set in a direction contrary to *evangelical justice and charity*, such as, for example, the use of the Bible to justify racial segregation, anti-Semitism or sexism whether on the part of men or of women. Particular attention is necessary, according to the spirit of the Second Vatican Council (*Nostra Aetate*, 4), to avoid absolutely any actualization of certain texts of the New Testament which could provoke or reinforce unfavorable attitudes to the Jewish peo-

---

about such actualization. For actualization must respect the progress made in interpretive methodology and must be based on a correct exegesis of the text, i.e. on the determinination of its *literal* sense. As examples of inappropriate actualization, the Commission cites the use of episodes drawn solely from the Old Testament (Exodus or 1–2 Maccabees) as models for a modern Christian struggle for liberation.

## 3. *Limits*

Three obvious limits of actualization are set forth: (a) Tendentious interpretations, i.e. readings or understandings that serve only narrow and extrinsic ideological purposes (as appears in the interpretation used by some sects). (b) Theoretical principles at variance with the basic orienta-

ple. The tragic events of the past must, on the contrary, impel all to keep unceasingly in mind that, according to the New Testament, the Jews remain "beloved" of God, "since the gifts and calling of God are irrevocable" (*Rom* 11:28-29).

False paths will be avoided if actualization of the biblical message begins with a correct interpretation of the text and continues within the stream of the living Tradition, under the guidance of the Church's Magisterium.

In any case, the risk of error does not constitute a valid objection against performing what is a necessary task: that of bringing the message of the Bible to the ears and hearts of people of our own time.

## B. Inculturation

While actualization allows the Bible to remain fruitful at different periods, inculturation in a corresponding way looks to the diversity of place: it ensures that the biblical message take root in a great variety of terrain. This diversity is, to be sure, never total. Every authentic culture is, in fact, in its own way the bearer of universal values established by God.

The theological foundation of inculturation is the conviction of faith that the Word of God transcends the cultures in which it has found expression and has the capability of being spread in other cultures, in such a way as to be able to reach all human beings in the cultural context in which they live. This conviction springs from the Bible itself, which, right from

---

tion of the Bible itself, e.g. rationalism (opposed to faith) or materialism (derived from atheism). (c) Interpretations contrary to evangelical justice and charity, e.g. fostering racial segregation, anti-Semitism, or sexism.

## B. Inculturation

The inculturation of the Bible can be seen as a specific form of actualization[207]. Every authentic culture, no matter how different from that in which the Bible has taken shape, reflects in its own way God's bounty to humanity. Since the Bible as the Word of God transcends all

---

[207] The Commission actually distinguishes them in terms of time (actualization) and place (inculturation), but in its discussion it realizes that the latter has itself been going on for a long time.

the book of Genesis, adopts a universalist stance (*Gen* 1:27-28), maintains it subsequently in the blessing promised to all peoples through Abraham and his offspring (*Gen* 12:3; 18:18) and confirms it definitely in extending to "all nations" the proclamation of the Christian gospel (*Matt* 28:18-20; *Rom* 4:16-17; *Eph* 3:6).

The first stage of inculturation consists in *translating* the inspired Scripture into another language. This step was taken already in the Old Testament period, when the Hebrew text of the Bible was translated orally into Aramaic (*Neh* 8:8-12) and later in written form into Greek. A translation, of course, is always more than a simple transcription of the original text. The passage from one language to another necessarily involves a change of cultural context: concepts are not identical and symbols have a different meaning, for they come up against other traditions of thought and other ways of life.

Written in Greek, the New Testament is characterized in its entirety by a dynamic of inculturation. In its transposition of the Palestinian message of Jesus into Judeo-Hellenistic culture it displays its intention to transcend the limits of a single cultural world.

While it may constitute the basic step, the translation of biblical texts cannot, however, ensure by itself a thorough inculturation. Translation has to be followed by *interpretation*, which should set the biblical message in more explicit relationship with the ways of feeling, thinking, living and self-expression which are proper to the local culture. From interpretation, one passes then to other stages of inculturation, which lead to the formation of a local Christian culture, extending to all aspects of life (prayer, work, social life, customs, legislation, arts and sciences, philosophical and theological reflection). The Word of God is, in effect, a seed, which extracts from the earth in which it is planted the elements which are useful for its growth and fruitfulness (cf. *Ad Gentes*, 22). As a consequence,

cultures and brings to all humanity a message in the very cultures in which people live, the interpretation of it has to cope with such diversity[208].

The process of inculturation of the Bible evokes three things: (a) The translation of the Bible into other languages may mean more than a simple

---

[208] The Commission cites passages from Genesis and the New Testament that support the universalist outlook: Gen 1:27-28, about the creation of humanity in God's image and likeness; Gen 12:3 and 18:18, about the blessing of "all the nations of the earth" in Abraham; Matt 28:19, about making disciples of "all nations"; Rom 4:16-17, about all who follow the faith of Abraham, the "father of many nations" (alluding to Gen 17:5); and Eph 3:6, about Gentiles as "coheirs" and "copartners" of the promise in Christ Jesus through the gospel.

Christians must try to discern "what riches God, in his generosity, has bestowed on the nations; at the same time they should try to shed the light of the Gospel on these treasures, to set them free and bring them under the dominion of God the Savior" (*Ad Gentes*, 11).

This is not, as is clear, a one-way process; it involves "mutual enrichment". On the one hand, the treasures contained in diverse cultures allow the Word of God to produce new fruits and, on the other hand, the light of the Word allows for a certain selectivity with respect to what cultures have to offer: harmful elements can be left aside and the development of valuable ones encouraged. Total fidelity to the person of Christ, to the dynamic of his paschal mystery and to his love for the Church, make it possible to avoid two false solutions: a superficial "adaptation" of the message, on the one hand, and a syncretistic confusion, on the other (*Ad Gentes*, 22).

Inculturation of the Bible has been carried out from the first centuries, both in the Christian East and in the Christian West, and it has proved very fruitful. However, one can never consider it a task achieved. It must be taken up again and again, in relationship to the way in which cultures continue to evolve. In countries of more recent evangelization, the problem arises in somewhat different terms. Missionaries, in fact, cannot help bring the Word of God in the form in which it has been inculturated in their own country of origin. New local churches have to make every effort to convert this foreign form of biblical inculturation into another form more closely corresponding to the culture of their own land.

---

transcription, since it may have to reconceptualize the biblical message as well as reformulate it. (b) An interpretation, which has to transfer the biblical ways of thinking, feeling, and living from the local culture of its matrix to others and cope with the variety of life, society, prayer, work, custom, law, art, science, and the mode of philosophical and theological reflection found in the diverse cultures of humanity. (c) A mutual enrichment, for diverse cultures may provide situations in which the Word of God can be differently planted, rooted, and allowed to bear fruit. Yet that process has to guard against a superficial adaptation of the biblical message, which might water it down to suit people, as well as the danger of syncretism[209].

---

[209] See Vatican Council II, *Ad Gentes* §22.

## C. Use of the Bible

### 1. *In the Liturgy*

From the earliest days of the Church, the reading of Scripture has been an integral part of the Christian liturgy, an inheritance to some extent from the liturgy of the Synagogue. Today, too, it is above all through the liturgy that Christians come into contact with Scripture, particularly during the Sunday celebration of the Eucharist.

In principle, the liturgy, and especially the sacramental liturgy, the high-point of which is the Eucharistic celebration, brings about the most perfect actualization of the biblical texts, for the liturgy places the proclamation in the midst of the community of believers, gathered around Christ so as to draw near to God. Christ is then "present in his word, because it is he himself who speaks when Sacred Scripture is read in the church" (*Sacrosanctum Concilium*, 7). Written text thus becomes living word.

---

## C. Use of the Bible

The Commission considers how the Bible functions rightly in four contexts: in the liturgy, in *lectio divina*, in pastoral ministry, and in ecumenism.

### 1. *In the Liturgy*

Many passages in the Bible itself come from a liturgical background: the psalter, canticles such as Jonah 2:3-10; Luke 1:46-55 (Magnificat); 1:68-79 (Benedictus), and passages in New Testament epistles (Phil 2:6-11; Eph 1:3-10) and the Book of Revelation (5:9-10; 11:16-18). Likewise, many items in the Bible have shaped the Christian liturgy and its liturgical calendar. This is especially true of the influence of Luke-Acts, with its emphasis on salvation-history, which helped to fashion the liturgical calendar[210].

---

[210] See further G. Dix, *The Shape of the Liturgy* (Westminster [London]: Dacre, 1945); J. Daniélou, *The Bible and the Liturgy* (Notre Dame, IN: University of Notre Dame, 1956); K. W. Stevenson, *The First Rites: Worship in the Early Church* (Collegeville, MN: Liturgical, 1989); E. H. van Olst, *The Bible and Liturgy* (Grand Rapids, MI: Eerdmans, 1991); C. Burgard, *Scripture in the Liturgy* (Westminster, MD: Newman, 1960).

The liturgical reform initiated by the Second Vatican Council sought to provide Catholics with rich sustenance from the Bible. The triple cycle of Sunday readings gives a privileged place to the Gospels, in such a way as to shed light on the mystery of Christ as principle of our salvation. By regularly associating a text of the Old Testament with the text of the Gospel, the cycle often suggests a scriptural interpretation moving in the direction of typology. But, of course, such is not the only kind of interpretation possible.

The homily, which seeks to actualize more explicitly the Word of God, is an integral part of the liturgy. We will speak of it later, when we treat of the pastoral ministry.

The lectionary, issued at the direction of the Council (*Sacrosanctum Concilium*, 35), is meant to allow for a reading of Sacred Scripture that is "more abundant, more varied and more suitable". In its present state, it only partially fulfills this goal. Nevertheless, even as it stands, it has had positive ecumenical results. In certain countries it also has served to indicate the lack of familiarity with Scripture on the part of many Catholics.

The liturgy of the Word is a crucial element in the celebration of each of the Sacraments of the Church; it does not consist simply in a series of readings one after the other; it ought to involve as well periods of silence and of prayer. This liturgy, in particular the Liturgy of the Hours, makes

---

The reading of Scripture in a liturgical setting dates from the early Church and was partly inherited by Christians from Jewish practice in synagogue-service[211]. In that setting most present-day Christians listen to the Word of God, especially in its Sunday form. The Commission speaks of it as a sacramental liturgy, because the Eucharist or other Sacraments are part of it. Yet, as it has been revised and when it is properly understood, it is all a liturgy both of the Word and of the Sacrament. For

---

[211] The Commission makes no reference to the debate about the date of the emergence of the synagogue in Judaism. No little part of the debate centers on the meaning of *synagōgē*, whether it designates a "congregation" of Jews or a "synagogue", i.e. a building distinct from others. According to many scholars, the latter appears in Palestine only in the third century A.D. See H. C. Kee, "The Transformation of the Synagogue after 70 C.E.: Its Import for Early Christianity", *NTS* 36 (1990) 1-24; R. E. Oster, Jr., "Supposed Anachronism in Luke-Acts' Use of *Synagōgē*: A Rejoinder to H. C. Kee", *NTS* 39 (1993) 178-208; H. C. Kee, "The Changing Meaning of Synagogue: A Response to Richard Oster", *NTS* 40 (1994) 281-83. Cf. J. Gutman (ed.), *The Synagogue: Studies in Origins, Archaeology and Architecture* (New York: Ktav, 1975); L. I. Levine (ed.), *The Synagogue in Late Antiquity* (Philadelphia, PA: American Schools of Oriental Research, 1987).

selections from the book of Psalms to help the Christian community pray. Hymns and prayers are all filled with the language of the Bible and the symbolism it contains. How necessary it is, therefore, that participation in the liturgy be prepared for and accompanied by the practice of reading Scripture.

If in the readings "God addresses the word to His people" (*Roman Missal*, n. 33), the liturgy of the Word requires that great care be taken both in the proclamation of the readings and in their interpretation. It is therefore desirable that the formation of those who are to preside at the assembly and of those who serve with them take full account of what is required for a liturgy of the Word of God that is fully renewed. Thus, through a combined effort, the Church will carry on the mission entrusted to it, "to take the bread of life from the table both of the Word of God and of the Body of Christ and offer it to the faithful" (*Dei Verbum*, 21).

## 2. Lectio Divina

*Lectio Divina* is a reading, on an individual or communal level, of a more or less lengthy passage of Scripture, received as the Word of God

---

in such a setting, above all, the Word of God is proclaimed, and the written Word becomes a living Word, "the word of faith that we preach" (Rom 10:8). Then too it is that Christ is present in his word to the Christian community, since "it is he himself who speaks when the holy Scriptures are read in the church" (*Sacrosanctum Concilium* §7). Recent liturgical reform has introduced the cycle of triennial readings, which relate passages of the Old Testament to New Testament readings and enable the former to bring their own message to Christians of today and to be interpreted christologically. Moreover, the purpose of the homily as an integral part of the liturgy is precisely to actualize the sacred Word just read and enable the assembled congregation to meditate upon it and build its prayers on it. For this reason the homily has to be a proper interpretation of God's message in the Word just proclaimed[212].

## 2. Lectio Divina

By this term is meant the meditative reading of a more or less lengthy passage of Scripture precisely as the Word of God, as one listens to the

---

[212] See R. P. Waznak, "The Catechism and the Sunday Homily", *America* 171/12 (22 October 1994) 18-21.

and leading, at the prompting of the Spirit, to meditation, prayer and contemplation.

Concern for regular, even daily reading of Scripture reflects early Church custom. As a group practice, it is attested in the 3rd century, at the time of Origen; he used to give homilies based on a text of Scripture read continuously throughout a week. At that time there were daily gatherings devoted to the reading and explanation of Scripture. But the practice did not always meet with great success among Christians (Origen, *Hom. Gen.*, X.1) and was eventually abandoned.

*Lectio Divina*, especially on the part of the individual, is attested in the monastic life in its golden age. In modern times, an Instruction of the Biblical Commission, approved by Pope Pius XII, recommended this *lectio* to all clerics, secular and religious (*De Scriptura Sacra*, 1950: *EB*, 592). Insistence on *Lectio Divina* in both its forms, individual and communal, has therefore become a reality once more. The end in view is to create and nourish "an efficacious and constant love" of Sacred Scripture, source of the interior life and of apostolic fruitfulness (*EB*, 591 and 567), also to promote a better understanding of the liturgy and to assure the Bible a more important place in theological studies and in prayer.

The Conciliar Constitution *Dei Verbum* (25) is equally insistent on an assiduous reading of Scripture for priests and religious. Moreover — and this is something new — it also invites "all the faithful of Christ" to acquire "through frequent reading of the divine Scripture 'the surpassing knowledge of Christ Jesus' (*Phil* 3:8)". Different methods are proposed. Alongside private reading, there is the suggestion of reading in a group. The Conciliar text stresses that prayer should accompany the reading of Scripture, for prayer is the response to the Word of God encountered in Scripture under the inspiration of the Spirit. Many initiatives for communal

--------

prompting of the Spirit that the text itself will suggest for prayer and contemplation. This use of Scripture is traced to the early Church, especially to the time of Origen, whose homilies were based on a text of Scripture read continuously throughout a week[213]. In time, that mode of reading Scripture became a regular practice in monastic life and was in recent times recommended to all the clergy[214]. The Second Vatican Council extended the invitation to such prayerful reading to "all the

[213] See Origen, *Hom. in Genesim* 10.1; GCS 29.93; SC 7bis. 256; FC 71. 157-58.

[214] See the Biblical Commission, "De Scriptura sacra recte docenda", *AAS* 42 (1950) 495-505 (*EB* §582-610, esp. §592; *RSS* §582-610, esp. §592).

reading have been launched among Christians, and one can only encourage this desire to derive from Scripture a better knowledge of God and of his plan of salvation in Jesus Christ.

### 3. In Pastoral Ministry

The frequent recourse to the Bible in pastoral ministry, as recommended by *Dei Verbum* (24), takes on various forms depending on the kind of interpretation that is useful to pastors and helpful for the understanding of the faithful. Three principal situations can be distinguished: catechesis, preaching and the biblical apostolate. Many factors are involved, relating to the general level of Christian life.

The explanation of the Word of God in *catechesis* (*Sacros. Conc.*, 35; *Gen. Catech. Direct.*, 1971, 16) has Sacred Scripture as first source. Explained in the context of the Tradition, Scripture provides the starting-point, foundation and norm of catechetical teaching. One of the goals of catechesis should be to initiate a person in a correct understanding and fruitful reading of the Bible. This will bring about the discovery of the divine truth it contains and evoke as generous a response as is possible to the message God addresses through his word to whole human race.

Catechesis should proceed from the historical context of divine revelation so as to present persons and events of the Old and New Testaments in the light of God's overall plan.

To move from the biblical text to its salvific meaning for the present time various hermeneutic procedures are employed. These will give rise to different kinds of commentary. The effectiveness of the catechesis depends on the value of the hermeneutic employed. There is the danger of resting content with a superficial commentary, one which remains simply a chronological presentation of the sequence of persons and events in the Bible.

---

Christian faithful[215]", and the Commission now recommends the practice of such prayerful reading of Scripture both in private and in groups.

### 3. In Pastoral Ministry

Three forms of such ministry are recommended to pastors: (a) Catechesis, one of the aims of which should be to initiate people to a

---

[215] See *Dei Verbum* §25 (*The Documents of Vatican II*, 127).

Clearly, catechesis can avail itself of only a small part of the full range of biblical texts. Generally speaking, it will make particular use of stories, both those of the New Testament and those of the Old. It will single out the Decalogue. It should also see that it makes use of the prophetic oracles, the wisdom teaching and the great discourses in the Gospels, such as the Sermon on the Mount.

The presentation of the Gospels should be done in such a way as to elicit an encounter with Christ, who provides the key to the whole biblical revelation and communicates the call of God that summons each one to respond. The word of the prophets and that of the "ministers of the Word" (*Luke* 1:2) ought to appear as something addressed to Christians now.

Analogous remarks apply to the ministry of *preaching*, which should draw from the ancient texts spiritual sustenance adapted to the present needs of the Christian community.

Today, this ministry is exercised especially at the close of the first part of the Eucharistic celebration, through the *homily* which follows the proclamation of the Word of God.

The explanation of the biblical texts given in the course of the homily cannot enter into great detail. It is, accordingly, fitting to explain the central contribution of texts, that which is most enlightening for faith and most stimulating for the progress of the Christian life, both on the community and individual level. Presenting this central contribution means striving to achieve its actualization and inculturation, in accordance with what has been said above. Good hermeneutical principles are necessary to attain this end. Want of preparation in this area leads to the temptation to avoid plumbing the depths of the biblical readings and to being content simply to moralize or to speak of contemporary issues in a way that fails to shed upon them the light of God's Word.

In some countries exegetes have helped produce publications designed to assist pastors in their responsibility to interpret correctly the biblical texts of the liturgy and make them properly meaningful for today. It is desirable that such efforts be repeated on a wider scale.

Preachers should certainly avoid insisting in a one-sided way on the obligations incumbent upon believers. The biblical message must preserve its principal characteristic of being the good news of salvation freely of-

---

correct understanding and fruitful reading of the Bible so that they will respond generously to its teaching and to God's message addressed to them in it (hermeneutical directives are given to achieve such an aim). (b)

fered by God. Preaching will perform a task more useful and more con-
formed to the Bible if it helps the faithful above all to "know the gift of
God" (*John* 4:10) as it has been revealed in Scripture; they will then understand in a positive light the obligations that flow from it.

The *biblical apostolate* has as its objective to make known the Bible as
the Word of God and source of life. First of all, it promotes the translation
of the Bible into every kind of language and seeks to spread these translations as widely as possible. It creates and supports numerous initiatives:
the formation of groups devoted to the study of the Bible, conferences on
the Bible, biblical weeks, the publication of journals and books, etc.

An important contribution is made by church associations and movements which place a high premium upon the reading of the Bible within
the perspective of faith and Christian action. Many "basic Christian communities" focus their gatherings upon the Bible and set themselves a
threefold objective: to know the Bible, to create community and to serve
the people. Here also exegetes can render useful assistance in avoiding
actualizations of the biblical message that are not well grounded in the
text. But there is reason to rejoice in seeing the Bible in the hands of
people of lowly condition and of the poor; they can bring to its interpretation and to its actualization a light more penetrating, from the spiritual
and existential point of view, than that which comes from a learning that
relies upon its own resources alone (cf. *Matt* 11:25).

The ever increasing importance of the instruments of mass communication ("mass-media") — the press, radio, television — requires that proclamation of the Word of God and knowledge of the Bible be propagated
by these means. Their very distinctive feature and, on the other hand,
their capacity to influence a vast public require a particular training in
their use. This will help to avoid paltry improvisations, along with striking
effects that are actually in poor taste.

Whatever be the context — catechetics, preaching or the biblical apos-

---

Preaching, which should draw from ancient biblical texts the sustenance
needed by Christians today, especially in the homily in the course of the
liturgy. Since the homily cannot go into great exegetical detail, it has to
sum up the central meaning of the biblical texts read in order to stimulate
the proper response of the congregation to the written Word of God. But
proper hermeneutics and exegetical study are required in the one who
prepares the homily for the liturgy. (c) Biblical apostolate, which should
seek to translate the Bible into every language, fashion groups for the

tolate — the text of the Bible should always be presented with the respect it deserves.

## 4. *In Ecumenism*

If the ecumenical movement as a distinct and organized phenomenon is relatively recent, the idea of the unity of God's people, which this movement seeks to restore, is profoundly based in Scripture. Such an objective was the constant concern of the Lord (*John* 10:16; 17:11, 20-23). It looks to the union of Christians in faith, hope and love (*Eph* 4:2-5), in mutual respect (*Phil* 2:1-5) and solidarity (*1 Cor* 12:14-27; *Rom* 12:4-5), but also and above all an organic union in Christ, after the manner of Vine and branches (*John* 15:4-5), Head and members (*Eph* 1:22-23; 4:12-16). This union should be perfect, in the likeness of the union of the Father and the Son (*John* 17:11, 22). Scripture provides its theological foundation (*Eph* 4:4-6; *Gal* 3:27-28), the first apostolic community its concrete, living model (*Acts* 2:44; 4:32).

Most of the issues which ecumenical dialogue has to confront are related in some way to the interpretation of biblical texts. Some of the issues are theological: eschatology, the structure of the Church, primacy and collegiality, marriage and divorce, the admission of women to the ministerial priesthood, and so forth. Others are of a canonical and juridical nature; they concern the administration of the universal Church and of local

---

study of it, and foster that study by conferences, publications, books, basic Christian communities, and the use of mass-media.

## 4. *In Ecumenism*

The unity of the Christian Church, the goal of the ecumenical movement, is profoundly affected by the Bible and the study and interpretation of it. Any number of New Testament passages support that goal[216]. Many issues, with which the ecumenical movement has to deal, are related to the Bible and its interpretation, for they have grown out of it or out of the Tradition related to it: Church structure and organization, papal primacy and the Petrine office, validity of ministerial orders,

---

[216] The Commission refers to John 10:16 ("one flock, one shepherd"); 17:11 (Christ's prayer "that they may be one"); 17:22 ("that they may be one, as we are one"); 1 Cor 12:14-27 (the solidarity of Christians, "many, yet one body" [cf. Rom 12:4-5]); Phil 2:1-5; John 15:4-5; Eph 1:22-23; 4:4-6, 12-16.

Churches. There are others, finally, that are strictly biblical: the list of the canonical books, certain hermeneutical questions, etc.

Although it cannot claim to resolve all these issues by itself, biblical exegesis is called upon to make an important contribution in the ecumenical area. A remarkable degree of progress has already been achieved. Through the adoption of the same methods and analogous hermeneutical points of view, exegetes of various Christian confessions have arrived at a remarkable level of agreement in the interpretation of Scripture, as is shown by the text and notes of a number of ecumenical translations of the Bible, as well as by other publications.

Indeed, it is clear that on some points differences in the interpretation of Scripture are often stimulating and can be shown to be complementary and enriching. Such is the case when these differences express values belonging to the particular tradition of various Christian communities and so convey a sense of the manifold aspects of the Mystery of Christ.

Since the Bible is the common basis of the rule of faith, the ecumenical imperative urgently summons all Christians to a rereading of the inspired text, in docility to the Holy Spirit, in charity, sincerity and humil-

---

difference of canons of Scripture, universal Church and its relation to local Churches.

Biblical exegesis cannot solve such problematic issues on its own, but it can contribute greatly to their solution. Especially since the Catholic Church has sanctioned the historical-critical method, in the encyclical of Pius XII of 1943, its interpretation of the Bible has become very closely akin to that of the mainline Protestant Churches. This has meant a remarkable agreement in the way Scripture is now interpreted in the great body of Christian Churches. It has thus enabled Catholics and Protestants to transcend many of the divisive issues inherited from the sixteenth century[217].

---

[217] See J. Reumann and J. A. Fitzmyer, "Scripture as Norm for Our Common Faith", *JES* 30 (1993-94) 81-107. Cf. R. E. Brown et al. (eds.), *Peter in the New Testament: A Collaborative Assessment by Protestant and Roman Catholic Scholars* (Minneapolis, MN: Augsburg; New York: Paulist, 1973); *Mary in the New Testament: A Collaborative Assessment by Protestant and Roman Catholic Scholars* (New York: Paulist; Philadelphia, PA: Fortress, 1978).

Cf. E. Fleeseman-van Leer (ed.), *The Bible: Its Authority and Interpretation in the Ecumenical Movement* (Geneva: World Council of Churches, 1980); R. C. Rowe, *Bible Study in the World Council of Churches* (Geneva: World Council of Churches, 1969); W. A. Visser 't Hooft, "The Bible and the Ecumenical Movement", *United Bible Societies Bulletin* 56 (1963) 165-71.

ity; it calls upon all to meditate on these texts and to live them in such a way as to achieve conversion of heart and sanctity of life. These two qualities, when united with prayer for the unity of Christians, constitute the soul of the entire ecumenical movement (cf. *Unitatis Redintegratio*, 8). To achieve this goal, it is necessary to make the acquiring of a Bible something within the reach of as many Christians as possible, to encourage ecumenical translations — since having a common text greatly assists reading and understanding together — and also ecumenical prayer groups, in order to contribute, by an authentic and living witness, to the achievement of unity within diversity (cf. *Rom* 12:4-5).

---

In this regard, the ecumenical translations of the Bible in various languages have to be noted. They are a testimony to the common mode of translating and interpreting the Bible that is shared by both Catholics and Protestants[218].

> Since the Bible is the common basis of the rule of faith, the ecumenical imperative urgently summons all Christians to a rereading of the inspired text, in docility to the Holy Spirit, in charity, sincerity and humility; it calls upon all to meditate on these texts and to live them in such a way as to achieve conversion of heart and sanctity of life. These two qualities, when united with prayer for the unity of Christians, constitute the soul of the entire ecumenical movement.

---

[218] See J. Potin (ed.), *Traduction oecuménique de la Bible: Edition intégrale* (2 vols.; Paris: Cerf/Les Bergers et les Mages, 1975; repr., 1985); O. Knoch et al. (eds.), *Die Bibel: Einheitsübersetzung der Heiligen Schrift, Altes und Neues Testament* (Stuttgart: Katholische Bibelanstalt/Deutsche Bibelstiftung, 1979-80). These two translations have been highly praised, but the following has been less successful: *La Bibbia concordata: Tradotta dai testi originali, con introduzione e note* (ed. S. Cipriani et al.; Milan: Mondadori, 1968). Cf. J. A. Fitzmyer, *Scripture, the Soul of Theology* (New York/Mahwah, NJ: Paulist, 1994) 99-102.

## CONCLUSION

From what has been said in the course of this long account — admittedly far too brief on a number of points — the first conclusion that emerges is that biblical exegesis fulfills, in the Church and in the world, an *indispensable task*. To attempt to by-pass it when seeking to understand the Bible would be to create an illusion and display lack of respect for the inspired Scripture.

When fundamentalists relegate exegetes to the role of translators only (failing to grasp that translating the Bible is already a work of exegesis) and refuse to follow them further in their studies, these same fundamentalists do not realize that, for all their very laudable concern for total fidelity to the Word of God, they proceed in fact along ways which will lead them far away from the true meaning of the biblical texts, as well as from full acceptance of the consequences of the Incarnation. The eternal Word became incarnate at a precise period of history, within a clearly defined cultural and social environment. Anyone who desires to understand the Word of God should humbly seek it out there where it has made itself visible and accept to this end the necessary help of human knowledge. Addressing men and women, from the beginnings of the Old Testament onward, God made use of all the possibilities of human language, while at the same time accepting that His word be subject to the constraints caused by the limitations of this language. Proper respect for inspired Scripture requires undertaking all the labors necessary to gain a

---

## CONCLUSION

The Commission, in its conclusion to this long document, mentions three important aspects of the interpretation of the Bible in the Church that have to be kept in mind.

(1) Biblical exegesis performs in the Church an *indispensable task*, which cannot be overlooked. It is more than mere translation, and a

thorough grasp of its meaning. Certainly, it is not possible that each Christian personally pursue all the kinds of research which make for a better understanding of the biblical text. This task is entrusted to exegetes, who have the responsibility in this matter to see that all profit from their labor.

A second conclusion is that the very nature of biblical texts means that interpreting them will require continued use of the *historical-critical method*, at least in its principal procedures. The Bible, in effect, does not present itself as a direct revelation of timeless truths but as the written testimony to a series of interventions in which God reveals himself in human history. In a way that differs from tenets of other religions, the message of the Bible is solidly grounded in history. It follows that the biblical writings cannot be correctly understood without an examination of the historical circumstances that shaped them. "Diachronic" research will always be indispensable for exegesis. Whatever be their own interest and value, "synchronic" approaches cannot replace it. To function in a way that will be fruitful, synchronic approaches should accept the conclusions of the diachronic, at least according to their main lines.

But, granted this basic principle, the synchronic approaches (the rhetorical, narrative, semiotic and others) are capable, to some extent at least, of bringing about a renewal of exegesis and making a very useful contribution. The historical-critical method, in fact, cannot lay claim to enjoying a monopoly in this area. It must be conscious of *its limits*, as well as of the dangers to which it is exposed. Recent developments in philosophical hermeneutics and, on the other hand, the observations which we have been able to make concerning interpretation within the biblical Tradition and the Tradition of the Church have shed light upon many aspects of the problem of interpretation that the historical-critical method has tended to ignore. Concerned above all to establish the meaning of texts by situating them in their original historical context, this method has at times shown itself insufficiently attentive to the dynamic aspect of meaning and to the possibility that meaning can continue to develop. When historical-critical exegesis does not go as far as to take into account the final result of the editorial process but remains absorbed solely in the

---

fundamentalist disregard of it fails to comprehend the Bible's character as at once human and divine, indeed, a reflection of the Incarnation itself. Hence proper respect for the role of the Bible in the Church must embrace the labor and effort needed to grasp and comprehend its meaning in all its variety — a task which is entrusted in a special way to exegetes.

issues of sources and stratification on texts, it fails to bring the exegetical task to completion.

Through fidelity to the great Tradition, of which the Bible itself is a witness, Catholic exegesis should avoid as much as possible this kind of professional bias and maintain its identity as a *theological discipline*, the principal aim of which is the deepening of faith. This does not mean a lesser involvement in scholarly research of the most rigorous kind, nor should it provide excuse for abuse of methodology out of apologetic concern. Each sector of research (textual criticism, linguistic study, literary analysis, etc.) has its own proper rules, which it ought follow with full autonomy. But no one of these specializations is an end in itself. In the organization of the exegetical task as a whole, the orientation towards the principal goal should remain paramount and thereby serve to obviate any waste of energy. Catholic exegesis does not have the right to become lost, like a stream of water, in the sands of a hypercritical analysis. Its task is to fulfil, in the Church and in the world, a vital function, that of contributing to an ever more authentic transmission of the content of the inspired Scriptures.

The work of Catholic exegesis already tends towards this end, hand in hand with the renewal of other theological disciplines and with the pastoral task of actualizing and inculturating of the Word of God. In examining the present state of the question and expressing some reflections on the

---

(2) The nature of the biblical text, as the written testimony to a series of interventions in which God has revealed himself in history, requires the continued use of the *historical-critical method*. Since the biblical message is grounded in history, "diachronic" research is indispensable for the correct analysis of that message and the circumstances that shaped it, for which no "synchronic" approach can be a substitute. Yet various synchronic approaches, literary, rhetorical, narrative, etc., can refine that method and enable it to function better. Hence the historical-critical method cannot be monopolistic, but has to recognize its own limits and the shortcomings to which it is exposed, especially its insufficient attention to the dynamic aspect of the Bible.

(3) The Catholic interpretation of the Bible is a *theological discipline*, well defined in its own methodology and distinct from other modes of theological reflection, but it is not an end in itself. Its task is to contribute to the authentic and vital transmission of God's Word to his people and to a deepening of genuine Christian faith. Hence Catholic exegesis must

matter, the present essay hopes to have made some contribution towards the gaining, on the part of all, of a clearer awareness of the role of the Catholic exegete.

Rome, April 15, 1993.

---

work hand in hand with systematic theology in its reflection on God's revelation in all its aspects and with the pastoral task of actualizing and inculturating the Word of God that finds expression in the Bible.

# SELECT BIBLIOGRAPHY

Anon., "Die Auslegung der Bibel in der Kirche", *Bibel und Kirche* 49 (1994) 58-60.

Anon., "The Catholic Church & Bible Interpretation", *BRev* 10/4 (1994) 32-35.

Byrne, B., "A New Vatican Document on the Bible", *Australian Catholic Record* 71 (1994) 325-29.

Dulles, A., "The Interpretation of the Bible in the Church: A Theological Appraisal", *Kirche sein: Nachkonziliare Theologie im Dienst der Kirchenreform: Für Josef Pottmeyer* (ed. W. Geerlings and M. Seckler; Freiburg im B.: Herder, 1994) 29-37.

Fitzmyer, J. A., "The Interpretation of the Bible in the Church", *America* 169/17 (27 November 1993) 12-15.

Focant, C., "L'Interprétation de la Bible dans l'Eglise", *RTL* 25 (1994) 348-54.

Grelot, P., *Combats pour la Bible en Eglise: Une brasée de souvenirs* (Paris: Cerf, 1994).

Haag, H., "Bilanz eines Jahrhunderts: Ein Lehrschreiben der Päpstlichen Bibelkommission", *Orientierung* 58/11 (Juni 1994) 129-32.

Hebblethwaite, P., "New Scripture Document 'Thinking in Centuries'", *National Catholic Reporter* 30/21 (25 March 1994) 13-14.

Kremer, J., "Die Interpretation der Bibel in der Kirche: Marginalien zum neuesten Dokument der Päpstlichen Bibelkommission", *Stimmen der Zeit* 212/3 (March 1994) 151-66.

Vanhoye, A., "Il nuovo documento della Commissione Biblica", *Osservatore Romano* (27 November 1993) 7.

# INDEXES

## 1. Biblical

*Genesis*

| | |
|---|---|
| 1 | 6 |
| 1:27-28 | 177 |
| 1:27 | 165-66 |
| 1:28 | 135 |
| 2:24 | 76 |
| 4:10 | 129 |
| 12:3 | 177 |
| 15:7, 18 | 135 |
| 17:5 | 177 |
| 18:18 | 177 |

*Exodus*

| | |
|---|---|
| 12:24-27 | 58-59 |
| 14–15 | 123 |
| 15:1-18 | 123 |
| 15:17 | 135 |
| 16 | 174 |
| 16:4, 14-15 | 173 |
| 19:5-6 | 152 |
| 20:1-17 | 165 |
| 20:22–23:33 | 49 |

*Leviticus*

| | |
|---|---|
| 17–26 | 49-50 |
| 26:3-33 | 135 |

*Numbers*

| | |
|---|---|
| 21:9 | 129 |

*Deuteronomy*

| | |
|---|---|
| 5:6-21 | 165 |
| 6:4-6 | 152 |
| 6:20-25 | 58-59 |
| 12–26 | 49-50 |
| 26:5-11 | 58-59 |
| 30:11, 14 | 9 |

*Judges*

| | |
|---|---|
| 5:19-21 | 56 |

*2 Samuel*

| | |
|---|---|
| 7:12-16 | 135 |
| 7:12-13 | 126 |
| 23:5 | 135 |

*1 Kings*

| | |
|---|---|
| 2:4 | 135 |
| 2:27 | 126 |
| 3:6 | 135 |

*1 Chronicles*

| | |
|---|---|
| 17:11-14 | 126, 135, 137 |

*2 Chronicles*

| | |
|---|---|
| 25:20-23 | 135 |
| 36:21 | 126 |

*Nehemiah*

| | |
|---|---|
| 8:8-12 | 177 |

*1-2 Maccabees*    174-75

*Job*

| | |
|---|---|
| 10:1-7 | 135 |
| 13:3-28 | 135 |
| 23–24 | 135 |
| 38–42 | 135 |

*Psalms*

| | |
|---|---|
| 1:1-6 | 135 |
| 2 | 123 |
| 2:7-8 | 127, 135 |
| 2:7 | 137 |
| 2:8 | 138 |
| 8:6-9 | 135 |
| 37 | 135 |
| 44 | 135 |
| 45:7 | 137 |
| 78:3-4 | 58-59 |
| 78:24 | 173 |
| 89:20-38 | 135 |
| 95:8-11 | 135 |
| 110:1 | 135, 137 |
| 110:4 | 127, 135, 137-38 |
| 112:1-10 | 135 |
| 132:7-8 | 135 |
| 150 | 56 |
| 151 | 71 |

*Wisdom of Solomon*

| | |
|---|---|
| 3–5 | 135 |
| 9:2-3 | 135 |
| 10:2 | 135 |
| 11–19 | 124 |
| 16:20-29 | 174 |
| 16:20 | 173 |

*Sirach (Ecclesiasticus)*

| | |
|---|---|
| 24:12 | 82 |

*Isaiah*

| | |
|---|---|
| 2:4 | 95 |
| 7:13-14 | 135 |
| 7:14 | 130-31 |
| 40:8 | 171 |
| 41:17-20 | 123 |
| 42:10-13 | 123 |
| 43:16-17 | 123 |
| 53 | 135 |
| 53:7-8 | 16 |
| 57:1-4 | 82 |
| 66:18-21 | 171 |

*Jeremiah*

| | |
|---|---|
| 3:1–4:4 | 56 |
| 22:23 | 73 |
| 23:5-6 | 135 |
| 25:11-12 | 16, 135 |
| 29:10 | 16, 135 |
| 30:9 | 135 |
| 31:31-34 | 73 |

*Ezekiel*

| | |
|---|---|
| 34:24 | 135 |
| 37:24-25 | 135 |

*Daniel*

| | |
|---|---|
| 2:35, 44 | 135 |
| 7:14 | 135 |
| 9:2 | 16, 135 |
| 9:24-27 | 135 |

*Hosea*

| | |
|---|---|
| 3:5 | 135 |

*Joel*

| | |
|---|---|
| 4:10 | 95 |

*Amos*

| | |
|---|---|
| 9:11 | 135 |

## Jonah

| | |
|---|---|
| 2:1 | 129 |
| 2:3-10 | 179 |

## Micah

| | |
|---|---|
| 4:3 | 95 |

## Matthew

| | |
|---|---|
| 1:22 | 126 |
| 1:23 | 130-31 |
| 2:5, 15, 17, 25 | 126 |
| 5:3-11 | 77 |
| 5:3 | 153 |
| 5:17-19 | 139 |
| 5:17 | 137 |
| 5:20, 21-48 | 136 |
| 9:13 | 137 |
| 10:2-12, 17-27 | 136 |
| 11:5 | 153 |
| 11:11-13 | 138 |
| 11:25 | 152, 185 |
| 12:40 | 129 |
| 12:41-42 | 138 |
| 16:16 | 167 |
| 19:16-26 | 81 |
| 23:13 | 22 |
| 27:25 | 82 |
| 28:18-20 | 177 |
| 28:18 | 135 |
| 28:19-20 | 171 |

## Mark

| | |
|---|---|
| 2:15-17, 27-28 | 137 |
| 7:1-23 | 137 |
| 10:5-9 | 137 |
| 10:14 | 152 |
| 11:10 | 135 |
| 14:62 | 137 |
| 15:26 | 137 |
| 15:34 | 139 |
| 15:38 | 121 |

## Luke

| | |
|---|---|
| 1:2 | 144, 184 |
| 1:32-34 | 137 |
| 1:46-55, 68-79 | 179 |
| 2:19 | 10 |
| 4:18 | 153 |
| 6:20-22 | 77 |
| 6:20 | 153 |
| 7:22 | 153 |
| 10:21 | 152 |
| 11:52 | 22 |
| 12:35 | 120 |
| 24:25-27 | 138 |
| 24:32 | 152 |
| 24:44-45 | 138 |
| 24:45 | 10 |

## John

| | |
|---|---|
| 1:1 | 137 |
| 1:36 | 120 |
| 2:22 | 142 |
| 3:3, 4, 7 | 122 |
| 3:14 | 129 |
| 4:10-14 | 122 |
| 4:10 | 185 |
| 4:12-14 | 138 |
| 5:37 | 138 |
| 6 | 174 |
| 6:32 | 138 |
| 6:41 | 173 |
| 6:45 | 152 |
| 6:58 | 173 |
| 7:8 | 122 |
| 8:29 | 139 |
| 10:16 | 186 |
| 10:35 | 143 |
| 11:50-52 | 122 |
| 13–17 | 56 |
| 14:26 | 142 |
| 15:4-5 | 186 |
| 15:26 | 138 |
| 16:7 | 138 |
| 16:12-13 | 142 |
| 16:32 | 139 |
| 17:11, 20-23 | 186 |

| | |
|---|---|
| 19:27 | 10 |
| 20:28 | 137 |

*Acts of the Apostles*

| | |
|---|---|
| 1:1 | 144 |
| 2:36 | 137 |
| 2:44 | 186 |
| 4:32 | 186 |
| 8:30-35 | 16 |
| 13:33 | 123 |

*Romans*

| | |
|---|---|
| 1:1-2 | 138 |
| 1:2 | 143 |
| 1:3-4 | 137 |
| 1:3 | 126 |
| 3:20-21 | 138 |
| 3:28 | 139 |
| 4:16-17 | 177 |
| 5:12-21 | 131 |
| 5:14 | 129 |
| 6:9 | 126 |
| 6:14 | 138-39 |
| 10:8 | 181 |
| 11:28-29 | 176 |
| 12:4-5 | 186, 188 |
| 12:6-7 | 153 |
| 13:1, 3, 6 | 99 |

*1 Corinthians*

| | |
|---|---|
| 1:14-17 | 152 |
| 1:31 | 73 |
| 10:1-5 | 76 |
| 10:11 | 147, 149 |
| 11:23-25 | 59 |
| 12:14-27 | 186 |
| 12:18, 24 | 6 |
| 12:28-30 | 153 |
| 12:28 | 6 |
| 15:3-5, 11 | 136 |

*2 Corinthians*

| | |
|---|---|
| 1:13 | 121 |

| | |
|---|---|
| 3:7–4:6 | 76 |
| 3:14 | 70, 143 |

*Galatians*

| | |
|---|---|
| 2:15–5:1 | 138 |
| 3:27-28 | 186 |
| 3:28 | 99 |
| 4:21-31 | 76 |

*Ephesians*

| | |
|---|---|
| 1:3-10 | 179 |
| 1:22-23 | 186 |
| 2:8-9 | 139 |
| 3:4 | 156 |
| 3:6 | 177 |
| 4:2-6 | 186 |
| 4:11-16 | 153 |
| 4:12-16 | 186 |
| 5:25, 29 | 80 |
| 5:32 | 76 |

*Philippians*

| | |
|---|---|
| 2:1-5 | 186 |
| 2:6-11 | 179 |
| 2:10-11 | 137 |
| 3:8 | 182 |

*Colossians*

| | |
|---|---|
| 3:3 | 125 |

*1 Thessalonians*

| | |
|---|---|
| 2:13 | 151 |

*1 Timothy*

| | |
|---|---|
| 6:14 | 72 |

*2 Timothy*

| | |
|---|---|
| 3:16 | 143 |

*Titus*

|  |  |
|---|---|
| 2:13 | 72 |

*Hebrews*

|  |  |
|---|---|
| 1:8, 10-12 | 137 |
| 3:7–4:11 | 135 |
| 5:6-10 | 137-38 |
| 6:12, 18, 20 | 135 |
| 7:1-11 | 76 |
| 7:11-19 | 138 |
| 7:23-24 | 137-38 |
| 8:8-12 | 73 |
| 9:15 | 135 |
| 10:8-9 | 138 |
| 11:4 | 129 |
| 12:24 | 129 |

*James*

|  |  |
|---|---|
| 2:24 | 139 |

*1 Peter*

|  |  |
|---|---|
| 1:12 | 144 |
| 3:20-21 | 129 |

*2 Peter*

|  |  |
|---|---|
| 1:20-21 | 143 |
| 1:20 | 16 |
| 3:16 | 16, 143 |

*1 John*

|  |  |
|---|---|
| 1:1-3 | 144 |
| 4:8, 16 | 7 |

*Jude*

|  |  |
|---|---|
| 3 | 151 |

*Revelation*

|  |  |
|---|---|
| .5:9-10 | 179 |
| 11:16-18 | 179 |

## 2. Modern Authors

Anonymous, 47, 193
Aalders, J. G., 31
Abbott, W. M., 22
Ahern, B., 18
Alan, E. H., 103
Aland, B., 39
Aland, K., 39
Aletti, J.-N., 64
Alexander, P. S., 75
Allen L. H., 105
Allen, T. W., 27
Allenbach, J., 40
Alonso Díaz, J., 158
Alonso Schökel, L., 52, 56
Altaner, B., 145
Alter, R., 52, 59
Andrews, C., 34
Arnold, P. M., 107
Assmann, J., 34
Astell, A. W., 80
Astruc J., 28, 30
Auerbach, E., 52
Auvray, P., 129

Baird, W., 23
Barbour, R. S., 42
Barnes, W. E., 41
Barr, J., 68, 106
Barth, G., 33
Barth, K., 112
Barthes, R., 64
Barton, J., 41-42, 68
Bauckham, R., 84
Bauer, B., 45
Baur, F. C., 45
Bea, A., 121
Beardslee, W. A., 42, 53

Benedict XV, Pope, 2, 20, 133
Benedictines of San Girolamo, 39
Berger, K., 42
Bergeron, R., 107
Berlin, A., 59
Bernardino, A. di, 148
Betz, H. D., 55
Biblical Commission, Pontifical, 1, 2,
   5-6, 8, 10, 14-26, 30, 33, 44, 47-50,
   53-54, 57, 60, 62, 66-70, 72-73, 78,
   81-82, 85, 90, 92, 94, 97, 100-101,
   106, 108-9, 111, 114-15, 117-27, 129-
   31, 133, 137-40, 145, 147-55, 158,
   160, 166-67, 170, 172-73, 175-77,
   179-80, 182-83, 186, 189
Bloch, R., 76
Blomqvist, J., 27
Bluhm, H., 29
Boismard, M.-E., 31
Boone, K. C., 103, 105
Bordreuil, P., 35
Bornkamm, G., 33
Bourke, M. M., 47
Bowker, J. W., 75
Brandi, M., 17
Braun, F.-M., 154
Bream, H. N., 74
Brent, J. S., 107
Brockington, L. H., 39
Brooke, A. E., 39
Brooke, G. J., 75
Brooks, C., 51
Brooks, R., 74
Brown, D., 28
Brown, R. E., xiv, 110, 122, 130, 168,
   187
Brown, R. M., 116

Browne, H., 27
Bruce, F. F., 76
Brunner, P., 28
Buchanan, G. W., 45
Bühler, P., 60
Bulhof, I. N., 110
Bultmann, R., 32-33, 42, 46-47, 109-15
Burgard, C., 179
Burton, E. D., 83
Bussmann, C., 94
Butler, H. E., 54
Butler, J. T., 80
Byrne, B., 193

Carlen, M. C. 17-18
Carmody, D. L., 98
Carroll, R. P., 68
Carson, D. A., 124
Case, S. J., 83
Cassidy, R. J., 84
Cassuto, U., 31
Cauthen, K., 83
Cazelles, H., 49
Ceresko, A. R., 94
Champollion, J. F., 34
Charlesworth, J. H., 74-75
Childs, B. S., 47, 68, 70
Cholewiński, A., 50
Cipriani, S., 188
Clarke, D. S., 64
Clements, R. E., 41, 84
Coggins, R. J., 47
Cohenel, D., 19
Cole, S. G., 103
Coleman, J. A., 107
Collins, J. J., 36, 74
Collins, R. F., 19, 28
Commission on Theology and Church
    Relations, 45
Congar, Y. M.-J., 149, 168
Conzelmann, H., 33
Coppens, J., 130
Corner, M., 94
Cotter, A. C., 17
Countryman, L. W., 107
Cousin, J., 54
Cox, D., 89

Crouzel, H., 125
Curtin, T. R., 45
Cypser, C. E., 98

D'Angelo, M. R., 100
Dahl, N. A., 115
Daly, M., 97
Damrosch, D., 59
Danby, H., 78
Daniélou, J., 125, 129, 179
Darrow, C., 105
Davies, M., 56
Dean, W., 83
Delattre, A.-J., 154
Deltizsch, F., 30
Demers, P., 98
Denzinger, H., xiii
Dibelius, M., 32, 46
Dillmann, A., 30
Dilthey, W., 109-10
Dinsmore, C. A., 52
Dix, G., 179
Donahue, J. R., 165
Doubrovsky, S., 51
Dozeman, T. B., 55
Drewermann, E., 89
Dreyfus, F., 47
Duke, J., 110
Dulles, A., 192
Dungan, D. L., 31
Dupont, J., 21

Ebeling, G., 110
Eco, U.; 64
Eichhorn, J. G., 31
Eissfeldt, O., 30-31, 38
Eliot, T. S., 51
Eliott, J. H., 84
Elliger, K., 39
Elliott-Binns, L. E., 50
Empson, W., 51
Epp, E. J., 39
Erbse, H., 27
Esler, P. F., 84
Exum, J. C., 52, 59, 98

Farmer, W. R., 31

Fehrenbacher, G., 89
Ferguson, D. S., 110
Fernández, A., 130
Fewell, D. N., 59
Field, F., 27
Fiore, B., 55
Fishbane, M., 52, 74, 124
Fitzmyer, J. A., xiii, 22, 31, 36, 45, 75-77, 126, 139, 187-88, 193
Flannery, E. H., 82
Fleesman-van Leer, E., 187
Focant, C., 53, 193
Fogarty, G. P., 133
Ford, D. F., 55
Forstman, J., 110
Fossion, A., 64
Foster, B. R., 35
Fox, M. V., 34
Freedman, D. N., xiii
Friedman, R. E., 30
Friedrich, J., 34
Frye, N., 52
Fuchs, E., 110
Funk, R. W., 110, 112
Furniss, N. F., 103

Gabel, J. B., 52
Gadamer, H. G., 109-14
Galindo, F., 103
Galot, J., 168
García Martínez, F., 36
Gardner, H. L., 53
Garfinkel, S., 74
Garrett, S. R., 84
Gatewood, Jr., W. B., 105
Geerlings, W., 193
Gerstner, J. N., 82
Gilbert, M., 17, 154, 158
Gilby, T., 125
Ginger, R., 105
Giroud, J. C., 64
Gnilka, J., 79
Gögler, R., 125
Gooding, D. W., 39
Goppelt, L., 129
Gottcent, J. H., 52
Gottwald, N. K., 84, 94

Graeme Auls, A., 74
Grant, F. C., 42, 83
Grant, P., 53
Grant, R. M., 100
Grayson, A. K., 35
Green, W. S., 76
Greenfield, J. C., 35
Greenlee, J. H., 39
Greenspahn, F. E., 74
Greimas, A. J., 63-64
Grelot, P., 20, 193
Griboment, J., 148
Griesbach, J. J., 29, 31
Grimké, S., 97
Groethuysen, B., 110
Gros Louis, K. R. R., 59
Grotefend, G. F., 34
Gruchy, J. W. de, 82
Güttgemanns, E., 64
Gunkel, H., 31, 34
Gunn, D. M., 59
Gutman, J., 180
Gwilliam, G. H., 40

Haag, H., 193
Habel, N. C., 41
Habermacher, J.-F., 60
Hailperin, H., 29
Hallo, W. H., 35
Hamilton, G. J., 18
Hanks, T. P., 94
Hanson, A. T., 126
Hartdegen, S., 17
Hartleben, H., 34
Haughton, R., 98
Hay, J., 70
Hayes, J. H., 41
Hayter, M., 100
Hebbelthwaite, P., 152, 193
Heidegger, M., 46, 109-12
Held, H. J., 33
Hengel, M., 38
Henn, T. R., 52
Hennelly, A. T., 94
Hincks, E., 34-35
Hinneberg, P., 32
Hirsch, E. D., 120

Hodges, H. A., 110
Holmberg, B., 84
Horgan, M. P., 124
Horsley, R. A., 84
Houlden, J. L., 47
Hupfeld, H., 30
Hynes, W. J., 83

Ihde, D., 111
International Theological Commission, 166-67
Iversen, E., 34

Jacob, B., 31
Jacobs, L., 74
James, R., 46
Jasper, D., 53
Jeanrond, W. G., 23
Jellicoe, S., 39
John Paul II, Pope, 1-10, 18-19, 125
Johnson, A. R., 32
Johnson, Jr., A. M., 64
Judd, R. H., 126

Kalita, T., 29
Kamesar, A., 28
Karakash, C., 89
Keating, K., 107
Kee, H. C., 84, 180
Kegley, C. W., 112
Kelly, J. N. D., 28
Kelsey, G. D., 82
Kennedy, G. A., 55-56
Kenyon, F., 27
Kermode, F., 52, 59
Kimmerle, H., 110
King, L. W., 35
Klatt, W., 32
Kleinhans, A., 21
Klostermann, A., 50
Knierim, R., 41
Knight, D. A., 42
Knoch, O., 188
Koch, D.-A., 41
König, E., 56
Kornfeld, W., 50
Kort, W. A., 59

Kraus, H.-J., 38
Kremer, J., 193
Krentz, E., 38
Kümmel, W. G., 38
Kundsin, K., 42

Lachmann, C., 31
Laffey, A. L., 98
Laghi, P., 17
Lagier, C., 34
Lagrange, M.-J., 154
Lambrecht, J., 55
Lampe, G. W. H., 129
Lane, J. L., 107
Lang, B., 88
Lange, N. R. M. de, 76
Lategan, B. C., 110
Lausberg, H., 54
Le Déaut, R., 75
Lefébure, M., 23
Leo XIII, Pope, 1-2, 5-6, 10, 13, 17-20, 23, 46, 158
Lepsius, R., 34
Lera, J. M., 158
Lessing, G. E., 45
Levenson, J. D., 74, 96
Leverenz, E. W., 45
Levie, J., 18
Levine, L. I., 180
Levine, L. W., 105
Licht, J., 59
Lightfoot, R. H., 33
Lindars, B., 124
Linnemann, E., 45
Loades, A., 52
Lods, A., 30
Lohfink, N., 43, 94
Lohmeyer, E., 33
Long, B. O., 59
Longmann III, T., 52
Lotman, Iu. M., 64
Lubac, H. de, 118, 125
Lukyn Williams, A., 82
Luzzi, G., 20

McConnell, F., 59
McGowen, T., 105

McKim, D. K., 110
McKnight, E. V., 41, 52
McLachlan, D. R., 103
McLain, M., 52
McLean, N., 39
McNamara, V., 165
Macquarrie, J., 111-12
Mahan, B., 98
Maier, G., 45
Maier, J., 52
Maier, W. A., 42
Majercik, R., 55
Malet, A., 112
Malevez, L., 112
Malina, B. J., 88
Marcheselli-Casale, C., 89
Marlé, R., 110, 112
Marrou, H. I., 27
Marrow, S. B., 107
Marti Ballester, J., 80
Martin, G., 116
Marxsen, W., 33
Mathews, S., 83
Meland, B. E. 83
Mercati, G., 38
Metzger, B. M., 29, 39-40, 71, 144
Meynet, R., 58
Michaelis, J. D., 38
Miegge, G., 112
Migne, J., xiv, 40
Miller, A., 21
Milne, P. J., 100
Miranda, J., 96
Möller, W., 31
Mollenkott, V. R., 98
Monléon, J. de, 80
Montanari, F., 27
Moore, S. D., 53
Morales, J. L., 80
Mosala, I. J., 82
Moulton, R. G., 51
Mudge, L. S., 111
Mueller-Vollmer, K., 110
Muilenburg, J., 54, 56
Munhall, L. W., 102
Murphy, R. E., 70-71, 74, 80
Murphy, R. T., 17

Musto, R. G., 94
Myers, J. M. 74
Myres, J. L., 27

Nautin, P., 125
Neirynck, F., 31, 77
Nestle, E., 39
Neuhaus, R. J., 168
Neumeister, C., 54
Neusner, J., 76, 79
Neyrey, J. H., 84
Nineham, D. E., 47
Norden, R. F., 45
Norton, D., 51

O'Doherty, E., 30
Ogden, S. M., 47, 112
Ohly, F., 118
Oliver, W. H., 82
Olst, E. H. van, 179
O'Neill, J. C., 23
Oosthuizen, M. J., 59
Oppert, J., 35
Orr, L., 64
Osiek, C. A., 84
Oster, Jr., R. E., 180

Packer, J. I., 103
Palmer, R. O., 110
Panier, L., 64
Paple, M., 107
Pardee, D., 35
Patte, D., 64
Patterson, P., 46
Paulus, H. E. G., 45
Per Bilde, T. E.-P., 27
Perkins, P., 63
Perrin, N., 42
Peshitta Institute of the University of
    Leiden, 40
Petersen, N. R., 53
Pfeiffer, R., 27
Pius X, Pope, 2
Pius XII, Pope, 1-4, 10, 13, 18-21, 23,
    43, 120, 126, 132-33, 150, 187
Platnauer, M., 55
Poland, L. M., 52

Porten, B., 35
Porton, G. G., 76
Potin, J., 188
Pottmeyer, J., 193
Powell, M. A., 52, 59
Price, J. A., 105
Prickett, S., 52
Pritchard, J. B., xiii, 34-35
Puech, E., 77
Pusey, P. E., 40

Quasten, J., 125, 145

Rahlfs, A., 39, 71
Rahner, K., 145, 169
Ransom, J. C., 51
Rashkow, I. N., 89
Rast, W. E., 42
Ratzinger, J. (Card.), 1, 13-14, 143
Rausch, D. A., 82
Rawlinson, H. C., 34-35
Redlich, E. B., 41
Reimarus, H. S., 45-46
Renan, E., 45
Reumann, J., 187
Rhodes, E. F., 39
Richards, I. A., 51
Richesin, L. D., 98
Ricœur, P., 109-11, 113-14
Riedl, W., 79
Riedlinger, H., 80
Rienstra, M. V., 98
Robbins, V. K., 41
Roberts, B. J., 39
Robertson, D. A., 52
Robertson, D. W., 28
Robinson, R. B., 45
Rogerson, J. W. 23, 88
Rollins, W. G., 89
Rosenblatt, J. P., 59
Rowe, R. C., 187
Rowland, C., 94
Rowley, H. H., 32
Rudolph, W., 39
Ruiz, G., 158
Ruotolo, D., 19
Russell, L. M., 98

Ryken, L., 52-53

Sadowski, F., 149
Sandeen, E. R., 103
Sanders, J. A., 68-70, 144
Sandmel, S., 70
Sands, P. C., 52
Sass, H. M., 110
Saussure, F. de, 63
Scalise, C. J., 69
Schaeffer, F. A., 103
Scherrer, S., 46
Schleiermacher, F. D. E., 109-10
Schleifer, R., 64
Schmid, J., 38
Schmidt, K. L., 32, 46
Schmithals, W., 112
Schneiders, S. M., 110
Schönmetzer, A., xiii
Scholes, R. E., 64
Schrieber, P. L., 94
Schüssler Fiorenza, E., 55, 98, 100
Schultenover, D. G., 20
Schwartz, R. M., 52
Schweitzer, A., 46
Schweizer, E., 38
Scofield, C. I., 105
Seckler, M., 193
Secondin, B., 103
Seeliger, H. R., 89
Segalla, G., 100
Segbroeck, F. van, 77
Sevrin, J.-M., 47
Sheppard, G. T., 68
Shereshevsky, E., 29
Sherman, E. J., 34
Siegman, E. F., 21
Silverstein, B., 103
Simon, M., 79
Simon, R., 27, 30
Simon, U. E., 59
Simonetti, M., 149
Sitterson, Jr., J. C., 59
Ska, J.-L., 52, 59
Spadafora, F., 17
Spicq, C., 29
Spiegel, Y., 89

Spong, J. S., 106
Stalker, J., 52
Stanton, E. C., 97
Steinmann, J., 30
Steinmetz, D. C., 29
Stemberger, G., 78, 173
Stenhouse, P., 107
Sternberg, M., 59
Stevenson, K. W., 179
Stevick, D. G., 106
Stibbe, M. W. G., 60
Strack, H. L., 78, 173
Strauss, D. F., 45-46, 112
Strauss, G., 28
Streeter, B. H., 31
Stuhlmacher, P., 45
Stuiber, A., 145
Stummer, F., 30
Sun, H. T. C., 50
Sundberg, Jr., A. C., 70
Swete, H. B., 27

Talbert, C. H., 45
Tamez, E., 94
Taylor, V., 32
Teeple, H. M., 107
Thackeray, H. St J., 39
Theissen, G., 84
Thompson, R. C., 35
Tischendorf, C. von, 29
Tollers, V. L., 52
Topping, R. R., 68
Tournay, R. J., 80
Tov, E., 39, 52
Trible, P., 98
Trigg, J. W., 149
Tucker, G. M., 41
Tuckett, C. M., 31

Vaccari, A., 118
Valk, M. H. van der, 27

Vanhoye, A., 17, 47, 136, 139, 193
Vargas-Machuca, A., 158
Vaux, R. de, 30
Villa-Vicencio, C., 82
Vincent, L.-H., 154
Visser 't Hooft, W. A., 187
Volkmann, R. E., 54
Vorgrimler, H., 143

Wallis Budge, E. A., 34
Walters, P., 39
Walz, A., 118
Warner, M., 58
Watson, N., 53
Waznak, R. P., 181
Weber, R., 40, 71
Weinfeld, M., 50, 52
Weisse, C. H., 31
Wellek, R., 51
Wheeler, C. B., 52
White, H. J., 40
Wikenhauser, A., 38
Wilder, A. N., 55
Wilke, C. G., 31
Williams, R. J., 34
Williamson, H. G. M., 124
Wilson, R. R., 84
Wimsatt, Jr., W. K., 51
Winterbottom, M., 54
Wolff, H. W., 88
Woollcombe, K. J., 129
Wordsworth, J., 40
Wrede, W., 46
Wuellner, W., 58
Würthwein, E., 39

Yarbro Collins, A., 98
Young, F., 55

Zenger, E., 38, 69

# 3. Topical

Abraham, 118, 135
Actualization, 9, 170-76, 191
Adam, 131
Akkadian (Language), 34
'*Al tiqrê*', 173
Alexandria
  Library, 27, 39
  School, 147
Allegory, 76-77, 126, 147, 149, 173-74
American Biblical Congress, 103
Analogy of Faith, 149-50
Analysis of Biblical Text, *see* Approach(es) to Scripture
Anthology, 77
Anti-Semitism, 81-82, 176
Antioch, School of, 118, 146, 148
Apocrypha, 71, 77
Approach(es) to Scripture, 24
  Anthropological, 87-89
  Canonical, 68-74, 156
  Diachronic, 20, 23
  Feminist, 96-101
  Liberationist, 92-96, 174-75
  Linguistic, 40-41, 191
  Literary, 3, 23, 27, 29-30, 33, 36, 41-42, 50-53, 114, 191
  Narrative, 20, 23, 58-63, 191
  Philological, 40-41, 191
  Psychoanalytic, 20, 89-92
  Psychological, 23, 89-92
  Rhetorical, 23, 53-58, 191
  Semiotic, 63-67
  Sociological, 20, 23, 83-87
  Structuralist, 63
  Synchronic, 20, 22-23, 191
Aquila, 27
Aramaic, 28, 75, 105, 160, 177

Archaeology, 3, 18
Aristarchus of Samothrace, 27
Aristotle, 54, 146
Astruc, Jean, 28, 30
Athanasius, 147
Atheism, 176
Atonement, 103
Augustine of (Dacia) Denmark, 117
Augustine, St., 27-28
Authenticity, 3
Author, 114, 120-22, 124, 130-31, 139, 148, 163
  Implied, 60
  Real, 60

Babylonian (Language), 34
*Barnabas, Ep. of*, 118
Basil, 147
Bible, *see* Scripture, Holy
Biblical Apostolate, 185
Biblical Commission, Pontifical, 1-2, 6, 8, 10, 14-15, 20, 24
  As author, *see* Index 2
  Responses, 20-21
Biblical Institute, Pontifical, 1-2
Bishops, 151, 158
Bisitun Stone, 34
Body of Christ, 153
Bryan, William Jennings, 105

Caiaphas, 122
Calvin, Jean, 29, 118
Canon, 47, 68-74, 131, 143-45, 156, 166, 187
  Alexandrian Jewish, 70
  Catholic, 71-72
  Eastern Orthodox, 71-72

Palestinian Jewish, 70-71, 79
Protestant, 70, 72
Canopus, Decree of, 34
Catechesis, 58-59, 183-84
Chicago School, 83-84
Christ, Mystery of, 156, 173-74, 180, 187
Church, 2, 5, 8-10, 15, 17-19, 22-24, 28, 47-48, 62-63, 69, 72, 75, 77, 80-81, 99-100, 107-8, 117-18, 141-42, 149-50, 152, 154-57, 162, 170-88
Cicero, 54
Clement of Alexandria, 147
Counter-Reformation, The, 108, 132
Covenant Code, 49
Criticism,
    Canonical, 68-74
    Form, 22, 32, 35, 41, 83-84, 111
    Higher, 41
    Historical, 5, 8, 13, 19, 22-23, 26-51, 61, 67-68, 84, 99, 102, 114, 117, 119, 122-23, 150, 154, 156, 160-61, 190
    Literary, 3, 23, 27, 29-30, 33, 36, 41-42, 50-53, 114, 191
    Lower, 41
    Redaction, 33, 36, 42
    Scientific, 3-4, 21-22, 139, 153
    Source, 27, 29-30, 33, 41, 45
    Textual, 3, 18, 27, 29, 36, 38-40, 153, 191
    Tradition, 42
Cyril of Alexandria, 147

Darius I, King, 34
Darrow, Clarence, 105
David, King, 135
Deacons, 151
Dead Sea Scrolls, 36, 75
Decalogue, 86, 165
Demotic, 34
Demythologization, 32-33, 46, 112-13, 115
"Diachronic" Defined, 20
Dialogue with Scripture, 141
Diaspora, 75
Dicta probantia, 167

Didymus the Blind, 147
Diodore of Tarsus, 146
Dionysius the Great, 147
Discoveries, Archaeological, 18, 33
Divino afflante Spiritu, 1-8, 13, 18, 20, 23, 48, 120-21, 126, 128-29, 132-33, 150, 153, 159, 187
Divorce, 165, 186
Documentary Hypothesis, 30-31
Dogma, 46
Dream(s), 77
Dynamic Aspect of Biblical Text, 122, 127, 191

Ecole Biblique, 154
Ecumenical Translations of the Bible, 188
Ecumenism, 10, 186-88
Egypt, 34
Egyptian (Language), 34
Eisegesis, 125
Elamite (Language), 34
Enlightenment, The, 29, 46, 102-3
Enoch, First, 75
Eschatology, 186
Ethiopian Eunuch, 16
Eucharist, 59, 151, 173, 179, 184
Exegesis, 44, 48, 72, 100, 109, 114-15, 117, 159-62, 166, 168-69
    Advocacy, 92
    Catholic, 3, 5-9, 24-25, 47, 108, 132-69, 191
    Historical-Critical, 5, 8, 13, 19, 22-23, 26-51, 61, 67-68, 84, 99, 102, 114, 117, 119, 122-23, 150, 154, 156, 160-61, 190
    Jewish, 47, 74-79, 173
    Liberal, 3, 102-3, 166-67
    Liberationist, 92-96, 174-75
    Materialist, 14, 174-75
    Medieval, 117
    Mystical, 4-5, 147
    Patristic, 14, 125, 145-50
    Psychoanalytic, 20, 89-92
    Psychological, 14, 23, 89-92
    Rationalistic, 3, 18, 46, 176
    Scientific, 3-4, 21-22, 139, 153

Exegetes, 153-62, 164, 166, 170, 189
Existentialism, 112-13, 115

Faith, Christian, 6, 15, 22-23, 44, 47, 68, 72, 78, 107, 115-16, 127, 140, 145, 151, 154-55, 162, 167, 176
Father, God the, 5, 130
Fathers of the Church, 114-15, 145-50, 173-74
  Unanimous Consent of, 150
*Fides quaerens intellectum*, 161
*Florilegium*, 76-77
*Formgeschichte*, 32, 35; *see* Criticism, Form
Forms, Literary, *see* Genres (Forms), Literary
4QBeatitudes, 76
Fulfilment of Scripture, 126-28, 144
Fundamentalism, 101-8, 163
  Catholic, 107-8
  Five Points of, 102-3
  Islamic, 103

*Gattungsgeschichte*, 31
*Genesis Apocryphon*, 75
Genres (Forms), Literary, 5, 20, 32, 41, 43, 48, 102, 104, 121, 153, 160
*Gĕzērāhšāwāh*, 173
Gospel Tradition, 22, 106, 113
Grammar, 109-10
Grammatical Analysis, 40
Greek, 27-28, 34, 75, 106, 160, 177
Gregory of Nyssa, 147
Gregory the Great, 147
Griesbach, J. J., 29, 31
Gutenberg, J., 29

Hadrianos, 38
Hebrew, 27-28, 105, 148, 160, 177
Hermeneutics, 44-45, 47, 80, 98, 109-32, 156, 173-74, 187, 190
Historical-Critical Method,
  Description, 38-44
  Evaluation, 44-50
  History, 26-36
  Origin, 26-27
  Principles, 37

Tainted, 45
*Historical Truth of the Gospels*, *see* *Sancta Mater Ecclesia*
Historicity, 3
History of Salvation, 58-59, 61, 72, 164, 179
Holiness Code, 49
Homer, 26-27
Homily, 77, 180, 184-85
Human Sciences, 82-92
Hymns, 77, 119, 181

Incarnation, 3-8, 189
Inculturation, 9, 176-78, 191
Inerrancy, 20, 103-5
Inspiration, 6, 69, 104, 117, 120, 122, 130, 144, 162, 177, 182
*Instructio de historica evangeliorum veritate*, *see* *Sancta Mater Ecclesia*
Intention of the Author, 120
International Theological Commission, 166-67
Interpretation of the Bible, 15 *et passim*
  Allegorical, 28-29, 124, 126, 149-50, 173
  Canonical, 68-74
  Catholic, 2, 18-19, 108, 132-69
  Christological, 124-26, 138, 148, 156-57
  Diachronic, 42, 49, 58, 62, 190
  Existentialist, 111-12
  Historical-Critical, 5, 8, 13, 19, 22-23, 26-51, 61, 67-68, 84, 99, 102, 114, 117, 119, 122-23, 150, 154, 156, 160-61, 190
  Jewish, 47, 74-79, 173
  Liberationist, 92-96, 174-75
  Literary, 3, 23, 27, 29-30, 33, 36, 41-42, 50-53, 114, 191
  Liturgical, 125
  Marxist, 96
  Materialist, 14, 175-76
  Medieval, 117
  Meditative, 19
  Metaphorical, 120
  Patristic, 14, 125, 145-50
  Precritical, 19, 36

Psychological, 14, 23, 89-92
Rabbinic, 77, 126, 129, 173
Rationalist, 3, 18
Sociological, 20, 23, 83-87
Spiritual, 3-4, 19, 23, 117-18, 124-29,
    138, 147, 173
Structuralist, 14
Subjective, 4, 23, 111, 116, 122, 124-
    25, 128, 149
Synchronic, 42, 49, 58, 62, 190
Tendentious, 44-45, 100, 175
Theological, 163-64
Typological, 124, 129, 149
Intertestamental Literature, 75
Intertextuality, 136
Introductory Questions, 38
Israel, Ancient, 48, 58-59, 72, 85, 128,
    134, 140, 157, 162

Jehovah's Witnesses, 175
Jerome, St., 2, 18, 20, 27-28, 76-77,
    145, 148, 153-54
    *Hebraica veritas*, 148
Jesus of Nazareth, 5, 10, 22, 46, 106,
    116, 118, 120-21, 136-37
    Christ, the, 28, 78
    Death, 58-59, 137
    Disciples, 85-86, 142
    Divinity, 22, 102-3
    Last Supper, 56, 59
    Message, 106, 152, 177
    Ministry, 59
    Miracles, 22
    Resurrection, 22, 58-59, 103-4, 137
    Sermon on Mount/Plain, 55, 136
    Son of God, 5, 78, 130
    Virginal Conception, 22, 103
Jewish Literature, Extracanonical, 75
Jewish Traditions of Interpretation, 74-
    78
John Chrysostom, 146
John of the Cross, St., 80-81
*Jubilees*, 75
Judah the Prince, Rabbi, 78

Kerygma, 59, 112
King James Version, 105

Kingdom of God, 88, 152

Lagrange, O.P., Marie-Joseph, 153-54
Language, Human, 9, 15, 26, 104, 122
Law(s), 119
Law, Mosaic, 86, 139, 164
*Leben-Jesu-Forschung*, 45
*Lectio Divina*, 181-83
Linguistic Analysis, 40-41, 191
Literalism, 102, 104, 106, 119, 121, 161
Literature,
    Assyrian, 34-35
    Babylonian, 34-35
    Deuterocanonical, 70
    Egyptian, 34
    Hebrew, 36
    Jewish, 75-78
    Sumerian, 35
    Ugaritic, 35-36
Liturgy, 167, 179-81
    Of the Word and the Sacrament,
        180-81
    Of the Hours, 180-81
Logic, 109
Lucian of Antioch, 146
Luther, Martin, 29, 118

Macarism(s), 76
Magisterium, 3-4, 7, 69, 151, 154, 167,
    172, 176
Manipulation of the Biblical Text, 172
Manna, 173-74
Marcellus of Ancyra, 146
Mary, Virgin, 10
Medellin, 93
Messiah, Messianic, 123, 137
Method(s) of Interpretation, 24; *see* In-
    terpretation of the Bible
Midrash(im), 76-77, 173
Midrash Rabbah, 78
Millenarianism, 81-82
Ministers of the Word, 151-52
Mishnah, 78
Modernism, 19-20, 132
Monkey Trial, 105
Moses, 28, 30, 128
Myth(s), 160-61

Narrative(s), 20, 23, 58-63, 191
Nathan, 135
Nestorius, 146
New Criticism, 51-52, 68
Niagara Bible Congress, 102
Nicholas of Lyra, 28, 118

Origen, 27-28, 76-77, 118, 125, 145,
    147-48, 153-54, 182
  Hexapla, 27-28
Original Sin, 131

Palestinian Jewish Background of the
    New Testament, 36
Parable(s), 77, 88, 119
Paschal Mystery, 72-73, 124-29, 138,
    144
Pastoral Ministry, 183-86
Pentateuch, 27-31, 35
Persian, Old (Language), 34
Pesher, 76-77, 124
Peshitta, 40
Pharisaism, 78
Philology, 3, 40-41, 44
Plato, 54, 147
Praeparatio evangelica, 73
Prayers, 181
Précompréhension    (Vorverständnis),
    111-12, 132-33, 161
Prehistory of the Biblical Text, 48
Presuppositions of Interpretation, 8,
    44, 46-47, 111-12, 115, 132-33, 161
Priests, 151-52, 186
Proverbs, 119, 121
Providentissimus Deus, 1-4, 6-8, 13, 17-
    18, 23, 158
Pseudepigrapha, 75
Publications, 160-61

Q (= Quelle), 30, 32
Quintilian, 54
Qumran, 8, 75

Racism, 81-82, 107
Rashi, 28
Rationalism, 46, 176
Re-reading, see Relecture(s)

Reader, Implied and Real, 60
Reading of Bible, Fundamentalist, 101-
    9, 119, 121, 132, 163
Reformation, The 20, 35, 102
Relation of New to Old Testament,
    136-39
Relecture(s), 75, 77, 106, 123-24, 134-
    35, 140-41, 171
Religions, History of, 3, 31, 45
Renaissance, The, 27-29, 35
Research, 104, 157-58, 162
Revelation, 9, 89, 104, 136, 142, 155
Rhetoric, 53-58
  Classical, 54-56
  New, 56-57
  Semitic, 56
Rosetta Stone, 33

Sancta Mater Ecclesia, 18, 21-23, 153
Scopes, John T., 105
Scripture, Holy (the Bible), 1, 7, 9, 14-
    15, 17-18, 21-22, 49, 58, 66, 79, 89-
    90, 95, 99, 102-3, 106-8, 114-16, 131,
    134, 136, 138-43, 148, 150-52, 154,
    156-57, 159, 162-63, 166-70, 174,
    176-77, 190-91
  As Norm, 145
  Scriptura Sola, 106
  Soul of Theology, 13, 158, 163
  Study of, 2, 6, 8, 18, 158, 163
Semiotics, 63-67
Sense of Old Testament, Christologi-
    cal, 126
Sense of Scripture,
  Accommodated, 125
  Alien, 124
  Allegorical, 28, 117-18, 147, 149, 150
  Anagogic, 117-18
  Christological, 124-26, 138, 148, 156-
    57
  Ecclesial, 156
  Fuller, see Sensus Plenior
  Historical, 5, 8, 13, 19, 22-23, 26-51,
    61, 67-68, 84, 99, 102, 114, 117,
    119, 122-23, 150, 154, 156, 160-61,
    190
  Literal, 4, 28, 43, 48, 106, 117-24,

127-28, 130, 153, 173-74
Moral, 117-18
Multiple, 117, 119, 122
Mystical, 4-5, 147
Spiritual, 3-4, 19, 23, 117-18, 124-29, 138, 147, 173
Typological, 124, 129, 149
*Sensus Plenior*, 124, 130-31
Septuagint, 27-28, 39, 71, 75-77, 130-31
Simon, Richard, 27, 30
Sinaiticus, Codex, 29
*Sitz im Leben*, 32, 35, 83-84, 162
Sixtus of Siena, O.P., 70
Song of Songs, 79-81, 140
Spirit, Holy, 5-7, 47-48, 69, 72, 104, 106-7, 116, 126-27, 130-31, 138, 142, 144-45, 149, 151-53, 162
*Spiritus Paraclitus*, 2, 20
Suspicion, Hermeneutic of, 98-99
Symmachus, 27
Synagogue, 179-80
"Synchronic" Defined, 20
Synoptic Gospels, 30-32
Syriac (Language), 28, 39

Talmud,
   Babylonian, 78
   Jerusalem, 78
Targum(s), 75-77, 173
*Tartê mišma'*, 173
Teaching, 150, 152-53, 158-59
Tertullian, 145
*Textus receptus*, 27, 29
Theodore of Mopsuestia, 146, 148
Theodoret of Cyrrhus, 146
Theodotion, 27
Theology, 161-69, 191
   Biblical, 48-49
   Dogmatic, 161, 163-64, 166
   Moral, 161, 164-66
   Systematic, 48, 162-64, 166, 168, 192
Thomas Aquinas, St., 119

Tradition, 7, 48, 67-82, 106-7, 114, 131, 145, 149-50, 154, 157, 162, 164, 176, 190-91
As Norm, 145
Biblical, 133-41
Church, 143-55, 164, 190
Double (in the Synoptic Gospels), 30
Jewish, 74-78
Triple (in the Synoptic Gospels), 30
Trent, Council of, 20, 130-31, 150
Trinity, Holy, 130
Two Source Hypothesis (of Synoptic Gospels), 30-31,
Typology, 129, 173-74, 180

Ugaritic (Language), 35

Vatican Council I, 150
Vatican Council II, 1-2, 14, 93, 151, 158, 165, 175, 179-81, 183, 188
   *Dei Verbum*, 2, 4, 7, 9, 13, 18, 22-24, 48, 72, 74, 143, 145, 150, 152, 154, 157-59, 163-65, 172, 182-83
*Vetus Itala*, 148
*Vigilantiae*, 5-6, 20
Vision(s), 77
Vulgate, Latin, 28, 39, 148
   Sixto-Clementine, 71

*Wirkungsgeschichte*, 79-81
Wisdom compositions, 77
*Woman's Bible, The*, 97
Word of God,
   Incarnate, 10, 148
   Preached, 46, 180-81, 184-85
   Written, 5, 15, 20, 26, 66, 86, 95, 103-4, 114, 116-17, 124, 138, 142, 151, 156-57, 159-61, 163, 168-70, 176, 181-82, 189, 191-92

Zenodotus of Ephesus, 27

Finito di stampare il 31 marzo 1995
Tipografia Poliglotta della Pontificia Università Gregoriana
Piazza della Pilotta, 4 – 00187 Roma